Caddyshack

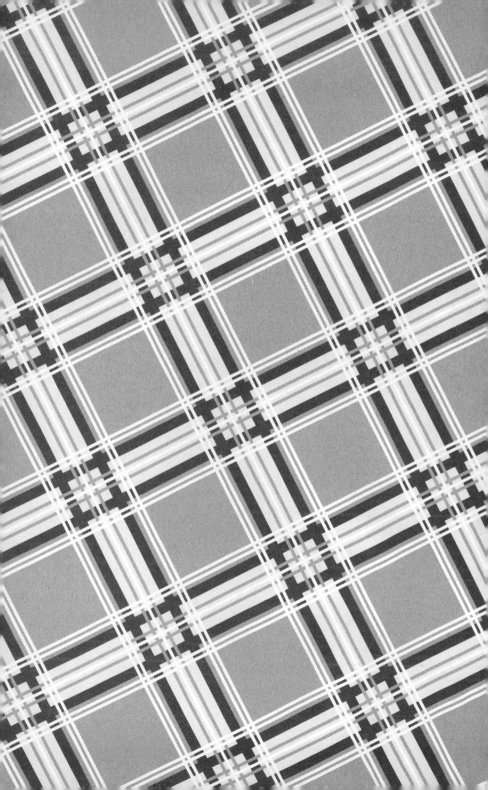

CHRIS NASHAWATY

Caddyshack

The MAKING *of a* HOLLYWOOD
CINDERELLA STORY

FLATIRON
BOOKS
NEW YORK

www.flatironbooks.com

Photographic section credits:
p. 1 (top): Copyright © 1966. The Harvard Lampoon, Inc. Used with Permission; (bottom): Getty Images
p. 2 (top): Courtesy of The Second City; (bottom): Courtesy of Michael Gold
p. 3 (top): Photographer Unknown; (middle): Courtesy of *National Lampoon*; (bottom): Courtesy of *New York* magazine
p. 4 (top): Getty Images; (bottom): Photofest
p. 5: Everett Collection
p. 6 (top): Everett Collection; (middle): Photofest; (bottom left and right): Courtesy of Orion/Warner Bros.
p. 7 (top and bottom): Courtesy of Orion/Warner Bros.; (middle): Everett Collection
p. 8: Courtesy of Michael Shamberg

Designed by Jonathan Bennett

The Library of Congress Cataloging-in-Publication Data is available upon request.

ISBN 978-1-250-10595-0 (hardcover)
ISBN 978-1-250-10597-4 (ebook)

Our books may be purchased in bulk for promotional, educational, or business use. Please contact your local bookseller or the Macmillan Corporate and Premium Sales Department at 1-800-221-7945, extension 5442, or by email at MacmillanSpecialMarkets@macmillan.com.

First Edition: April 2018

10 9 8 7 6 5 4 3 2 1

In loving memory of Keith, my first and best friend

Contents

A flute with no holes is not a flute.
A donut with no hole is a Danish.

—Basho, seventeenth-century Zen philosopher

Prologue

A FEW DOZEN NEWSPAPER REPORTERS, film critics, television talking heads, and studio publicity flacks were gathered outside Dangerfield's comedy club on the Upper East Side of Manhattan. It was the morning of July 12, 1980, and just after 9:00 a.m., the doors were unlocked and the group was led inside to meet the cast and crew of the soon-to-be-released comedy *Caddyshack*.

It had already been a long, hot summer. And the depressing state of the world somehow made the days feel even longer and more oppressive. The Iran hostage crisis was in its eighth month, with no end in sight. Detroit was laying off tens of thousands of line workers as Japan became the world's largest auto-producing country. Even the feel-good respite of a Summer Olympics had been taken away after the United States decided to boycott the 1980 Moscow Games in protest of the Soviet Union's invasion of Afghanistan. The presidency of Jimmy Carter was limping to the finish line.

Inside, Dangerfield's wasn't much sunnier. With its faux wood paneling and pungent aroma of stale ashtrays and spilled beer, the club had an air of seedy, down-at-the-heels squalor. It had opened for business in 1969, and it looked as if nothing had been updated since. At night, with stand-up comics firing off jokes to out-of-town tourists, that was one thing. But at this ungodly hour of the morning, as blinding shards of morning light sliced in through the front door from First Avenue, it was another. The place looked downright funereal. A fitting site for what would end up becoming a wake of sorts.

One by one, the movie's stars and above-the-line talent slowly rolled in, each looking more bleary-eyed and hungover than the last. Bill Murray, in pale pink shorts and a striped polo shirt that looked pulled from the bottom of the hamper, had a week's worth of shaggy stubble on his face. His bloodshot eyes sought relief behind a pair of oversize sunglasses. He walked into the club with a what-me-worry grin and a grease-stained pizza box in his hands. He'd been pretty much on permanent vacation since his final season on *Saturday Night Live* had ended, in May.

Chevy Chase, in cream-colored linen pants and a matching silk shirt and driving cap, didn't attempt to hide his red-rimmed eyes, which were little more than pinholes. If he looked edgy and deflated, he had reason. His latest movie, a disposably inane comedy called *Oh! Heavenly Dog*, had opened the previous day to reviews that were so devastating they read like kiss-off notes from a scorned ex. How had he, the same man who just a few short years earlier had been the biggest star on late-night television, allowed himself to be in a picture where he was reincarnated as the movie mutt Benji?

Rodney Dangerfield, on his home turf as the dingy club's celebrity proprietor, pinged around the room with nervous, caffeinated energy. He was already sweating through a khaki cabana shirt that strained to contain his bulbous potbelly as he glad-handed the media, tossing off his signature seltzer-spray one-liners. After decades spent tirelessly grinding it out on the stand-up circuit, Dangerfield was now fifty-eight, and thanks to a recent string of live-wire appearances on *The Tonight Show*, was more popular than he'd ever been. The self-effacing comic, who chronically complained about getting no respect, was finally getting some. *Caddyshack* was Dangerfield's first big role in a studio film. The money hadn't been great, but if he managed to win over the critics and the movie turned out to be a hit, it might just lead to a new, cushier chapter in his career.

Only the teetotaling Ted Knight, with his Pacific Palisades tan, immaculate swept back head of silver hair, and pressed blazer, looked like someone who actually wanted to be there on this morning. Maybe because he was one of the few who hadn't been up all night getting bombed.

Less than twenty-four hours earlier, the press had gotten their first look at the new snobs-versus-slobs country club comedy at the Loew's State Theatre in Times Square. The reaction had been lukewarm at best. And lukewarm was not what everyone had been hoping for. The film's financier, Orion Pictures, and its distributor, Warner Bros., had hoped that *Caddyshack* might be their sleeper hit of the summer—a counterpunch to Universal's *The Blues Brothers* and Paramount's *Airplane!* But the stingy smattering of laughs and halfhearted applause that greeted the end of the film let them know it wouldn't be the box office triumph they'd signed up for when they green-lighted its $6 million budget.

After the early-evening preview, some of the cast and crew returned to their hotel on Central Park, where they drowned their disappointment in drink and drugs. By then, it had become something of a tradition for many on the *Caddyshack* team. For them, alcohol, marijuana, and especially cocaine had been the diet of choice during the film's wild eleven-week shoot in Florida, back when director Harold Ramis, producer Doug Kenney, and the pair's writing partner, Brian Doyle-Murray, still believed they were making another *National Lampoon's Animal House.* Ramis and Kenney had written that frat-house smash that had opened two years earlier. And not only did it end up buying them new houses, it wound up on the cover of *Newsweek* after becoming the biggest movie comedy of all time.

But now that seemed like a long time ago.

The past six months of postproduction back in Los Angeles had been a series of nightmarish setbacks. What had begun as a loose, laid-back, inmates-running-the-asylum revel just outside Fort Lauderdale had curdled into a toxic stew of bitter compromises, bruised feelings, and bare-knuckle power plays. The drugs certainly hadn't helped.

Still, the film was finally finished (or as close to finished as it was going to get), and now everyone agreed that it was what it was. Everyone except for Kenney. The toll of so many creative concessions still weighed on him heavily. As the others partied late into the night after the disastrous preview, Kenney grew more and more depressed, looking for some kind of solace (or perhaps oblivion) in the white powder he was vacuuming up his nose.

In his short life, the thirty-three-year-old writer and producer had already accomplished an extraordinary amount, but he'd yet to really experience failure firsthand. He'd begun *Caddyshack* as Hollywood's latest can't-miss prodigy—a charmed but troubled genius who turned everything he touched into money. A decade earlier, he'd edited the legendary *Harvard Lampoon* and parlayed its smartass, Ivy League sensibility into the start-up publishing sensation the *National Lampoon*, sparking a subversive New Wave of slash-and-burn satire. Five years later, he cashed out and became an overnight millionaire. For his encore, he cowrote the screenplay for *Animal House*, which earned $140 million on a budget of just $2.7 million. Kenney was a comedy rock star—brilliantly witty and combustibly self-destructive.

On that July weekend in New York, however, his run finally

seemed to be coming to an end. Or so he feared. As morning light broke over the park outside his hotel-room window, he knew that it was too late to try to close his eyes and sleep. He was too wired anyway. So he went for a walk. But he couldn't stop his mind from whirring with a million nagging questions. *How had he let his film get away from him so completely? Had he lost his touch? Had he even deserved his success in the first place?* Eventually, Kenney found himself at the corner of First Avenue and 61st Street, where he looked at the entrance to Dangerfield's and steeled himself for what awaited.

Inside, Chase and Murray drifted to opposite corners of the room. The relationship between the two men had always been . . . *complicated*. They had gotten along well enough while making *Caddyshack* in Florida, but there was still a leftover chilliness—a frosty distance that lingered from a bitter backstage tussle between the two at *Saturday Night Live*, when Chase returned to guest-host in 1978 with what many considered a lack of humility and a swollen head. Insults were exchanged. Punches were thrown. Both had made up and moved on—to a point.

As the morning's round-robin of quickie interviews was about to begin, Kenney slumped into a chair in the back of the room, still buzzed from the night before. He ordered a drink. Then another. His simmering anger was about to boil over.

Ramis, Doyle-Murray, and the film's four stars—Chase, Murray, Dangerfield, and Knight—grimly death-marched up to the Dangerfield's stage and took their seats. A young Warner Bros. publicist welcomed the reporters and thanked them for having come so early in the day. Attempting to stoke the media's enthusiasm, the flack asked if they had enjoyed the previous night's screening.

"Wasn't it great?"

Then, he jokingly added, "And who thought it sucked?"

Kenney's voice rose from the back of the room to break the uncomfortable silence: "Yeah, it sucked!! Didn't everyone think it was *terrible?!*"

The nervous publicist, awkwardly trying to recover from Kenney's burst of friendly fire, assured the crowd that the man in the back was just kidding around. Then, just to prove that he wasn't, Kenney stood up and told everyone in the club to go fuck themselves. He slumped back down into his chair and passed out with his head on the table. Kenney's parents, who'd traveled into Manhattan from Connecticut that morning, walked over to their son and hugged him before quietly leading him out of the room.

Chase, the man who'd grown closest to Kenney during the making of *Caddyshack*, couldn't believe what he was witnessing. Not that he didn't understand Kenney's frustration. And certainly not because he'd never seen him loaded before. He just thought it was bizarre that Kenney would lash out here of all places—at the very people who held the fate of the movie in their hands. He was sabotaging his own film at the precise moment that he should be putting on a phony smile and hyping it.

When the Dangerfield's press conference was mercifully over, a friend pulled Chase aside and suggested that he take Kenney away on a vacation after the film's upcoming premiere to help him clean up. Preferably somewhere where they could avoid the film's sure-to-be-negative reviews. And more important, someplace where it wouldn't be so easy to score cocaine.

Chase thought that he should be the *last* person to ask. He'd been running just as hard and using just as much coke as Kenney. The idea of him being anybody's—least of all his drug buddy's—voice of reason and sober coach seemed absurd.

Later, when Harold Ramis heard the plan, he thought it sounded like a terrible idea. It was like putting a box of matches

next to a pile of oily rags. When Kenney asked Ramis if he
wanted to join him and Chevy in Maui for a few weeks, he recalled having thought, "Oh, man, that's the *last* thing I need."

• •

Looking back now, it would be understandable to think that
Caddyshack was both a huge box office hit and an instantly ac-
knowledged comedy classic from the moment it opened on 656
screens on July 25, 1980. But it would also be wrong. The film was
a modest success. By the end of 1980, it stood as the seventeenth-
highest-grossing film of the year, light-years behind *The Empire
Strikes Back* and sandwiched between *Cheech and Chong's Next
Movie* (at No. 16) and *Friday the 13th* (at No. 18).

The reviews for the film ran the gamut from slightly mixed
to scathingly negative. While *The New York Times*'s cranky
fifty-five-year-old critic, Vincent Canby, seemed to like it more
than most, his peers dismissed *Caddyshack* as uneven, lowbrow,
and sophomoric. Some seemed to enjoy Rodney Dangerfield's
outsize performance as the crass, nouveau riche boor, Al Czervik. But, almost across the board, they regarded Bill Murray's
deranged, camouflage-clad assistant greenskeeper, Carl Spackler, as unsubtle, sub-mental, and perverted. David Ansen in *Newsweek* wrote, "The writers have saddled themselves with a bland
hero and a perfunctory drama that will be of interest only to the
actors' agents." And in *New York* magazine, David Denby wrote
that first-time director Harold Ramis had cobbled together "a
perfectly amiable mess." Backhanded, sure. But it was also one of
the most complimentary things anyone said at the time.

The critics weren't right, of course. But they weren't exactly
wrong, either. *Caddyshack was* an amiable mess. Ramis was the
first to admit that his debut behind the camera was less than assured. In fact, he'd later refer to it as his learn-on-the-job "six
million-dollar scholarship to film school." But what those critics

failed to recognize at the time was that it was *Caddyshack*'s imperfections that ended up making it so perfect.

Part coming-of-age comedy, part class-warfare commentary, *Caddyshack* was rooted in the teenage experiences of the blue-collar Murray clan. Growing up, Brian and his younger brother Bill had spent their summers thanklessly working their way up the minimum-wage ladder from lowly driving-range shag boys to concession-stand slaves to those tip-hungry beasts of burden—caddies, hauling the bags of the well-to-do on some of the snootiest golf courses along Chicago's suburban North Shore. For both them and Kenney (whose father had supported the family for years as a club tennis pro), *Caddyshack* was deeply autobiographical—an affectionate look back at the most outrageous and formative summers of their lives.

It was a personal story but also a universal one. After all, every private club in the ritzier pockets of America had a starched-shirt WASP dictator like Ted Knight's Judge Elihu Smails (*"How 'bout a Fresca?"*), a wealthy playboy wastrel like Chevy Chase's Ty Webb (*"Be the ball . . ."*), an uncouth loudmouth like Rodney Dangerfield's Al Czervik (*"Did someone step on a duck?"*), and, as they knew firsthand, working-class kids like Michael O'Keefe's Danny Noonan (*"Do you take drugs, Danny?" "Every day."*).

The *Caddyshack* script would go through a number of drafts and overhauls, but when it was finally shot, in the fall of 1979, it was something quite different from the usual Hollywood comedy of the time. Like *Animal House*, it reflected a brash anti-authoritarian worldview, targeting the lily-white Republican citadels of the Greatest Generation. It looked at the conservative, calcified, and complacent adult world and put it in its ruthlessly ironic crosshairs.

As the 1970s rounded the bend into the '80s, the country was changing. Watergate and Vietnam were receding into the rearview. Nixon was long gone, licking his wounds back in Yorba Linda. But he had been replaced by the spiritual retrenchment of the cardigan-clad Carter years and a malaise of tapioca mildness. The country had made a slow and steady march to the boring center.

The movie industry had already been turned upside down in the late '60s and early '70s by a New Hollywood generation led by maverick directors such as Dennis Hopper (*Easy Rider*), Francis Ford Coppola (*The Godfather*), and Martin Scorsese (*Mean Streets*). But those filmmakers had trafficked mostly in existential dramas, not comedies. They offered brutal truths and bleak endings. What they didn't seem to possess was a sense of humor about the world or themselves—or just a sense of humor, period. By the tail end of the '70s, many of them had also run out of gas.

The critics had been so busy celebrating the New Hollywood that they were slow to spot the revolution *after* the revolution—the rise of the baby boomers. Suddenly there was an entirely new generation of postwar teenagers and college students who'd grown tired of the '60s and all of its dialectical arthouse earnestness. While no one had been looking, they'd mainlined the first season of *Saturday Night Live*, dialed into the Second City improv scene in Chicago, and subscribed to the nothing-sacred philosophy of the *National Lampoon*, which had famously put an adorable mutt with a gun pointed to its head on the cover of its January 1973 issue along with the sick-joke ultimatum: "If You Don't Buy This Magazine, We'll Kill This Dog." Hollywood had been caught napping.

This new generation no longer wanted to see George Burns geriatrically yukking it up in *Oh, God!*, or Burt Reynolds cracking redneck jokes in *Smokey and the Bandit*, or Clint Eastwood palling around with an orangutan in *Every Which Way but Loose*. They wanted big-screen comedies that were newer and edgier—

the kind that could sting and leave a welt. They wanted the scalpel-sharp satire that Kenney, Ramis, Chase, and Murray had practiced at the *Lampoon*, Second City, and *SNL*. They wanted another *Animal House*.

Caddyshack would not be another *Animal House*. At least, not at first. It would take years for the film to build its audience—and take its rightful place in the canon of timeless movie comedies. But in a way, its delayed success and continued popularity make it much more interesting than if it had been an immediate hit. In the nearly four decades since its release, *Caddyshack* has become one of those rare contradictions: a mainstream piece of pop culture that, to its fans, still somehow manages to feel like a cult movie.

This is the story of how that film got made. But it's also the story of *who* made it, *why* they made it, and *when* it got made. It's the story of a very specific and very special ten-year period in American comedy when a brilliant group of authority-defying merry pranksters somehow found one another, pushed one another to new heights, and ended up bluffing their way onto the studio lots. It's the story of a group of outsiders grappling with the idea of becoming insiders. And it's the story of a film that was distinctly of its time but would end up speaking the loudest after that time had passed.

It's what you'd call a Cinderella Story.

The Algonquin Round Table with a Couple of Wobbly Legs

THEY CAME FROM THE COUNTRY'S finest families and belonged to its most exclusive clubs. Yet in 1966, it was exceedingly difficult for a member of *The Harvard Lampoon* to get laid. It wasn't just because of their withering sarcasm, bookish awkwardness, and fumbling, pre–sexual revolution anxiety (although that certainly didn't help). It was also because the place where they spent most of their waking hours didn't allow women.

Built in 1909 thanks to the deep pockets of William Randolph Hearst, The Castle is a three-story, medieval-looking tower with leaded-glass windows and fortress-grade wooden doors smack in the middle of Bow Street in Cambridge. Perched atop its domed roof is the figure of an ibis—an ancient Egyptian bird that doubles as the *Lampoon*'s cryptic mascot. In the light of day, the strange building looks like a cross between a squat, brick lighthouse and some half-mad architect's idea of a practical joke. The *Lampoon*'s history, however, goes back even further than Hearst's East Coast Castle. Established in 1876, *The Harvard Lampoon* is the country's oldest college humor magazine, with a roster of famous alumni that includes such urbane wits as Robert Benchley, George Plimpton, and John Updike.

The *Lampoon*'s headquarters had always been an insular place, a sort of patrician social club of high IQ gentleman smart-asses biding their time before they graduated and headed off to Wall Street or to join the family law firm. The summer of 1966 was no different. As antiwar demonstrations broke out on college campuses across the country, the undergraduate rascals inside The Castle were more likely to thumb their noses at the patchouli-scented protesters outside than march alongside them. When not occasionally putting out a magazine, they held to the hermetic, tribal traditions of the past: secret weekly black-tie dinners, Caligulan feats of alcohol consumption, and the fine art of delivering a perfectly crafted cutting remark—an intellectual one-upmanship that bordered on a blood sport. Catching a glimpse of a willing woman in the nude, however, was not one of these extracurricular activities. For that, one had to buy a copy of *Playboy*.

By the mid-'60s, Hugh Hefner's glossy men's lifestyle monthly was nearing the peak of its popularity, with 6 million subscribers. There were Playboy Clubs from Los Angeles to London and Miami to Manila, all operating on the swinging CEO's pipe-and-silk-pajamas "Playboy Philosophy." If the members of *The Harvard Lampoon* didn't possess the savoir faire to embody that hedonistic worldview, why not do the next best thing—the thing that they did better than anyone else: make fun of it?

The *Lampoon* had a long tradition of shooting satirical spitballs at stuffy, mainstream publications. It was like *Mad* magazine with elbow patches instead of Yiddish puns. But by the '60s, their one-off parodies were still pretty parochial affairs—essentially private jokes told within the seven-square-mile echo chamber of Cambridge. Now, with a target as big and buxom as *Playboy*, ambitions were scaled up. What if they put out a professional-looking publication to be sold on newsstands from coast to coast? Walker Lewis, who was then the president of the *Lampoon*, and

Rob Hoffman, the son of a well-to-do Dallas family with a mind for business as precise as a Swiss watch, approached *Playboy* gauging how receptive it might be to some good-natured ribbing. They fully expected the answer to be: Not very. Either that or: Go to hell. As they predicted, The Bunny threatened swift legal action. Lewis fired back, saying they looked forward to all of the free publicity that a lawsuit would bring. Not long after, the phone rang inside The Castle. Hugh Hefner was on the line.

After giving it some thought, Hefner had recognized the value of free publicity on his end, too. Not to mention the priceless measure of Ivy League literary respectability a *Lampoon* parody might bring. He not only gave his blessing; he offered to whip out his checkbook and help finance it. Hoffman's Dallas connections had already agreed to underwrite the printing bill, but they did take Hef up on the offer of using his distributor. An unprecedented and wildly optimistic 500,000 copies of the *Lampoon*'s *Playboy* parody (featuring a Little Orphan Bosom comic, a photo of Henry Kissinger splayed out on a bearskin rug in a thong, and a pinup model in a slightly scanty jester's costume on the cover) landed on newsstands on Labor Day weekend in 1966. It sold out in a week.

Henry Beard, one of the issue's key contributors, who, along with Doug Kenney, was also one of the *Lampoon*'s rising young stars at the time, recalls walking with Hoffman to a bank in Harvard Square with a check for $155,000 to be deposited into the *Lampoon* account. "The whole way we kept saying, 'What happened here? This could be the start of something!' It opened our eyes to the possibility of doing a national humor magazine."

◆ ◆

After the *Playboy* parody, three things quickly happened at *The Harvard Lampoon*. The Castle, which had fallen into utter disrepair, got sorely needed updates to its wheezy heating and electrical systems that had basically been left untouched from the days of the Depression. Second, its subscriber base finally spread beyond mere Harvard alumni to a national audience. And third, Beard and Kenney were anointed as the magazine's resident enfants terribles. The whip-smart yin-and-yang hopes for the next generation. They couldn't have been more different.

Henry Beard (class of '67) was, in fact, the genuine WASP article. The great-grandson of James Buchanan's vice president, John C. Breckinridge, he grew up in the Westbury Hotel on the Upper East Side of Manhattan. His father was a Yale-educated Wall Street accountant who was the heir to a family woolen mill in Canada. Before enrolling at Harvard, he attended the prestigious Taft School, where he gave the impression of being a middle-aged curmudgeon while still in his teens. He looked like an exotic baby bird in horn-rimmed glasses, baggy Brooks Brothers tweed blazers, and a pipe clenched between his teeth. There wasn't a lick of irony in the pose.

Doug Kenney (class of '68) had a decidedly different background. He grew up in the improbably named Cleveland suburb of Chagrin Falls, Ohio, where his Irish-Catholic father was a tennis pro. Or, at least, that's how Kenney chose to tell it. In truth, his father had long given up a career of stringing rackets and taken a position as a corporate personnel manager. But his murky blue-collar background made for vivid self-mythologizing. Either way, Kenney had spent his high-school summers working at private clubs, a middle-class kid waiting on blue-blood members not unlike the Beards. Despite Kenney's brilliance, his father had deeply preferred Doug's older brother Daniel—a beloved all-American type who would pass away from kidney failure in his twenties. Doug worshiped him and felt as though his parents saw him as a pale consolation prize—that he should have been the one to die rather than Daniel. At school and at home, he felt like an unloved misfit.

If Beard was a model of wry, cerebral preppy sobriety, Kenney was a hard-to-pin-down wild card, enthralled by the carnal libertinism of the Summer of Love and the dope smoking that came with it. When he entered Harvard in 1964, grass was a taboo recreation punishable by a steep jail sentence. Just a few years later, you couldn't walk down Massachusetts Avenue without getting a contact high. Plus, marijuana seemed to calm Kenney's manic, ever-pinwheeling mind. He could expound on eighteenth-century English literature one minute and astound you with his signature party trick of sticking his entire fist in his mouth the next. While Kenney could inhabit the role of the Gatsby-esque swell as if it were his birthright, he was a chameleon—fair-haired, hysterically funny, and a genius . . . but a troubled one.

Flush with the success of its *Playboy* send-up, the *Lampoon* briefly flirted with the idea of moving full-time into the parody business. Their follow-up was a riff on *Life* magazine, Henry Luce's photo-heavy standard-bearer of square, Middle American vanilla complacency. If Hefner's centerfold bible was a buzzed-about cultural lightning rod, *Life* was the polar opposite. It was so staid and past its prime, it gave off the scent of mothballs. It was a magazine no one much cared about anymore. Parodying it was like picking on the most invisible schoolyard kid at recess.

It didn't help that the country wasn't exactly in the mood for levity. By the fall of 1968, when the *Lampoon*'s "End of the World" *Life* parody issue appeared, Martin Luther King and Bobby Kennedy had been gunned down; the street-hassle beatings at the Democratic National Convention in Chicago had exposed the toxic rot of the Silent Majority, which was now speaking quite loudly with police batons; and the Black Panthers had taken up arms in Oakland. Then there was the election of Richard Milhous Nixon. It truly did feel like the end of the world. The *Life* parody would only sell half of its newsstand run, losing nearly $75,000 and sinking The Castle back into the red. But one good thing lay at the bottom of the *Lampoon*'s fiscal sinkhole: Beard and Kenney had been introduced to Matty Simmons.

Simmons was an old-school, cigar-chomping Brooklyn self-promoter with brash gambler's instincts, an outsize, heliocentric sense of himself, and a Barnum-esque flair for hype. It was hard to imagine someone *less* Ivy League. He'd been part owner of the woeful Philadelphia Warriors basketball team, had once purchased a stable of harness-race horses, and had made a small fortune in stock with Diners Club, the world's first credit card giant, where he published the company's vanity magazine with a partner named Leonard Mogel. When Simmons and Mogel left Diners Club in 1967 and sold their interest, they used the windfall to launch Twenty First Century Communications, a start-up publishing company that, in short order, failed to get a psychedelic magazine called *Cheetah* off the ground and eventually found a steady money maker (albeit not a very sexy one) in *Weight Watchers Magazine*. Simmons was hungry to expand what he was bold enough to call his empire.

In the summer of 1968, as Kenney and Beard were putting together their *Life* parody, and Rob Hoffman was hustling up and down Madison Avenue trying to gin up advertisers, Simmons got a call from Harold Chamberlain, a mutual publishing-industry acquaintance, asking if he would help out these three Harvard students on the business end of their latest venture. Simmons was in the middle of his weekly poker game at his apartment at Park Avenue and 83rd Street. Wanting to keep the conversation short and return to what he thought was a winning hand, Simmons agreed to meet "the boys."

"I was enormously impressed by them," says Simmons. "Rob Hoffman was the business man of the group and did most of the talking. Henry was from a family of millionaires. He was a genius, but quiet. And Doug . . . Doug was harder to peg. He was outgoing and handsome and charming, but I don't think I ever thought that he would end up becoming the foremost humorist of his generation."

It was a little late in the game for Simmons to be of much help with the *Life* parody. By that point, costs had already spiraled out of control and it was more or less doomed. But he was intrigued, and maybe a little dazzled, by these kids who were young enough to be his sons. The idea of teaming up to start a national humor magazine came up, but it was quickly tabled. After all, Kenney and Beard had bigger concerns weighing on their minds.

Like a lot of college students at the tail end of the '60s, they were terrified of the draft. Kenney and Beard had enrolled in ROTC at Harvard (figuring it was better to wind up in the Army Reserves than be shipped off to the front lines). But not surprisingly, both wound up getting kicked out. In Beard's case, the expulsion was for failing to attend the military ball and giving a poorly received lecture on why the US could not win the war in Vietnam. They both had to figure out quickly how to avoid being called up. Beard admits that he might have slid a small amount of money to an officer to regain a place in the Reserves, while Kenney hatched a more devious scheme.

Having heard rumors that the one disqualifying ailment that couldn't be medically diagnosed was epilepsy, Kenney began studying the *Merck Manual*, memorizing the medical reference book's laundry list of disorders and symptoms. He would become the most convincing non-epileptic epileptic the Army had ever seen. He visited a shady Boston doctor to get a prescription for Dilantin, an anti-seizure medication that he ingested with the commitment of a Method actor. He sat Beard down in the ratty postgraduate apartment they were sharing in Cambridge and briefed him on all of the telltale manifestations of his "condition" (foaming at the mouth, eyes going sideways). Kenney gave Beard's name as a reference to the draft board in case it needed a witness to back up his phony ailment.

In the end, it was moot. It turned out that Kenney's eyesight was so poor that he never would have been drafted in the first place. He was 4-F before he ever popped his first Dilantin. "He went through this whole charade for nothing," says Beard, who graduated a year ahead of Kenney. Both men felt as if they had dodged a bullet. And Beard felt doubly lucky having just been rejected by Harvard Law School, where he didn't want to go in the first place. With their undergraduate years behind them, the question became: What were they going to do now? They couldn't just hang around the *Lampoon* forever. Or could they?

By 1969, J.R.R. Tolkien's *The Lord of the Rings* had become mandatory reading for enlightenment-seeking college students between midterms and bong hits. An unlikely cult sensation written by an aging Oxford professor of medieval literature, the patience-testing saga set in Middle Earth was so self-serious and steeped in arcane furry-footed mythology that it was an obvious target to deflate. Kenney, a pop-culture savant with an occasionally cruel gift for mocking the things his peers felt most passionate about, quickly recognized that it would be their next victim. To him, Tolkien's book was the height of flaky stoner stupidity, its popularity utterly dumbfounding. Their title was as dead-on as it was pithy: *Bored of the Rings*.

Having already proved their financial and creative value to the *Lampoon*, Kenney and Beard were given small stipends to live on by the magazine after graduating. Their job was basically to brainstorm new parodies that might turn into the next *Lampoon* golden goose. In addition to their Tolkien takedown, they moved forward with a parody of the venerable *Time* magazine with Simmons and Mogel on board as partners. *Bored of the Rings* and *Time* came out within a week of one another, and both became huge hits. With a shamelessly commercial cover of a half-naked blonde underneath the heavy-breathing line "Does SEX Sell Magazines?," the *Time* one-off quickly earned $250,000 for *The Harvard Lampoon*. Its racy cover provided a lesson Kenney and Beard would tuck away for future use. The profits from *Bored of the Rings*, however, were of a totally different magnitude.

At Hoffman's suggestion, Kenney and Beard had penned a fawning fan-boy letter to Tolkien careful to namedrop some of the *Lampoon*'s more hallowed alumni, essentially asking for his blessing. The subtext of the letter, of course, was that if they got that blessing, it would protect them from whatever copyright issues popped up from Tolkien's litigious publisher. To their surprise, Tolkien wrote back, saying that he had no idea why anyone would want to parody his book, but by all means, have at it and God bless.

"We sat across from each other at a double desk at the Harvard library, and each of us had a portable typewriter facing one another," says Beard. "Doug would type 1,000 words just like that. I've never seen anything like it. He could make 2 plus 2 equal not 4, but 22. He basically wrote that book. It was staggering. I think we wrote the whole thing in four or five weeks. We just clicked."

Beard recalls that when he and Kenney went to New York to deliver the manuscript to their publisher, "It was like he wanted to pick it up with fireplace tongs. He didn't even want to hold it, he thought the idea was so horrible." In their slim, pun-packed paperback, for example, Bilbo Baggins is named Dildo Bugger. Thirty-two editions later, *Bored of the Rings* has sold 750,000 copies and has been translated into more than ten languages.

By June of 1969, Simmons had become more sold than ever on the idea of kick-starting a national humor magazine. The boys were on a hot streak, and the time to strike was now. He summoned Kenney, Beard, and Hoffman back to New York. It was time to figure out their next move. In the back of his mind, he surely thought: Why should these guys make *The Harvard Lampoon* rich when they could be making *me* rich?

The three young men arrived at the cramped Broadway offices of Twenty First Century Communications with Hoffman, the sharpest negotiator of the three, assigned to do the talking. Simmons proposed a deal in which he would put up all of the seed money (about $350,000) and in return would get 75 percent ownership of the fledgling publication. Kenney, Beard, and Hoffman could split their 25 percent however they saw fit. Since they planned to call their new venture *National Lampoon*, they hammered out a side agreement to give *The Harvard Lampoon* a small royalty from the magazine's newsstand sales.

The Harvard Three worried that with a minority stake, editorial control might be a problem—a notion that was especially disconcerting since Simmons's hopelessly square idea of humor seemed to run along the lines of Bob Hope and Milton Berle. So Hoffman, a deceptively boyish-looking pit bull in a J. Press suit, countered with a buyout clause that allowed Kenney, Beard, and himself to cash out their shares at the end of five years at eighteen times the magazine's earnings. It was like a prenuptial agreement between two parties who weren't convinced that they wanted to say "I do" in the first place. Not to mention that it bullishly assumed that the *National Lampoon* would be earning anything at all in five years—or even be around. Simmons, desperate for a flagship magazine for the empire he envisioned, reluctantly agreed.

Five years later, he'd end up kicking himself.

Calling Hoffman a "tough, unrelenting Yuppie," Simmons now admits that he was outmaneuvered. "Rob Hoffman was smarter than me. No question about it."

◆ ◆

Doug Kenney and Henry Beard moved to New York at the beginning of October 1969, sharing two floors of a brownstone on East 83rd Street. They each paid $400 a month. By then, Kenney had grown his dirty-blond hair past his shoulders, letting his freak flag fly. He'd transformed yet again, this time from ersatz WASP into instant hippy in wire-rimmed granny glasses and a burning joint rarely out of reach. Kenney lived on the second floor with his girlfriend and soon-to-be wife, Alex Garcia-Mata, the daughter of a South American financier. The monastic Beard lived just above them. They were play-acting at being grown-ups in the big city.

The most pressing of their newly acquired adult responsibilities was assembling a staff of off-kilter, like-minded humorists who could crank out copy at a breathless clip—pitched somewhere between the juvenile idiocy of *Mad* and the sophisticated wit of *The New Yorker*. They needed people who were willing to work herculean hours and fill ninety-six blank magazine pages every month. And for cheap. At the time, the magazine business was exploding. The newsstands were fat with advertising. New niche publications such as *Circus* and *Creem*, which aimed at the same baby-boomer market that Jann Wenner had tapped into with *Rolling Stone* a few years earlier, were constantly popping up. But few were able to duplicate the innovative New Journalism of Wenner's rock 'n' roll bible or its plugged-in authenticity. Kenney and Beard knew the *National Lampoon* had to speak in their voices, not Simmons's or anyone else's.

Kenney and Beard initially shared a claustrophobic office at Twenty First Century Communications's midtown headquarters before the whole shop moved to 635 Madison Avenue shortly after the New Year. They began casting the net for outside agitators and simpatico bomb throwers, asking friends and friends of friends for writers who were willing to gamble on what Beard only half-jokingly called "one of the ten worst business ideas of 1969." That's when two old Harvard pals, Christopher Cerf and George Trow, first mentioned the name of Michael O'Donoghue.

O'Donoghue was the son of an industrial engineer from Buffalo. Expelled from the University of Rochester in his junior year for failing to attend classes and stealing a campus police car, he had a dark streak as wide as the Niagara River and should have come with a warning sign that read CAUTION—DOES NOT PLAY WELL WITH OTHERS. Cerf, the son of famed Random House founder Bennett Cerf, had thought that O'Donoghue's taste for the jugular might make an interesting counterweight to the Harvard grads' brainy irreverence. His street smarts might add a serrated edge to their book smarts.

O'Donoghue was slightly older than Kenney and Beard, and he looked like an urban guerilla in a torn Army surplus jacket, thinning unkempt hair, and a slim brown More cigarette constantly dangling from his mouth. He had made an underground splash writing for *Evergreen Review* and by publishing a lewd, off-beat comic strip parody of adventure stories called *The Adventures of Phoebe Zeit-Geist* (which Garry Trudeau would later cite as an inspiration for *Doonesbury*). But O'Donoghue thought of the Cambridge crowd as "a bunch of Harvard snot faggots who thought it was wrong to shed blood." He preferred to think of comedy as a cruel, venomous attack on propriety—a baby-seal hunt in which no subject, no matter how taboo (cancer, the Holocaust, . . . *baby seals*), was off-limits. He was especially fond of saying that "making people laugh is the lowest form of humor." It was generally agreed that if Kenney and Beard wielded a surgical satirical scalpel with their writing, O'Donoghue used a chain saw.

Desperate to mock up the first issue of the *National Lampoon* by the early spring of 1970, Kenney and Beard were relieved to discover that O'Donoghue had, for years, kept methodical metal filing cabinets full of unpublished pieces and ideas for pieces that had never found an outlet. The three of them essentially wrote all of the magazine's first issue, with Kenney writing the whacked-out dirty stuff, Beard writing the rapier-edged intellectual stuff, and O'Donoghue writing the corrosively outrageous, dangerous stuff. They were part Three Musketeers and part Three Stooges. On their good days, at least. On their worst, Kenney was prone to mysterious disappearances and the short-fused O'Donoghue to ripping phones out of walls when he detected some petty slight against his inarguable genius. Beard was left to mediate, the calm center of the storm.

Eventually, other malcontents and literary sadists would find their way to 635 Madison. In addition to contributions from Christopher Cerf (now an editor at his father's shop, Random House) and George Trow (cozily ensconced at *The New Yorker* and writing under the pseudonym Tamara Gould), there would be the wicked-witted boyfriend-girlfriend tag team of Michel Choquette and Anne Beatts; the absurd, bow-tied eccentricity of Brian McConnachie (who, Kenney insisted, was so strange that he hailed from a distant alien planet); the surly, Cambridge-educated British former stand-up performer Tony Hendra; the gonzo retro visual genius Bruce McCall; and Chris Miller, a gifted short story writer with a sweet tooth for filthy-bordering-on-pornographic male sexual fantasies.

Sean Kelly, an Irish-Catholic college professor in Montreal who would join the ranks shortly after the *National Lampoon*'s inception, recalled that "meeting Henry was like meeting Holden Caulfield. He had that preppy disheveled thing going on, sucking on a pipe. And Doug was obviously some kind of superstar. When you met him you knew that he was not average. He was the brightest star in whatever room he was in. But he was *so* uncomfortable in his own skin. There was nothing he couldn't do, but he was always second-guessing himself. I think he probably always thought he was getting away with something."

With Kenney, Beard, and O'Donoghue working around the clock (Rob Hoffman, always more of a businessman than a writer or editor, was receding into the background), the fourth floor of 635 Madison would soon start to feel like the Island of Misfit Toys—the Algonquin Round Table with a couple of wobbly legs. Just as the *National Lampoon*'s debut issue was about to hit newsstands, in April 1970, *Newsweek* ran a four-paragraph story about the brash publishing-world newcomer under the headline "Postgraduate Humor." It was a pretty rote *Lampoon* origin story, but it wraps up on an oddly cynical, downbeat note. The *Newsweek* writer predicts: "Putting out a monthly that will entertain the nearly-30s may make the three youthful editors old fast."

The article wasn't wrong. The debut "Sexy Cover Issue" in April features a come-hither model wearing a dark, military-green one-piece bathing suit in front of a visually muddy orange-brown background with a cartoon duck leering off to the side (Kenney's misguided attempt to mimic *Playboy*'s bunny mascot). The first issue was aggressively ugly, and its contents more sophomoric than smart or titillating. It sold less than half of the 500,000 copies that had been run off the press. Inside, though, what would soon become the *Lampoon*'s DNA of generational in-jokes and sacred-cow slaughtering was evident, if a little unfocused. There was Aristotle Onassis's lost, pidgin-English love letters to Jackie Kennedy, a gallows-humor piece titled "The Case for Killing Our Aged" (penned by O'Donoghue, naturally), and a lewd, self-pleasuring Dr. Seuss character named Seymour the Splurch. The two brightest standouts were a pair of Kenney contributions: the fictitious Letters page (from correspondents such as fusty Nobel Prize–winning author John Galsworthy, and Renaissance portraitist Hans Holbein begging for smutty pictures) and "Mrs. Agnew's Diary"—a column ostensibly penned by Vice President Spiro Agnew's wife, Judy, that paints the inhabitants of the White House as paranoid, tight-assed rubes who dine on meat loaf and cottage cheese. Both would become recurring features.

Back at Harvard, Kenney and Beard's stumble out of the gate was met with a not-surprising degree of schadenfreude. A recap of the debut issue in *The Harvard Crimson* reads, "It seems that *The National Lampoon* staff culled the poorest secondary school bathroom graffiti to paste together their April issue." It continues, "*The National Lampoon* will be chalked up as a business failure unless the overall quality of the publication improves soon. Plain curiosity helped sell the first issue. The May edition will need some original ideas and more mature humor in order to hold its own on the nationwide newsstands."

Things would get worse before they got better. With Simmons calling the shots on the business side, Hoffman decided to return to Harvard and get an MBA before joining his father's soft-drink-bottling business. Meanwhile, Doug Kenney and Henry Beard were, just as *Newsweek* predicted, getting old very fast indeed, scrambling to fill the magazine every month.

"That was the hardest time," says Beard. "It felt like you had a deadline every eleven days. It was so constant and frantic. The question wasn't: Should we publish this? It was: Can we get two more just like it?"

That June, Kenney and Garcia-Mata got married at her parents' home in the wealthy, white-bread suburb of New Canaan, Connecticut. The two had met as undergraduates while Garcia-Mata was studying at Radcliffe. She was smart, beautiful, and cosmopolitan in a manner to which a self-conscious working-class kid from Chagrin Falls could only aspire. Still, all of Kenney's friends couldn't fathom why he would want to walk down the aisle at twenty-three, especially with someone who couldn't seem to keep pace with his rocket-fueled sense of humor. Kenney himself wasn't quite sure either.

His best man was the musician Peter Ivers, one of his closest friends and confidants at Harvard (in 1983, Ivers would be found in his LA apartment mysteriously bludgeoned to death with a hammer at the age of thirty-six). Lucy Fisher was Ivers's girl-friend at the time, and she recalls asking Kenney shortly before his wedding day why he was getting married so young. "I'll never forget it," she says. "He said, 'I have no idea.' I remember feeling even then that he already seemed a little lost." On the morning of the nuptials, Ivers and Kenney smoked a joint and Ivers offered to call off the wedding, all Kenney had to do was say the word. But, in the end, he went through with it.

"It was a product of momentum rather than determination or intent. One thing leads to another and suddenly you're up there and someone's saying, 'Do you take this woman . . .' and you're like, 'Wait, *what?!*' " remembers Henry Beard.

In a sense, Kenney now had two spouses wrestling for his attention: Garcia-Mata and the magazine where he was now spending ninety to one hundred hours every week. The first five issues of the *Lampoon* would be soul-crushing commercial and creative disappointments. That would all change, though, with the September 1970 issue, the magazine's sixth. Simmons had decided that the magazine's original art directors, an underground band of long-haired, knicker-wearing hash smokers from Cloud Studios who operated out of an East Village storefront, had to go. In came Michael Gross—a twenty-six-year-old Pratt Institute graduate with more aboveground credentials, including a stint at *Cosmopolitan*.

The shake-up instantly cleaned up the magazine's design. The duck mascot was eighty-sixed. The focus sharpened. The covers started to pop. In fact, the cover of that month's "Show Biz" issue was adorned by the image of Minnie Mouse opening her dress like a 42nd Street flasher and revealing a pair of microscopic rodent breasts covered by daisy-shaped pasties. It jumped off the newsstands but not without causing a major headache for Simmons.

The Walt Disney Company sued Twenty First Century Communications for $8 million—way more than the highly leveraged company had in the bank at the time. Not used to humbling himself, Simmons reluctantly groveled at Disney's feet, promising never to parody one of its wholesome characters again. Privately, though, he delighted in the gallons of free ink that the dustup with the Mouse House had produced. It was a marketing masterstroke. Nothing was sacred, not even Minnie freakin' Mouse. *National Lampoon* was suddenly *dangerous*. Circulation began to slowly take off, and within three months the *Lampoon* would finally nudge its way into the black. Advertisers, who had once turned up their noses, were beginning to circle back and sniff around.

By late 1970 and into the first half of 1971, the *Lampoon* was on a roll, smashing taboos and breaking fine china with each new issue. "It was like there was this big ironbound wood door that said 'Thou Shalt Not!,'" says Beard. "We touched it, and it just fell off its hinges. It was incredible." The new misfit-toy recruits were humming with inspired ideas that were tweaked, jazzed up, and spit-polished by Kenney. Although Nixon and his posse of inept West Wing cronies were frequent and obvious targets, liberals (from John Lennon and Yoko Ono to the radical student left) weren't immune from the staff's merciless piñata swings.

"Some people thought the *Lampoon* was a counterculture magazine," says Chris Miller. "God knows we went after Nixon tooth and claw. But we also raked Teddy Kennedy over the coals. It wasn't like we were anti-Republican, pro-Democrat . . . we were just anti-asshole."

Between the exhausting all-nighters, Kenney's increased consumption of alcohol and pot, and a tense marriage that seemed to skip the honeymoon phase altogether, made him begin to show disconcerting signs of becoming unglued. It didn't help that he'd carelessly launched into an indiscreet affair with a female coworker that had become public knowledge around the office. The guilt ate at him. For the most part, he stayed away from home. Beard urged him to slow down. His wife urged him to see a psychiatrist. Instead, Kenney just stepped on the gas pedal.

By early summer, the *Lampoon*'s editorial staff was beginning to brainstorm ideas for its upcoming August "Bummers" issue at its favorite drinking hole, a rank-smelling dive called The Green Man. One of the ideas being kicked around was a hilariously offensive takedown of our neighbors to the north, titled "Canada, the Retarded Giant on Your Doorstep." For the issue's cover, the staff decided to take a cheeky swipe at *Esquire*'s now-infamous 1970 portrait of a smiling Lt. William Calley Jr. posing with Vietnamese children. Calley was a US Army platoon leader who was convicted of murdering 109 unarmed, innocent South Vietnamese civilians in the My Lai Massacre. In the

Lampoon version, Calley would be portrayed by gap-toothed *Mad* magazine poster boy Alfred E. Newman, whose famous catchphrase ("What, me worry?") was turned into: "What, My Lai?" It was right in the *Lampoon's* wheelhouse: stealthily thought-provoking, slightly profane, and more than a little offensive.

Unfortunately, before the issue hit newsstands there would be a more serious bummer closer to home.

2

If You Don't Buy This Magazine . . .

ON THE MORNING of July 4, 1971, Henry Beard woke up to find a note pinned to the mantel over the fireplace written in Doug Kenney's scrawl. It cryptically referred to "the great eye in the sky" and said that he needed to split town.

"Doug was basically saying, I'm gonzo, I'm out of here," says Beard. "My reaction was, you know, What the fuck? He had basically been the strongest presence in the office anytime he was there and suddenly he was gone. He was just burned out. He'd been working like a monkey. But there was a sense of, What the hell are we going to do now?"

Some thought that Kenney's strange, paranoia-laced missive was a suicide note. But Beard suspected otherwise—that his partner had simply been working without a break for a year and a half by that point, secretly (or perhaps not so secretly) buckling under the constant, helter-skelter rhythm of putting out a monthly magazine. He was in the midst of a full-fledged midlife crisis at the age of twenty-four. Still, no one had any clue where the *Lampoon*'s boy genius had vanished to.

Without telling anyone, including his wife, Kenney had boarded a flight to Los Angeles, carrying nothing more than a knapsack, his *Lampoon* American Express card, and exactly one change of underwear. All he knew was that he had to get away; he didn't know for how long. When Kenney arrived at LAX, he took a taxi to the Laurel Canyon home that his friends Peter Ivers and Lucy Fisher were renting. But they hadn't moved in yet. They were still in Berkeley, the last pit stop on a cross-country road trip from Cambridge. So Kenney sweet-talked the landlord into letting him crash there until his friends arrived. When they finally showed up, Ivers and Fisher were greeted at the front door by a smiling Kenney: "Hi, Mom and Dad, I'm home!"

Kenney's lost weekend in LA would last for two months, give or take. Fisher remembers Kenney as seeming like a lost soul— a wounded Peter Pan who wanted only to be taken care of and mothered. Ivers and Fisher did just that. They had breakfast at Schwab's almost every day; Fisher read him bedtime stories; he and Ivers had cap-gun fights in the Hollywood Hills; they went to Disneyland. Kenney was trying to go back to his childhood. Clothes were rarely worn around the house. It was all very early-'70s California.

"This was before anyone had ever heard of the words 'addict' or 'rehab,' " says Fisher. "In our minds, there were no alarm bells with Doug." Fisher knew that Beard and Simmons (not to mention his wife) had to be worried, so she purchased a handful of postcards and urged Kenney to let everyone know he was OK. He finally gave in, scribbling a note to his boss, Simmons. It consisted of just five words: "Next time, try a Yalie!"

Back at the magazine, there was confusion, concern, and more than a little disappointment among the *Lampoon*'s staff. But there were still deadlines to meet. Other writers shared Kenney's workload. The magazine, which had just begun to hit its stride, didn't stumble, thanks to Beard, who was forced to step up as editorial ringleader—a role he didn't particularly want. When Kenney returned, in September, the mood at 635 Madison had turned. The magazine was no longer his; it was Henry's. Kenney skulked into an office full of resentment and tension, mumbling apologies and saying all the right things. Yet a trust had been violated. The man who managed to get along with everyone so effortlessly that Chris Miller had once compared him to "type O blood" was now toxic. Could he be depended on? "The guys were really pissed at him when he came back," Simmons recalls. "They felt Doug had betrayed them."

Recalls Beard, "It wasn't like 'You stabbed us in the back, you piece of shit!' But there was a certain tentative quality . . . Are you *really* back?"

Shortly after returning, Kenney and his wife, Garcia-Mata, began the process of getting a divorce. The marriage had lasted just over a year. Simmons, desperate to find a way to keep his biggest and brightest star happy and committed, sent Kenney on a grassroots speaking tour of college campuses to help spread the *Lampoon* gospel. Kenney was eager to hit the road and leave his messy life behind. Speaking in front of lecture halls packed with *Lampoon* adoring undergraduates who were still swept up in the new freedoms of the late '60s, Kenney was treated like a rock star—a counterculture prophet dropping head-shop references and cracking down-with-Nixon jokes. He decided that he could get used to the showbiz glare of klieg lights and fame.

At one stop at UCLA in March of 1972, Kenney gave a rambling and often hilarious speech about the magazine's success, some of its greatest hits, and the squares that didn't understand his generation of longhairs. The students ate it up. It felt like a manic and (literally) half-baked stand-up routine. When asked by one UCLA student about his plans for the future, Kenney responded, "My plans are these: I'm going to stick around the magazine for two and a half more years and try to rip off as much money as possible. Then write a book, which should take about six months, called *Teenage Commies From Outer Space*, and then smoke a lot of dope."

Eventually, Simmons called Kenney back to New York, where his gonzo ideas and inimitable writing voice were needed, and where the iciness toward him had thawed a bit. The prodigal son dutifully returned. Briefly.

In the fall of '72, Kenney would disappear again. This time, no one was surprised. It was just Doug being Doug. True to his UCLA career forecast (although not its timetable), Kenney high-tailed it to Martha's Vineyard to work on his era-defining literary masterpiece, *Teenage Commies From Outer Space*. He predicted that it would be nothing short of "the best recollection of youth ever written"—a mix of *Huckleberry Finn* and *The Catcher in the Rye*, but with a trippy sci-fi twist.

Kenney camped in a tent on a remote piece of land in the woods of West Tisbury owned by singer-songwriter James Taylor. There he dropped copious amounts of LSD looking for inspiration. As winter kicked in, and tent living became unfeasible, he moved to a house on a windy bluff on the westernmost point of the island in Gay Head, where he toiled on his novel in total seclusion and rarely bothered to eat anything that didn't come in blotter form.

While Kenney was AWOL, three things happened back at the *Lampoon*: First, the magazine finally started to make serious inroads with advertisers. While it had been headquartered *on* Madison Avenue, it was never *of* Madison Avenue. The big ad agencies and their deep-pocketed clients had initially been put off by the *Lampoon*'s tasteless monthly orgies of anti-establishment grenade-lobbing and playground gross-out humor. Now, with circulation finally spiking past 500,000 copies per month, the magazine had moved out of the underground. Advertisers lined up.

Second, Simmons was approached by RCA to come up with a *National Lampoon* comedy album—a genre that had suddenly become lucrative thanks to the hip "head" humor of George Carlin, Cheech and Chong, and the Firesign Theatre. Christopher Guest, a twenty-four-year-old musician-comedian with a knack for deadpan mimicry and a childhood friend of *Lampoon* publisher Gerry Taylor, was brought on board as a contributor on the strength of his hilarious, Xerox-sharp send-ups of sacred cows Bob Dylan and James Taylor. The resulting album, which was actually put out by Blue Thumb after RCA got cold feet from some of the record's edgier material, was *National Lampoon's Radio Dinner*, a freewheeling collage of savage song parodies such as the Beatles-inspired "Magical Misery Tour," which sniped at rock's most sanctimonious icons with marksman precision. Recorded in less than three days, it would go on to sell surprisingly well and win a Grammy.

Third, on December 10, 1972, the *Lampoon's* pirate's ship of verbal swashbucklers was anointed by none other than the Newspaper of Record, *The New York Times*. In a feature written by Mopsy Strange Kennedy, the core writers and editors put on a manic show of canned wordplay and clever-boy shtick. It would end up becoming great PR. But if you quickly scanned the article, it would have been easy to miss the one person absent from all of the naughty, quip-happy mirth. At least, until you get to a parenthetical halfway through the piece mentioning that Kenney was currently on a leave of absence while working on a book. The wording almost made his desertion sound like it was officially approved—that there were no hard feelings (which was definitely not the case). Still, with the *Times's* benediction, the *Lampoon's* profile was soaring and its staffers were starting to walk with a swagger.

A month later, with its January 1973 "Death" issue, the

Lampoon would produce the most famous cover in its history. The idea came from Ed Bluestone, an occasional contributor and cranky stand-up comedian from New Jersey with a weakness for comedy that left a bruise. The cover would feature an adorable black-and-white mutt with a revolver pointed to its head next to the headline: "If You Don't Buy This Magazine, We'll Kill This Dog." It was shocking, sick, subversive, and cruel. It sold out in days.

The *Lampoon* was doing just fine without Kenney.

• •

After the success of *Radio Dinner*, the *Lampoon*'s record label was hounding Simmons for a follow-up album. They quickly settled on *Lemmings*—a send-up of the 1969 Woodstock music festival that lacerated both the generation of zonked-out, easily herded hippies who saw it as a heavy, meaning-packed pilgrimage, but also the greedy musicians who lined their pockets while paying blissed-out lip service to peace and love. One thing that the *Lampoon* always had a gift for was calling out hypocrisy, even within its own ranks. They could dish it out *and* take it. And they knew that baby boomers were a lot more materialistic and gullible than they copped to.

Simmons believed that the concept would work better if the concert were performed in a live setting where you could hear people actually laughing rather than in a stifling and silent recording studio. So he booked the Village Gate, a cavernous cellar-level jazz club on the corner of Thompson and Bleecker Streets in New York, and handed *Lampoon* staffer Tony Hendra the directing reins while drafting Sean Kelly as his lieutenant. Since *Lemmings* would be loaded with rock music, Hendra wasted no time going back to Christopher Guest, his satirical songwriting ace (and future maestro of the mockumentary film genre). Hendra asked Guest if he could think of any other performers who might work in the cast of the stage show. If they knew how to play an instrument, even better. One person came to Guest's mind, a former Bard College classmate with a funny name who'd once played drums with an early incarnation of Steely Dan.

Cornelius Crane Chase was given the name Chevy in childhood by his grandmother on his father's side. It's unclear whether the nickname came from the posh Maryland suburb or the medieval English song, "The Ballad of Chevy Chase." Chase came from a privileged background. His father was a publishing executive and his mother a concert pianist who had been adopted as a child by her stepfather, the wealthy industrial heir Cornelius Vanderbilt Crane. Chevy grew up in a Park Avenue brownstone on the same block as New York mayor John Lindsay and attended a handful of tony private schools—most of which expelled him for acting up. After college, he worked for a time writing spoofs for *Mad* magazine and performing with an obscure underground video collective called Channel One (essentially a crude, shoestring forerunner to *Saturday Night Live*) that would go on to make a feature film comprising absurd skits, called *The Groove Tube*.

Despite Chase's lightning sarcasm and seemingly boundless confidence bordering on smugness, he always saw himself more as a writer than a performer. But Guest gave him the confidence to come out from behind the scenes. It didn't hurt that Chase also possessed the sort of athletic, dimple-chinned good looks that would stand out on a poster outside the theater.

Next, Hendra flew to Chicago to check out a twenty-two-year-old who he heard was burning up the stage with Second City, the famed improv troupe. John Belushi knew that the *Lampoon* scout was coming and he knew that he had to be ready. Ambitious and hungry for the break that would take him to New York, Belushi laid waste to the club that night, tearing up the stage like a

barrel-chested typhoon. That sort of me-first showboating—
hogging the spotlight, going for the selfish laugh at all costs—
went against everything Second City stood for, but Belushi wasn't
about to let this opportunity slip through his fingers. He could
apologize to his fellow performers later.

Started in 1959, Second City grew out of a 125-seat cabaret
on the Near North Side of Chicago. The space had previously
been a hat shop and a Chinese laundry. There, a new kind of
comedy was born. Rooted in improvisational theater techniques
and built on an all-for-one foundation of trust, risk-taking, and
listening to your scene partner and building off their ad-libs (their
credo was "Yes, and . . ."), Second City quickly became an in-
cubator for some of the sharpest minds in humor. It was comedy
without a net, where off-the-cuff scenes could just as easily go
disastrously wrong as electrically, hilariously right. The group
was named after a condescending 1952 article by A.J. Liebling in
The New Yorker, which dismissively referred to Chicago as a second city in contrast to New York. The troupe wore that mockery
as an underdog badge of honor.

The first generation of Second City performers grew out of
the Compass Players, a brainy group of University of Chicago
alumni that included Mike Nichols and Elaine May. And, in the
early years, their performances were arch, buttoned-down intellectual affairs, with jokes about Freudian analysis, Beatniks,
and the Cold War. But in the volatile late '60s and early '70s, as
the political mood in the country started to tack right and the
counterculture started to push back, a new generation of performers turned Second City into a vibrant, anything-goes forum for topical mayhem, druggie humor, and joy-buzzer flights
of wild pop culture absurdity. In addition to Belushi, the Next
Generation of satirists taking over Second City included Brian
Doyle-Murray (a blue-collar, lunch-pail Chicago prankster with

a voice like broken glass and a soft comic touch), Harold Ramis (a bookish-looking beanpole with owlish glasses, a big frizzy explosion of hair, and a taste for garish paisley shirts and bell-bottoms), and Joe Flaherty (a tall and gangly magician at conjuring oddball characters). "Back then, music was all that people were interested in," says Flaherty. "No one did comedy. A lot of us didn't like stand-up that much. They'd come on TV and be so corny. But the idea of getting a group of people together and improvising and creating scenes, it was an outlet. We wanted to say something, I guess. And we did that through comedy."

Belushi was the burly, bearded son of Albanian immigrants who had grown up in Wheaton, Illinois, where his father owned a pair of restaurants. He looked like a college middle linebacker whose off-season training consisted of eating hot dogs in front of the TV. He could be tremendously quiet and shy offstage, but he seemed to transform into an angry, cornered bull on it—an insane improv Jekyll and Hyde who threw his fireplug body around with no regard for either his own physical safety or the physical safety of his Second City partners. To him, comedy wasn't cerebral; it was a back-alley brawl.

Belushi joined Second City in 1971 and quickly eclipsed Ramis as the star of the troupe. Ramis might have been able to fire off more-highbrow references, but he was no match for Belushi's feral magnetism, desperate bravery, and live-wire unpredictability.

"John would start improvising, and everybody would look at their watches and say, 'Oh, Jesus,' and he'd be off," said Ramis. "But you forgave it, because you liked him and it was funny. He made us all look good. John lifted us all and took us with him."

Tony Hendra knew the moment that he saw Belushi take ownership of the Second City stage that he had found the star of *Lemmings*—and maybe more. "What appealed to me was that nothing was sacred to him. He was saying even Second City isn't sacred to me if I want something," says Hendra. "Belushi was pure street gut. Here was the generation: raw energy and instinctive skepticism, naive and knowing, an animal well aware that there were rules but yet to be convinced that they made any sense." Simmons would refer to Belushi as a "young Albanian hoodlum." Hendra rounded out the *Lemmings* cast with a roster of rising talents who had both music and performing chops, including Paul Jacobs, Garry Goodrow, Mary-Jennifer Mitchell, and Alice Playten. They would all quickly learn that there wasn't much room for ego or competitiveness in the show—Chase and Belushi already had that covered.

Lemmings opened at the Village Gate on January 25, 1973. The first half was a scattershot series of shticky *Lampoon* skits that didn't quite congeal. But the second half, which satirically focused on the fictitious Woodchuck festival, including cutting parodies of Joan Baez, James Taylor, Bob Dylan, and Joe Cocker, hit an exposed generational nerve. The mock concert was occasionally interrupted by Belushi's kamikaze master of ceremonies, who invited the audience to commit mass suicide—a dark, gallows-humor rebuke to the era's good vibes, curdling the Edenic notions of peace and love until they turned sour.

The day after *Lemmings* opened, the *New York Times* critic Mel Gussow weighed in, saying that the first act was "a headlong, supposedly comic assault on sex and politics [that] suffers from a serious case of the puerilities." But, he went on, "in the second act the show mercifully finds its wits for a wicked parody of the world of rock, spoofing the talented along with the pretenders, their absurdities, conceits, and affectations." Audiences in their teens and early twenties ate it up. Even the rock icons who were made fun of, like Dylan and Taylor, showed up either out of curiosity or to publicly show that they could take a joke. Originally scheduled to play for just three nights, *Lemmings* would run for 385 performances.

Belushi was hooked on his newfound recognition. It certainly beat doing eight shows a week at Second City back in Chicago. "I can remember coming out of my apartment on 13th Street and Third Avenue just after it opened, buying the papers and sitting down in a greasy spoon," he later said. "I opened *The New York Times* and there was something like 'new discovery, John Belushi.' I felt like I was three feet off the ground."

Soon the *Lemmings* crew started to come around the *Lampoon* office in their free time. Simmons, now a newly minted off-Broadway producer in addition to a successful magazine publisher and Grammy winner, began dreaming up grandiose new ways to extend the *Lampoon* brand. He settled on a syndicated weekly radio show to be spearheaded by Michael O'Donoghue that would make use of not only the *Lemmings* actors but also the *Lampoon* staffers, who were now beginning to see the seductive allure of fame.

Everyone agreed that the presence of the *Lemmings* performers around the office was a shot in the arm—a sorely needed jolt of new energy and enthusiasm after three years of grinding out a monthly magazine. But with them came a flaunting of recreational vices that had, for the most part, been indulged behind closed doors at the *Lampoon* office: marijuana, LSD, quaaludes, and occasionally cocaine, which was expensive enough to be considered a splurge. They weren't just impersonating rock stars onstage, they were living like them off of it. "You walked into the *Lampoon* office and you got a contact high," says Simmons. "Everyone was smoking pot. Especially when the show came, because Chevy and Belushi were heavily into drugs."

Kelly remembers sitting behind the typewriter in his office at the *Lampoon*, and like clockwork every afternoon, Belushi would poke his head in and say, "Get me high?"

"John loved drugs," says Kelly. "But he also loved alcohol and food and sex and acting. He was like an omnivore. He would smoke or drink whatever was available."

Doug Kenney would return to the *Lampoon* just in time.

◆ ◆

In the winter of 1973, Kenney showed up unannounced at 635 Madison. It had been nearly a year since the wunderkind editor had gone missing. He was thinner, his hair longer, and he carried a half-finished manuscript under an arm. He went into Beard's office and closed the door. Rather than make small talk or catch up with his old friend, Kenney handed him the stack of papers and asked him to read it. Beard was confused by the unfinished novel he was reading. Where was Doug's genius? Where was the promised "best recollection of youth ever written"? Beard tried to be tactful, but Kenney could tell by the puzzled expression on his face exactly what he thought.

"It sucks, doesn't it?" Kenney asked. But he seemed to already know the answer. Beard gave it to him anyway. It was a mess. Kenney picked up his one and only manuscript of *Teenage Commies From Outer Space* and threw it into the wastebasket. It was the first time in his life that something creative didn't come off easily and brilliantly for him on the first try. What now?

The fortunes of the *Lampoon* looked very different from when Kenney bolted off to play Robinson Crusoe on the Vineyard. They had put out an album, mounted a hit stage show, and become the fastest-growing magazine in America. Kenney was relieved that his unannounced departure hadn't left everyone in the lurch, but maybe also a bit deflated that the *Lampoon* had thrived in his absence. With his divorce finalized, Kenney moved out of the brownstone he shared with Beard and got a place of his own on Bank Street in the West Village. Soon he would be spending more and more time hanging out with the *Lemmings* cast whenever they'd pass through the radio studio, especially Belushi, who often crashed on Kenney's couch after a late-night bender. The two had an instant connection and a mutual fondness for getting high. The door to Kenney's apartment was always open to him. Literally. He never bothered locking it.

With Beard now single-handedly holding the editorial horsewhip, Kenney was able to stop worrying about being a leader (not that anyone would have followed him anywhere after his pair of vanishing acts) and just focus on writing. Simmons was eager to put his long-absent star back to work on his latest project: *The 1964 High School Yearbook Parody*. The assignment couldn't have played to Kenney's strengths better. After all, the 1950s and early '60s were Kenney's singular obsession. High school, in particular, seemed to have an especially strong psychological vise grip on him. It reached back to his lonely childhood in Chagrin Falls, the small, Norman Rockwellian Ohio town with a population of seemingly idyllic Ozzie-and-Harriet nuclear families with sons in varsity jackets and virtuous, virginal pom-pom-waving daughters. He had been an outcast there, but he knew its tribal rites and rituals in his marrow. Part of him seemed to long for its orderly Eisenhower-era simplicity (a time when his older bother was still young and vibrant and alive), and part of him seemed hell-bent on exposing its milquetoast conformity and middle-class hypocrisy and tearing it all down.

Kenney was partnered for the better part of a year on the *Yearbook* project with a recent *Lampoon* hire named P. J. O'Rourke—a young, chain-smoking renegade from Toledo with a vicious sarcastic streak. Based on an idea that Kenney and O'Donoghue had come up with together for the *Lampoon*'s November 1970 "Nostalgia" issue, the *Yearbook* would be a special stand-alone publication that elaborately replicated and riffed on the social hierarchies and archetypes of heartland adolescence at a fictional school named C. Estes Kefauver Memorial High School in Dacron, Ohio. The genius of it would lay in the jeweler precision of its details.

Kenney and O'Rourke combed through dozens of school newspapers and yearbooks, identifying the various social castes like zoologists classifying insects. Kenney would later say, "It was chilling to see how much they were all the same. Bully, clown, intelligent introvert, politician, proto-homosexual. It was Nazi social engineering. By weight of social pressure these people became these things." With the *Yearbook*, Kenney took those stereotypes and simply exaggerated them. He was cranking out some of the funniest and most pitch-perfect satire he'd ever written. The best inside joke, of course, was saved for last: the requisite "In Memoriam" page dedicated to a deceased classmate—the popular and handicapped Howie Havermeyer.

The picture of Howie is actually Kenney's own crew-cut high school yearbook photo. Across the picture someone has scrawled, "What a dipshit!" *Harper's Magazine* called the *Lampoon*'s *High School Yearbook Parody*: "A literary masterpiece. The best work of collective writing since the King James Bible." It would go on to sell more than a million and a half copies.

Kenney was back. . . .

And O'Donoghue was out. Increasingly prone to destructive, diva-like tirades, Michael O'Donoghue had finally had enough. After his girlfriend, Anne Beatts, had her office at the *Lampoon* taken away without sufficient respect shown or explanation given, O'Donoghue stormed out and never looked back. That summer, Simmons handed the *Lampoon Radio Hour* to Belushi, who had just finished a run with the *Lemmings* touring company. It was an odd choice. No one would have ever pegged Belushi as the management type, but Simmons was eager to keep him within the *Lampoon* orbit. Plus, Simmons was already beginning to flirt with the idea of another stage show and would need the breakout star of *Lemmings* as its marquee draw. Belushi now had to find a new stable of acting talent to fill the air every week. He didn't have to look far.

"John called me up and said that I needed to come to New York right away," said Harold Ramis. "He sounded like a gold prospector who'd hit a vein and was now saying that there were riches to be had for all of us. Come East! Come East! He invited me and Brian Doyle-Murray from Second City in Chicago and then he brought in Joe Flaherty and Gilda Radner from Toronto. The idea was that while we worked on the *Radio Hour* we'd develop a cabaret show to tour under the *Lampoon* name."

Ramis was itching for a new challenge. He had been performing at Second City on and off since 1968. Before that, the son of Chicago shopkeepers had grown up on Marx Brothers movies and attended Washington University in St. Louis. After graduating, he worked as an orderly in a mental institution, a substitute teacher, a freelance reporter at the *Chicago Daily News*, and eventually became *Playboy*'s party joke editor. By the time he arrived at the *Lampoon* in his late twenties, Ramis was already married and gave off the lanky, mellow, and slightly nerdy air of a suburban psychiatrist, albeit one with a playful, subversive streak. His eyes always seemed to be at half-mast, as if he had just woken up from a long nap or smoked a very potent joint— or perhaps both.

Although Second City and the *Lampoon* shared similar genetic strands, Ramis quickly learned that they were, in fact, quite different worlds. "There was a tremendous arrogance around the *Lampoon*," he said. "They believed they were—and maybe they were—the smartest people writing comedy at the time. They were really smart. It was almost frightening. And very cruel. They attacked anyone's weakness or sensitivity. It was a very predatory atmosphere. Second City was always more of a benign enterprise."

Brian Doyle-Murray had been at Second City with Ramis since 1968, the year that Chicago seemed to be erupting between the city's race riots in the spring, the tear-gas violence of the Democratic National Convention in the summer, and ultimately the surreal circus of the Chicago Seven trial. Doyle-Murray, who added "Doyle" (his grandmother's maiden name) so as not to be confused with a South African stage actor of the same name, grew up in Wilmette, a well-to-do suburb just north of the city. His Irish-Catholic father was a salesman at J. J. Barney Lumber Company, a profession that the six Murray boys and three Murray girls would joke (or half-joke) allowed him to bring home free wooden yardsticks to discipline them. Like several others of the Murray boys, Brian grew up caddying at private golf clubs in the swankier Chicago suburbs to earn tuition money for parochial school. Beneath Doyle-Murray's button-down Bob Newhart appearance and gravelly, rock-tumbler voice lay a barbed and merciless, sadistic sense of humor.

With Ramis, Doyle-Murray, Flaherty, and Radner now in New York, Belushi finally had a stock company. Doug Kenney was the first to start regularly hanging around the radio studio with the new arrivals. Part of it might have had to do with Kenney's own secret desire to become famous as more than just a writer, and part of it might have been that he felt that he was still on thin ice with the *Lampoon* staff after abandoning them. Either way, Kenney was again the office's transfusion of type O blood.

Kenney and Ramis first met during the taping of a *Moby-Dick* radio parody that Sean Kelly had written. They immediately hit it off. Belushi played the part of Ahab, Ramis was Starbuck, and

Kenney portrayed a random sailor who finds an apple in a worm barrel.

"Doug liked our company," said Ramis. "He was as smart as anyone I ever knew. I remember once he came over to my apartment and he stood at my bookcase, closed his eyes, and randomly pulled a book out and turned to a page and started reading aloud. And at some point he started improvising and you couldn't tell where the book ended and Doug's improvising began. He could do it with any book on the shelf. It was his little parlor trick."

After a few months, the Second City crowd was beginning to blend in at the *Lampoon* office. They were all becoming one organic unit. Then, one morning, Sean Kelly recalls, he got off the elevator on the eleventh floor to open the radio studio and found something strange in the reception area. "There was a dude curled up asleep on the couch," he says. "My first thought was that someone had let in a homeless guy because he looked pretty rough and ragged and he was snoring. He might have smelled too. That's how I met Bill Murray."

Live from New York

JOHN BELUSHI HAD SUMMONED BILL Murray from Chicago. He'd called the twenty-three-year-old at Second City and told him to pack his bags and take the overnight bus to New York that evening. "Belushi was really instrumental in dragging everyone out," says Murray. "He said there's easy pickings out here in New York. So one by one we came out, and we found that we could survive there and liked it there. Actors from Chicago either had to go to New York or LA. And at Second City we thought of ourselves as *serious actors*, and serious actors went to New York."

Belushi had given Doyle-Murray's little brother the address of the *Lampoon* building—but nothing more than that to go on. So, after getting off the bus at the Port Authority terminal, Bill headed for 635 Madison, talked his way past security, and took the elevator up to the eleventh floor, where he found the closest thing to a bed he'd seen in days. That's where Sean Kelly first set eyes on "the most unkempt, fucked-up looking human I'd ever seen." In one short year at Second City, Murray had established himself as Belushi's heir apparent—an instant star who gave off an anything-could-happen sense of lunatic danger every time he bounded on stage. He had certainly taken a circuitous route to get there.

Five years younger than Brian, Bill was the fifth of the nine Murray kids tightly packed in at 1930 Elmwood Avenue in Wilmette, a three-bedroom house on a tree-lined street across from the Sisters of Christian Charity convent. In school, when he wasn't getting his knuckles rapped by the priests, he developed an interest in theater, mainly because it was the only way to meet girls while at Loyola Academy, his all-boys Catholic school. Other than that, his only experience performing had been trying to make his father laugh at the dinner table. Like his brothers, Bill worked at nearby golf clubs in the summer to earn money for tuition. It was the Murray way.

"I started as a shag boy at Indian Hill in Winnetka when I was ten," says Murray. "A guy would hit balls from the driving range, and I'd run out and collect them. You were basically a human target. They'd hit the ball right at you. And you wouldn't be able to pick it up until it was too late, so you'd block them with your body. That's how we paid our way through Loyola. Then you'd work your way up to caddie. First, B caddie where you carried one bag and didn't get paid much. Then A caddie, where you got paid full freight because you carried doubles. Being a caddie, you learned how to treat people. Most people don't have a job where you're asked to carry a heavy load no matter the weather and don't speak unless spoken to. It was an extraordinary education."

Hard work was something that Murray's father drilled into his kids before he passed away from diabetes, in 1967. He was forty-six; Bill was just seventeen. "I remember the first time I met Bill," said Ramis. "Brian and I were in Second City together and he said, 'Why don't you come up and have dinner at my mother's house?' And we stopped off at the golf course. Bill had just graduated high school and his job at the time was running the hot dog stand on the ninth hole of the Wilmette public course."

Recalls Murray, "Harold was like a mythical creature back then, because he'd once had a job as a joke writer for *Playboy!* He even had an apartment! He was in a very different category from the rest of us when I first met him."

If Murray looked up to Ramis, he absolutely idolized his older brother Brian. Bill could make people laugh, but he wasn't sure he had what it took to do it in front of a crowd in the Second City footlights. After graduating from high school, Murray enrolled at Regis College in Denver as a premed student. True to his work ethic, he also got a sideline job that brought in a lot of money: dealing weed. In 1972, on his twentieth birthday, Murray was arrested while boarding a TWA flight out of O'Hare airport. Unable to produce ID to show that he was young enough to qualify for an under-twenty-one discount fare, Murray joked, "That's too bad. I wanted to get on 'cause I got two bombs in my suitcase." The joke didn't go over very well. Murray walked away and tried to stash his luggage in a locker, but he didn't have any change. The police caught up with him and searched his bag. They found eight-and-a-half pounds of marijuana, worth roughly $20,000. Murray spent the rest of his birthday in jail. "It was stupid, but I guess I was turning myself in," said Murray. "I did do one good thing: I ate a check this guy had given me that was in the suitcase, and that guy owes me his life and reputation."

Released on probation, Murray dropped out of school and returned to Chicago, where he auditioned for one of Second City's improv workshops. He bombed the tryout. Then, a short while later, he had a run-in that would change his life. "It was Christmastime. Bells were ringing. There under the clock at Marshall Field, I met the head of the workshop, and he said, 'We'd like to offer you a scholarship, if you want to come back.' The bells were going *bong, bong, bong,* and I figured it was a miracle."

Following in his brother's footsteps, he soon landed a spot on Second City's main stage. His most famous character there was a side-talking doofus he called the Honker. Murray would jut his lower jaw out, twist his lips, and speak with a deranged mush-mouthed lisp, sounding drunk or brain-damaged or both. Murray would slip into his Honker alter ego whenever the mood struck him, whether he was on stage at Second City, accosting random people in the streets, or simply running into a busy Chicago intersection and randomly deciding to direct traffic.

When Murray showed up at the *Lampoon* office in New York, he brought the Honker and an arsenal of other outsize characters he'd been working on, such as an early, oily version of Nick the Lounge Singer. He proved right away that he was a gifted improviser on the air—that he belonged with the brain trust of older, more seasoned *Radio Hour* performers. "Bill turned out to be tremendous in the studio," says Sean Kelly. "He was marvelous ad-libbing when the tape was running, especially when he was with Christopher Guest. They were like Peter Cook and Dudley Moore. And to be able to keep it deadpan like they did. What they could do was rare."

Murray also quickly developed a reputation as being temperamental and having a short, sometimes violent, fuse. He could fly into black rages at the slightest provocation. One time, Murray barged into Matty Simmons's office demanding to know why $1.20 was missing from his paycheck. Simmons told him to go to the accounting department, but Murray wouldn't leave. Simmons eventually stood up from his desk and fired him on the spot. He hired him back the next day.

But if Murray had one personality trait that seemed to dominate it was his attitude of casual indifference. He just didn't seem to care whether you liked him or not. It didn't even seem to weigh on his mind. When Murray was still at Second City, Ramis was visiting from New York. The show's producer asked the improv veteran if he would talk to Murray about his bullying volatility with his fellow performers. "I remember sitting down with Bill and saying, 'You know, a lot of people in the cast are pissed off at you,'" said Ramis. "And he said, '*Yeeee-eah.*' I said, 'Do you care?' He said, '*Nnn-o.*' So I said, 'Okay, good talk.' And that was it. That kind of defined him."

By the fall of 1974, the new Second City arrivals had been moonlighting between putting out a weekly *Lampoon* radio show and writing and rehearsing the follow-up to *Lemmings*, creatively titled *The National Lampoon Show*. The cast comprised Belushi, Doyle-Murray, Radner, Flaherty, and Ramis. Doug Kenney wrote a Patty Hearst sketch for the show, but most of the material was hatched by the Second City actors themselves. When the revue headed to Philadelphia to kick off a series of one- and two-night stands, Bill Murray was left behind, relegated to the role of understudy and tasked with holding down the fort at the radio studio with Kenney. The two hit it off. "Doug was one of the great guys," says Murray. "He enabled so many people to succeed. People like Chevy, Chris Guest, and myself. At the *Lampoon*, at one time, there was more talent in that building than anywhere else in the world."

Out on the road, it didn't take long for problems to bubble up. Belushi, the de facto leader of the troupe (based on both the hard-charging hurricane force of his personality and the seniority of his tenure under the *Lampoon* banner), was trying to out-*Lampoon* the *Lampoon* by ratcheting up the venom in the show. His instincts always seemed to tell him to push the boundaries further and further until the audience either bent to his will or snapped and walked out. "The *Lampoon* and Belushi had their own approach to comedy, which was basically insulting the audience," says Flaherty. "Belushi said they loved it, but I couldn't get into it. We were taking potshots at everybody."

In particular, Flaherty points to a sadistic musical parody of Cole Porter's "You're the Tops" called "You're the Pits," aimed at the very people who had paid to see the show. Flaherty eventually decided to leave and go back to the calmer waters of Second City. Making matters more complicated, Doyle-Murray had fallen into a lopsided romance with Radner on the road. The sting of unreciprocated love was too much for him to bear every night, so he returned to the *Radio Hour* and let his little brother take his spot. Like Belushi, Bill Murray had no problem dishing out abuse from the stage on a nightly basis.

In Toronto, *The National Lampoon Show* was booked for two weeks at a club called the El Mocambo. It was a friendlier audience—and also marked a homecoming of sorts, since the city had its own Second City outpost that included Eugene Levy and John Candy. After the show, the cast would party late into the night at a tiny after-hours bar owned by another young Second City Toronto cast member named Dan Aykroyd. Also in the crowd at the El Mocambo was Ivan Reitman, a hungry Canadian movie producer who knew Radner and was knocked back on his heels by what he was seeing.

"In the late '60s, my generation took itself a little too seriously," says Reitman. "We were pretty fucking earnest. And finally, you had this group that just seemed like the future of comedy. Watching them was like grabbing an electrical wire. I knew that this was it. It spoke to me in a way that nothing else ever had."

At twenty-seven, Reitman had already produced a handful of disreputably schlocky and mildly risqué B movies in Canada. He'd also directed a 1973 horror-movie parody called *Cannibal Girls*. His résumé didn't quite jibe with a serious and slightly nerdy demeanor that was, no doubt, informed by a bleak child-hood. Reitman's mother was an Auschwitz survivor, and his father had fought with the Resistance during World War II. The family had fled Czechoslovakia when Ivan was four. Reitman's biggest professional success had been as a producer of *The Magic Show*, a hit Broadway extravaganza starring the corny Canadian illusionist Doug Henning. It ran for five years.

Sitting in the El Mocambo, being jolted into revelation by the *Lampoon's* electric current, Reitman knew that what he was wit-nessing was the future—and he needed to be a part of it. Reitman cold-called Simmons at the *Lampoon* office in New York and laid out a proposition. He offered to produce *The National Lampoon Show* when it returned to New York for its stage run there in exchange for the opportunity to adapt the show into a movie which he would direct. He thought it could be his ticket to Hollywood. "I don't think Matty was particularly impressed by my credits," says Reitman. "But he was impressed by the fact that I'd done a very successful Broadway show."

Simmons was eventually worn down by Reitman's pushy per-sistence and agreed. The Canadian desperately wanted to work with *The Lampoon Show*'s cast. But the feeling was hardly mu-tual. When Reitman arrived for his first day of rehearsal in New York, he wore a wool hat, a long scarf, and a heavy parka. He walked into the room and smiled, flashing his oversize piano-key teeth, and introduced himself to the performers while tak-ing off his jacket. When he was finished, Bill Murray put an arm around his shoulder, picked up the clothes he'd taken off, and put them back on him piece by piece. He steered Reitman to the door, gently guided him out like a stray, and slammed the door shut behind him. Reitman couldn't muster the nerve to come back for two days.

After its run of out-of-town previews, a retooled version of

The National Lampoon Show finally opened on March 2, 1975, at the New Palladium, a cabaret underneath the Time & Life Building near Rockefeller Center in midtown Manhattan. During one memorable evening, the comedian Martin Mull was sitting at a table near the stage talking loudly and derisively with some friends as Murray was in the middle of his Honker routine. According to Simmons, Murray shot Mull a deadly look. But it didn't put an end to Mull's heckling. So Murray jumped off the stage and lunged into the audience, where he grabbed Mull by the throat and shook him until Belushi had to restrain him.

The reviews for *The National Lampoon Show* were mixed, mostly comparing it unfavorably with *Lemmings*. In *The New York Times*, Mel Gussow wrote, "Often there is a great gap, a comic void, between idea and execution." The one cast member that the *Times* critic singled out was its whirling dervish leader, Belushi. Still, the actors weren't trying to appeal to the *Times* or its establishment subscribers. They were speaking to a rowdier, younger audience who thought along the same frequency. The show would end up running for 180 performances over four months. The twin streams of Second City and the *National Lampoon* had finally formed a single river whose current would prove to be unstoppable for the next decade. "We all felt very confident that we were somehow going to be the next wave of comedy," said Ramis. "That somehow our style would begin to dominate."

He wasn't the only one who thought so. Sitting in the audience at the New Palladium on several consecutive nights was a young Canadian writer-producer in a corduroy blazer and a Hawaiian shirt. His name was Lorne Michaels.

◆◆

Back at the magazine, as 1974 was drawing to a close, it was dawning on Matty Simmons that the deadline for the buyout clause he had hammered out with Kenney, Beard, and their business-minded consigliere Rob Hoffman during the *Lampoon's* founding five years earlier was rapidly approaching. It couldn't have come at a more inconvenient time. The good news was that the *Lampoon* was solidly in the black. Circulation was mushrooming and earnings were soaring. The bad news was that the contract called for Simmons to cough up a now-ludicrous sum that he didn't have. Thanks to a crash in the stock market the previous year, the Harvard Three stood to receive a payday in the neighborhood of $6 million. In a sense, Simmons had been a victim of his and the magazine's own success.

Simmons and his partner, Len Mogel, sat down with Kenney, Beard, and Hoffman (who came up from Dallas, where he was now working for his father). Hoffman would do the negotiating just as he had five years earlier, although this time he had much more leverage. Simmons appealed to their sense of fairness, explaining how the swooning stock market had put him in a financial pickle. He asked if they could wait until the market bounced back. Hoffman, playing hardball, said no. Simmons floated other, more creative payout structures. But again, no sale. The negotiations turned tense. Essentially, it boiled down to an unpalatable binary decision for Simmons: He could either hand over control of the magazine to the three men and work for *them*, or find a way to pay up.

Kenney and Beard had stayed silent through all of the back-and-forth. They went out of the room and talked it over. "We simply couldn't find a middle ground," says Beard. "And at one point, Doug said to me, 'Look, it's your call. If you want to go on with this and basically run the magazine, I'll sign on.' I thought about it and said, 'I think we better take the money and run.'"

According to Simmons, when the three men came back into the room, Kenney started jumping up and down, screaming,

"*I want my money! I want my money!*" Mogel got up and threatened to punch him in the nose. After a few heated beats, all five men in the room started cracking up. Simmons picked up the phone and called his friend Steve Ross, the chairman of Warner Communications, and arranged for a loan to cover the payout.

When all of the *i*'s were dotted and *t*'s crossed, the Harvard Three would all become overnight millionaires. Kenney and Beard received $2.8 million each, and Hoffman headed back to Dallas $1.9 million richer. Simmons admits that Hoffman simply out-negotiated him. Said Kenney later, "Hardly anyone reads contracts. I certainly don't. We lucked into something that I don't even totally understand."

Although the buyout occurred behind closed doors and directly involved only five people, the aftershocks were felt throughout the entire *Lampoon* office. The magazine was basically out of cash. There would be no raises for any of the other staff members who weren't lucky enough to hit the lottery (although some were secretly pleased to see Simmons get fleeced). Belts and budgets would be tightened. And morale took a serious blow. "Matty would walk around the office referring to Doug and Henry as 'the Pirates,'" says Sean Kelly, "like they'd boarded his galleon and taken all of his gold."

Kelly says that during the drawn-out period when the payout was being negotiated, Henry Beard would occasionally make veiled promises over drinks to some of the more senior staffers that they would get a slice of the pie and that their kids wouldn't have to worry about college. But Kelly just assumed that that was the wine talking.

"We thought maybe he'd remember, but no," says Kelly. "What I resented is that it meant the magazine had no money and we had to crank out an amazing amount of work. We had to keep the ship afloat."

On the day that the deal was finalized, Tony Hendra and Kelly walked into Beard's office to congratulate him on his seven-figure windfall. Both were shocked by what happened next. As they sat down, Beard leaned back in his chair, laced his fingers behind his head, and announced, "I haven't felt this happy since the day I got out of the Army." Everyone knew that Beard had been working insane hours putting out the magazine every month, but he had never expressed any resentment about it or complained. He was the rock, the father figure in a madhouse of squabbling children. Had he been miserable all this time? So unhappy in all of their company? It hit them that they'd never really known their friend at all. Hendra and Kelly were both stunned and devastated as they exited his office. They didn't know it then, but that was the last time they would see Henry Beard for years. That day, he left *The National Lampoon* and never looked back.

Kenney, the one who had made such a peculiar habit of periodically disappearing, decided to stick around—perhaps out of some small sense of guilt for having run the magazine into such dire financial straits in the first place. To some, he joked that his first big splurge would be a trip to Disneyland. But, in the end, he went someplace much closer. With hair down to his shoulders, a scraggly beard, and jeans that were more holes than denim, Kenney walked into a Manhattan Porsche dealership and bought a red 911 Targa, telling the shocked salesman that he intended to pay for it in cash. He also bought his parents a house in Connecticut, sent his sister to a fancy boarding school in Virginia, and began picking up the check wherever he went. He was careless with money simply because he'd never really had any. His friend Peter Ivers later recalled flipping through the pages of a book in Kenney's apartment only to have an uncashed check for $186,000 spill out. The date on it was four months old.

Kenney's reaction was typical Doug: "Oh, I was wondering what happened to that."

Another thing that Kenney could now afford was more expensive drugs.

◆ ◆

By 1975, television still looked a lot like it had a decade earlier. Despite a handful of prime-time shows that dared to grapple with progressive themes and hot-button issues, such as *All in the Family, The Mary Tyler Moore Show*, and *Maude*, network programmers largely ignored what was going on in the world beyond the idiot box. They were more interested in the soap-opera twists of *Rich Man, Poor Man*, the unscientific science fiction of *The Bionic Woman*, and the cornpone family-values nostalgia of *Happy Days* and *The Waltons*. In late night, things weren't much hipper. The Big Three networks offered a disposable and geriatric wasteland of wheezy reruns, movies of the week, and Johnny Carson sitting behind the desk on *The Tonight Show*—a desk he'd been manning like a suntanned mummy since 1962. To the college-aged readers of the *Lampoon*, it was Squaresville, USA (population: your parents).

NBC had been doing just fine in the Nielsens by airing Carson reruns at 11:30 on Saturday nights. But that was basically the only time slot where the limping, third-place network was succeeding. Plus, Carson was becoming weary of the weekend repeats. He thought they diluted his brand and he wanted them pulled. Peacock president Herb Schlosser had poached a hungry young executive from ABC named Dick Ebersol and tasked him with finding a new weekly show for Saturday nights at 11:30—something that could one day (preferably sooner rather than later) become a money-minting franchise. Ebersol landed on the idea of going after the elusive and coveted youth demographic that would never in a million years be caught dead watching Johnny banter with his even more embalmed sidekick, Ed McMahon. Advertisers would pay a premium just to reach them.

Some months earlier, another NBC executive thinking along similar lines had approached Matty Simmons about a *Lampoon*-inspired late-night satire show. But Simmons, already feeling stretched thin between the magazine, the radio show, and his stage experiments, demurred. NBC wasn't the only one to make Simmons a TV overture. ABC was hatching its own top secret Saturday-night project: a variety show to be hosted by the verbose sports broadcaster Howard Cosell. But it got only slightly further with Simmons before negotiations broke down. In the end, NBC and Ebersol decided to hand the reins over to a twenty-nine-year-old Canadian, a veteran of *Laugh-In* and a handful of Lily Tomlin comedy specials named Lorne Michaels. He was ambitious but calculated enough not to *seem* ambitious.

Born on a kibbutz in British-occupied Palestine in 1944 with the given name of Lorne Lipowitz, Michaels's family moved to Toronto when he was a child. After graduating from the University of Toronto, he became half of a stand-up comedy act with a former law student named Hart Pomerantz. The duo performed on CBC radio and television shows under the name Hart and Lorne (before changing his name to Michaels, Lorne half-jokingly flirted with changing it to Lorne Ranger or Lorne Zwelk). The team proved to be too political for the government-owned network, so they left and began submitting jokes for other comedians, such as Woody Allen.

In 1968, Michaels moved to Los Angeles to work as a writer on a lousy Phyllis Diller variety show and then *Laugh-In*, where he saw his funniest, most off-the-wall ideas blendered into pap devoid of their intended flavor. From there, he got a job as a writer on a 1973 Lily Tomlin special, which won him an Emmy. He was bumped up to coproducer on subsequent Tomlin specials during which time he conceived the idea for his dream show: a rule-breaking late-night sketch program comprising a crazy quilt of absurd Python-esque skits, parody commercials, live music, and cutting-edge guest hosts anchored by a regular cast of young, dangerous comic actors—actors not unlike the ones he had seen at the New Palladium. It would be a variety show that satirized and subverted the notion of traditional variety shows. It would be television made for the first generation who'd been weaned on television. Both a celebration of the medium's possibilities and an antidote to its plastic, commercial phoniness. When Dick Ebersol met with Michaels, he liked the innovative sound of the Canadian's pitch. Now he just had to get NBC and its resident King of Late Night, Johnny Carson, to sign off on it.

On April 1, 1975, Michaels was officially hired as the producer of *NBC's Saturday Night* (the "Live" would eventually be added in 1977, since ABC's in-the-works Cosell vehicle had already registered a version of the name *Saturday Night Live*). Michaels was given a salary of $115,000 and the imperative to turn NBC's graveyard slot into must-see TV for baby boomers—the largest generation in American history. Raised on rock 'n' roll and recreational drugs, he couldn't have been a more ideal candidate for the job. Michaels had told Ebersol that he wanted *Saturday Night's* viewers to walk away with the impression that the network's suits had gone home and a bunch of kids had slipped into the studio to put on a show. And when NBC told him that they wanted to air the show live, Michaels wasn't rattled, he was turned on by the unpredictability of it. Now, with just six months before his new show's debut, he had to find his team of writers and performers—his kids.

Michaels first focused on the *Saturday Night* writers' room. One of the first people he pursued was the prickly prince of darkness Michael O'Donoghue, who had more or less spent the year since he'd left the *Lampoon* turning up sofa cushions for spare change. Although O'Donoghue and his girlfriend and fellow *Lampoon* veteran Anne Beatts made a point of telling Michaels how little they cared for TV, they were won over by the Canadian's vision of the show, and signed on. Next, Michaels recruited another familiar face from 635 Madison, Chevy Chase. Chase, who had been living with Christopher Guest in Los Angeles since *Lemmings* ended, was writing for the Smothers Brothers' latest stab at a comeback. One night, while waiting in line for a midnight screening of *Monty Python and the Holy Grail*, he met Michaels and impressed him with an impromptu display of his wit, including a pratfall. Michaels hired Chase soon after.

When it came to casting his new show's on-screen repertory company, Michaels's main requirement was that the performers not have any actual *experience* in television. He felt that comedy was too important to be left to the professionals. The second requirement: They had to be willing to work for next to nothing. Michaels's top priority was landing Gilda Radner, who'd knocked him out in both a Toronto production of *Godspell* and, more recently, in *The National Lampoon Show*. Then he moved on to Laraine Newman (a performer in LA's Groundlings improv troupe whom he'd already known from one of his Lily Tomlin specials) and Garrett Morris (who was originally hired as a writer). Michaels then met with Belushi. It didn't go well.

"I thought all television was shit and I let Lorne know it," Belushi later said. "My own set at home was often covered with spit. The only reason I wanted to be on it was because Michael O'Donoghue was writing for it and it had a chance to be good."

With Belushi yet to be cast and three spots left to fill (he'd since reconsidered Chase's status and moved him over to the performing side), Michaels held auditions on August 12 and 13,

1975. Roughly two hundred comedians showed up. With her WASPy appearance disguising a caustic sense of humor, Jane Curtin quickly got the nod on day one. That left two openings to be filled on day two. Belushi, sensing the magnitude of the moment as he had when Tony Hendra came to scout him for *Lemmings* back in Chicago, broke out his A material, including his samurai character. He slayed. There was one final vacancy to be given, to either Bill Murray (who auditioned with a monologue as the Honker) or Dan Aykroyd (who showed up, flustered, in a derby hat and upper-crust British accent). Michaels couldn't make up his mind.

As weeks went by, Aykroyd became more and more convinced that he wasn't going to get the gig. So he went off to join Joe Flaherty at Second City's newest club, in Pasadena. "Danny drove all the way down from Toronto," recalls Flaherty. "And the day he got there, he got a call from Lorne in New York. Danny asked, 'What do you think, should I do it?' We didn't know what it was going to be. We certainly didn't know it would take the world by storm. All we knew was that we were doing this stupid-ass show in Pasadena that no one was coming to. So he went." Michaels had his Not Ready for Prime Time Players. Later, he said, "We wanted to redefine comedy the way the Beatles redefined what being a pop star was."

Murray may have been disappointed, but he wasn't out of work for long. He, his brother Brian, and Guest would all quickly be scooped up by ABC's prime-time competitor. They had no clue what they were walking into. *Saturday Night Live with Howard Cosell* premiered at 8 p.m. on September 20, 1975, three weeks before Michaels's NBC show. The nasally sportscaster was his usual stiff self—a toupeed cadaver stiffly pantomiming the role of dog-and-pony vaudeville emcee. The show's hipness quotient was reflected in its kickoff episode's roster of celebrity guests:

Frank Sinatra, Shirley Bassey, Paul Anka, Jimmy Connors, John Denver, Siegfried & Roy, and, as its musical act, the Bay City Rollers.

The show was mercifully put to sleep after eighteen episodes. "Everybody else was on the other show," said Murray. "So we were on TV, and they were on TV. But they were *the show*, and we were on with the Chinese acrobats and elephants and all sorts of crazy acts, and we would get cut almost every other week."

Just as Lorne Michaels was about to give the world the Beatles of comedy, the Murrays were stuck as the opening act for the Bay City Rollers.

◆ ◆

At 11:29 p.m. on October 11, 1975, the air in NBC's newly renovated Studio 8H was choked with anxiety, pungently aromatic smoke, and frayed-nerve electricity. The revolution was about to be televised. Five million Americans had just watched their local newscasts wind down and had no idea what they were in store for.

In the week leading up to the first episode of *Saturday Night*, up in his spacious seventeenth-floor office, Michaels's face had broken out from nerves. There had been a series of bare-knuckle battles with NBC's censors over the skits he wanted to air. The first week's host, George Carlin, had reportedly been coked-up in the week leading up to the debut. There had been talk among the network brass of adding a delay of several seconds to his monologue in case any obscenities happened to fly out of his mouth on live TV. The only concession they would ever get from Carlin was making him wear a suit jacket over his T-shirt.

Then, at 11:30, the audience saw two men they'd most likely never laid eyes on before sitting in a pair of high-backed chairs for the show's cold-open sketch. There was no introduction to the show, no credits. Belushi played an Eastern European immigrant who had come for an English lesson at the home of an instructor played by Michael O'Donoghue, who wrote the piece. O'Donoghue tells his student to repeat phrases after him—phrases such as "I would like . . . to feed . . . your fingertips . . . to the wolverines" and "I'm afraid . . . we are out . . . of badgers, would you accept . . . a wolverine . . . in its place?" Then O'Donoghue grabs his chest and keels over, stricken by a heart attack. Belushi looks puzzled for a beat, then grabs his chest, too, and throws himself to the floor. Just then, Chase enters from stage right playing the hapless floor manager, wearing a headset and holding a clipboard. He looks at the camera, smiles, and announces, "Live from New York, it's *Saturday Night!*"

An hour and a half later, as the end credits rolled, it was clear to those watching at home that something ineffable had changed in the culture. How did this get on network TV? *Saturday Night* was defiantly topical, wildly satirical, and unabashedly political with an absurd, skunk-weed counterculture vibe. For the first time, the boomers had seen themselves—their tastes, their sensibilities, their attitudes—reflected back at them in a way that felt personal and intimate. For ninety minutes, at least, the underground went mainstream.

Back at the *Lampoon*, Simmons saw red, correctly realizing (albeit too late) that all of the talent that had been under his roof less than a year ago had not only been cherry-picked by Michaels, but would also now be giving away for free what the *Lampoon* was still charging a dollar an issue for. Yes, he had once raided talent himself from Second City, but now *Saturday Night* was screwing *him*, and he didn't like it. All he could do was wait it out. It would be a very long wait.

Most of the nation's critics weren't immediately sure what to make of Michaels's strange small-screen comedy insurrection. A month after his initial pan in *The New York Times*, John J.

O'Connor made an about-face, writing, "NBC has found itself a source for legitimate pride, a commodity in scarce supply at any network these days." He continued: "The future of *Saturday Night* is uncertain—intentionally so. Mr. Michaels and company are especially anxious about avoiding the pitfalls of being slick, coy, or predictably routine. . . . For however long it lasts, *Saturday Night* is the most creative and encouraging thing to happen to American TV comedy since *Your Show of Shows*."

Of course, critical love was beside the point. While the early weeks of *Saturday Night* brought only a small improvement ratings-wise over NBC's *Best of Carson* reruns, it gave the network a whiff of insider cool. "*SNL* spoke to the whole generation," says Ivan Reitman. "For the first time, somehow they were letting people like us on TV."

Director John Landis, whose path would soon cross with the *Saturday Night* cast's, added, "By the end of the first season, *Saturday Night* had a tremendous cachet of hipness. Not everyone was talking about it, but the *right people* were talking about it."

As the outlaw show slowly began to snowball into a bona fide cult hit, picking up viewers and buzz each week, jealousy began to surface at the *Lampoon*. There had been an exodus of talent there, and now those refugees were thriving elsewhere. Michaels wasn't shy about taking full credit for discovering his new stars—something that annoyed Simmons to no end. O'Donoghue and Beatts had left, and eventually *Lampoon* mainstays Brian McConnachie and Sean Kelly would join the *Saturday Night* writers' room, too. You could almost feel the creative energy being slowly sucked from 635 Madison and moving a few blocks south and west to 30 Rock. *Saturday Night* was now the cool place to be. It had that same start-up excitement and reckless abandon that the *Lampoon* had had in 1970.

Within a few weeks of its debut, it was clear that Chevy Chase had become the breakout star of the show. In its first few epi-sodes, the show's lineup of Not Ready For Prime Time Players had been forced to take a backseat to Michaels's zeitgeisty guest hosts, such as Paul Simon, Lily Tomlin, and Richard Pryor. They had even taken a backseat to the Muppets—Jim Henson's menagerie of felt-covered creatures that, in an environment that could exist only in the '70s, had somehow managed to find their way into the show's still-evolving mix of eclectic attractions.

Two unspoken truths had become clear from the earliest days of *Saturday Night*. First, Michaels had cast himself in the role of a stern father figure who kept his paternal love at a distant, chilly remove. And second, though all of Lorne's children were equal, some were more equal than others. The cast had to compete for his affection and approval. Michaels, who aspired to the high life of a hip, plugged-in New York media power broker, seemed to carry the social-climbing ambitions of a man who looked in the mirror only to see Lorne Lipowitz staring back at him. To him, Chase was what he wanted to be—to the manor born, charming, effortlessly funny, undeniably good-looking, and comfortable in any social setting. O'Donoghue may have been the show's head writer, its self-crowned alpha dog, but Chase was the one who had his name on the marquee. Everyone seemed to know it. If they didn't, Chase would soon make it clear himself.

Jealousy and resentment were inevitable. And it didn't help that while the rest of the ensemble was standing around anony-mously mugging in humiliating killer-bee costumes, begging for on-air crumbs to be swept their way, Chase was being given the spotlight without having to even so much as ask for it. In season one, virtually every episode of the show opened with Chase tak-ing a pratfall either as the stumbling president, Gerald Ford, or as himself. It was hard to tell which of the two was more famous. Chase had also been handed the high-profile recurring show-

case of the "Weekend Update" anchor chair, which eventually
became a solo vehicle for glib, self-aggrandizing jokes. Chase's
soon-to-be signature opening for the segment ("Good evening.
I'm Chevy Chase, and you're not") wasn't just a funny punch
line (although it was that); it stung like an open-handed slap to
all the other cast members patiently waiting for their shot.

Belushi, who had always had a love-hate relationship with
Chase dating from the *Lemmings* days, seemed to internalize the
slight to his ego most acutely. He considered himself to be a
more dynamic performer and more talented improviser than
Chase, who seemed to succeed more and more the less and less
he tried. For the first time in his career, Belushi felt overshad-
owed. The consummate upstager was being upstaged. Belushi
would grouse about the secondary and tertiary roles he was given
each week, saying, "I go where I'm kicked. They throw me
bones dogs wouldn't chew on." To Belushi, Chase was becoming insufferable and smug, giving off the swollen-headed impression that he was bigger than the show.

In December 1975, in the middle of *Saturday Night's* third
month on the air, *New York* magazine published a cover story
on Chase. The cover line read: "And heeeere's TV's Hottest New
Comedy Star!" The article, written by Jeff Greenfield, hit 30
Rock like a hurricane. Even early on, *Saturday Night* had generated plenty of press attention. It was the darling of the Manhattan
media intelligentsia, but this was the first time that a publication had gone out of its way to single out *one person* to elevate
above the rest. It just happened to be the person with the most
memorable name and the shrewdest knack for repeating it while
the camera was on.

The article was a star-making air kiss to Chase, hailing him
as "the heir apparent to Johnny Carson." Chase, of course, had
some idea that the *New York* article was coming. After all, he'd

been interviewed for it. But he didn't know that he would be its focus, or that he would be on the cover. And he certainly hadn't gone out of his way to warn his costars about it. Years later, Chase would recall walking out of his Upper East Side studio apartment on the morning that the magazine hit newsstands. "A strange and fun moment," he said. "I remember buying it off one of those stands on 61st Street and saying to the guy, 'Look.' And he said, 'Yeah, that's you—you're famous!' I remember liking that." Chase later said that the cover story changed his life.

The *New York* story not only cited the thirty-two-year-old Chase as the reason *Saturday Night* had become an overnight sensation with its young audience; it suggested that Chase already had his wandering eye on bigger and better things: "On the surface, Chase is cut from the conventional TV mold: A rich, 'sincere' voice; neatly cropped hair; a pleasant, harmless face; jacket and tie a permanent part of his wardrobe. But when he comes onstage, strange things begin to happen." The article goes on . . . "This combination of reassuring form and outrageous content— the 'naughty boy' quality—has made Chevy Chase a hot property at NBC. Industry sources report that network executives see in Chase 'the first real potential successor to Johnny Carson when he gives up the "Tonight Show." ' "

Michaels didn't help quiet any potential storm that the article would create backstage, saying in the piece, "All of the players are brilliant—the difference is that Chevy is always doing himself. The others are in character, and they're not as accessible as Chevy." In case it hadn't already been clear enough to everyone on the show, there it was: Daddy publicly anointing his favorite son, a cold lesson about the ruthless mechanics of fame.

The *New York* article further went on to detail a development deal that NBC was in the midst of preparing that would elevate

Chase to becoming a guest host for Carson. Back in Malibu, Carson was more than annoyed. He felt blindsided. This was all news to him. Chase was now in a position to ask the network for anything he wanted. His bargaining position was only strengthened by the fact that he had signed only a one-year deal when he got the *Saturday Night* job (all of the other cast members had initially signed on for five years). He was barraged with movie offers. For its part, NBC tried to woo him with a $2 million deal to produce his own prime-time specials for the network. Chase hadn't told anyone yet, but he'd already made up his mind that he would be moving on—and moving West.

After the first season of the show ended, on July 31, 1976, Chase was finally free to publicly announce that he was leaving *Saturday Night*. By then, he'd already become more famous than the celebrity guest hosts he was ostensibly there to serve each week. Michaels would later say that it was clear after the first season that the show could only go in one of two directions: "Was the show going to become the Chevy Chase show or was it going to stay an ensemble show? I think he'd become too big a star." Everyone assumed that Chase was heading to Hollywood for fame and fortune. But he always denied it, insisting that he left because of a woman.

During his time on *Saturday Night*, Chase had been wrestling with a stormy long-distance relationship with a model and aspiring actress named Jacqueline Carlin. The two had got engaged. "I was conflicted with love," says Chase. "I wanted to marry this girl who everybody else knew was the wrong one except me. It didn't last. And she wouldn't move from LA to New York. So she gave me the ultimatum to come back after a year on the show. Otherwise, I very well may have stayed."

Chase would officially leave *Saturday Night* on October 30,

1976, after the sixth episode of season two. Two months later, he and Carlin were married and moved in together on Mulholland Drive.

"Everyone from *Saturday Night* came out for the wedding," says Chase, "which, of course, was hilarious. John Belushi got so drunk that he started making out with my mother. It was very funny." The marriage between Chase and Carlin would be a brief and unhappy one, during which he began his long affair with cocaine.

"Lorne used to say that coke was God's way of telling you that you have too much money," Chase later said. Seventeen months after Chase and Carlin exchanged I do's, she sued for a divorce. Chase would later say that he deeply regretted leaving *Saturday Night* when he did.

◆ ◆

When Chase left *Saturday Night*, Michaels saw his exit as more than just one of his protégés moving on to bigger and better things. He lost his closest friend on the show. Some said that the hurt went even deeper—that he felt stabbed in the back and regarded Chase's departure as an almost Shakespearean act of betrayal. Whether or not that's the case, the fact is *Saturday Night* would do just fine without its biggest and buzziest name. With Chase gone, Belushi and the other remaining cast members were free to assert themselves and establish their own on-air identities, becoming household names themselves. But they were still a man down.

Bill Murray, whom Michaels had initially passed over for the inaugural *Saturday Night* lineup in favor of Dan Aykroyd, was asked to join the show. He was finally being called up to the majors. Michaels had always admired Murray's loose, anarchic style and his lack of the kind of craven neediness so many comedians have. Plus, Murray already had a built-in history with many of his *Saturday Night* costars thanks to his time at Second City and the *Lampoon*. But NBC wasn't sold on the replacement. They thought that the twenty-six-year-old wasn't telegenic and a bit too ragged around the edges—they were replacing the next Cary Grant with an Irish-Catholic Chicago street dog. Murray wasn't just the *new guy*; he was the new guy who was replacing *Chevy Chase*.

By that time, Doug Kenney had become such a regular presence backstage at Studio 8H that Michaels had offered him a writing job on the show. Kenney passed. He was done with deadlines. He'd recently fallen in love with a beautiful, sophisticated, and intelligent actress from Philadelphia named Kathryn Walker, to whom he had introduced himself at a party by biting into a crystal wineglass—part knight-errant, part carny geek. After the two began dating, Kenney had decided that it was time to move on from the *Lampoon*. He'd been there six years, which seemed like a decent run. When Kenney walked into Matty Simmons's office to break the news that he was leaving, Simmons panicked and blurted out the only thing he thought might make Kenney reconsider. "I said, 'You can't leave; we're making a movie!' I knew that would get his attention."

It did.

4

Knowledge Is Good

WHILE MATTY SIMMONS WAS DANGLING the carrot of a *Lampoon* movie in front of an antsy Doug Kenney, Ivan Reitman had separately moved forward with a similar plan. As part of the deal for Reitman to come to New York and oversee *The National Lampoon Show*, Simmons had promised him that he would get the first shot at directing a *Lampoon* movie—if and when one should ever happen. Not one to sit back and wait for opportunities to be handed to him, Reitman had recruited Harold Ramis to start hammering out a *Lampoon*-esque screenplay for him. He paid Ramis $2,500. They both agreed it was probably best to keep the project a secret from Simmons for the time being.

"Everyone had gone off to do either *Saturday Night Live* or the Cosell show," says Reitman. "Harold was the only one who got left behind, which I didn't understand. So we tried to put together a movie based on some skits from the *Lampoon Show* that had kind of a high school theme." Actually, Ramis based the first draft of his script on his own early-'60s fraternity experiences at Washington University in St. Louis. He was calling it *Freshman Year*. But after a few torturous months, Ramis and Reitman agreed that it wasn't clicking. It needed a shot of the

Lampoon's lethal comic edge. Reitman decided it was time to go to Simmons.

Since the most successful single publication that the *Lampoon* had ever put out was Doug Kenney and P. J. O'Rourke's *High School Yearbook* parody, Ramis floated the idea of partnering up with Kenney for another stab at cracking the screenplay. The two had become friendly while Ramis was working at the *Radio Hour,* and they both shared a wicked, wiseass outsider's sensibility even if, outwardly, they couldn't have been less alike. Ramis was professorial with an air of Zen calm, while Kenney was more like an ADHD-addled kid in the back of the classroom doing everything he could to get sent to detention. But somehow, they complemented each other. "One of my mottos is, you only want to collaborate with people who are at least as good as you are if not better," said Ramis. "And that's what I found with Doug. He was just as smart as anyone I ever knew."

The premise for Ramis and Kenney's movie was so out-there it could barely be contained in the crude form of a high-concept pitch. The closest that they could come up with was: Charles Manson in high school. Fueled by significant amounts of marijuana, the two imagined the mass-murdering SoCal Svengali as a demented and strangely seductive loner in Midwest suburbia corrupting the local youth and forming a depraved cult of flying-saucer-worshipping teenage zombies. They called it *Laser Orgy Girls.* "Every time they had a new idea, it had sex and drugs and everything," says Simmons. "I thought these guys were going to get me shot. Everyone was drunk or high in it. So I said we're going to have to move this to college so it's not quite as offensive."

As soon as the word "college" came out of Simmons's mouth, Kenney and Ramis immediately thought of Chris Miller. Miller had been the *Lampoon*'s in-house fraternity specialist. His hilariously lewd short stories such as "The Night of the Seven Fires" and "Pinto's First Lay" had leaned heavily on his own first-hand experiences as an Alpha Delta Phi brother at Dartmouth in the early '60s (in fact, the Pinto character was based on him—he was given the nickname in his fraternity allegedly due to the splotchy birthmarks on his penis). The stories had also been some of the most popular in the magazine's history. Kenney, in particular, was a huge fan of Miller's work. So he asked him if they could borrow his material and use it as the basis for his and Ramis's script.

"Doug went crazy over [my stories] because they didn't do shit like that at Harvard," says Miller. "I told them, Sure, they could use them, but what was *my* part in this? They offered to buy the stories from me, but I told them, No, I want to be one of the writers or I'll beat you to the script and write it myself."

The three amateur Hollywood wannabes met for a largely liquid brunch at a restaurant called Casey's in Greenwich Village and proceeded to spew forth every outrageous college story they could remember happening to them or anyone they knew over Bloody Marys. Each embroidered the others' experiences with his own, while Ramis took notes on a legal pad. By the time they left the restaurant, they were already calling their project *Animal House*. "We were there for hours just cracking up and ruining everyone else's meals," says Miller. "At the end, I remember saying: At the center of any great animal house is a great animal. And there was about a half second pause and we all looked at each other and said, '*Belushi!*' "

For the better part of 1976, they would work at the *Lampoon* office and periodically get together at Kenney's dorm-like West Village apartment to bang out a movie treatment, coming up with outrageous bits of dialogue, kicking around character sketches they'd based on everything from Archie and Jughead to *Our Gang*, and outlining ideas for scenes—many of which involved disgusting arias of gross-out humor. "Chris's fraternity was virtually a vomiting cult," said Ramis. "His fraternity would eat certain kinds of food to produce certain types of regurge. We had a lot of scenes that were almost orgies of vomit and hell-night scenes with frozen hot dogs in various orifices. We didn't back off anything. And, in our naïveté, we totally believed that we were going to lead some studio to the most successful comedy they had ever made."

What they ended up with was a treatment that was 114 pages long (a standard Hollywood treatment is somewhere between ten and thirty pages). "They gave me this thing and I didn't know what the hell to do with it," Simmons recalls. "It was funny as hell, but it was like *War and Peace*." Whenever Belushi would drop by Kenney's place, the writers would toy with him by saying, "Ooooh, do we have a movie part for you!" Belushi, who desperately wanted to parlay *Saturday Night* into a movie career, kept begging them to let him read it. It drove him nuts. Simmons and Reitman sent the strange, doorstop-size document to various studios, including Warner Bros., which quickly passed. Finally, the two men flew out to Los Angeles to meet with Universal Pictures president Ned Tanen, hoping for a deal but expecting another rejection.

Brilliant but erratic, the forty-four-year-old Tanen had already shepherded an impressive string of box office hits at Universal, including *American Graffiti*, *The Sting*, and *Jaws*. But like most other major studios in the mid-'70s, his was staffed largely with aging executives blindly chasing after what they thought young moviegoers wanted to see. Ever since the out-of-nowhere successes of *Bonnie and Clyde* and *Easy Rider* at the dusk-end of the '60s, Hollywood had been caught flat-footed by a revolution it didn't quite understand. "The studios were still controlled by moguls in their sixties and seventies," says Reitman. "Even when you think of a critical movie that represented our boomer generation like *Easy Rider*, well, it was pretty fucking earnest."

By the middle part of the '70s in Hollywood, up was down, black was white, and yesterday's surefire blockbusters were today's megaton bombs. Everything seemed to be in flux. The studios, including Universal, lived in daily terror of missing out on the next big thing—but they were too myopic to see what that next thing might be. In reaction to this atmosphere of uncertainty, Universal had created a Youth Division and put Tanen in charge of it. The operating philosophy of the unit was to spread the studio's production money around and place a lot of inexpensive, low-risk bets on risky movies with the hope that one or two of those wagers might pay off. Which, in theory, made a lot of sense. But it could also stand in the way of bankrolling a bigger, more ambitious movie such as *Star Wars*, which Tanen had, in fact, recently passed on.

Comedies had become especially tough to predict. With the exception of Robert Altman's *M*A*S*H* and a few others, the studios were still serving up the same old diet of middlebrow comedies by Blake Edwards and Neil Simon. Tanen, who was smart enough to know what he didn't know, had surrounded himself with a small staff of junior executives in their early twenties, such as Thom Mount and Sean Daniel—both of whom had been readers of the *Lampoon*. They worked out of a windowless basement office under the studio commissary.

When Matty Simmons and Ivan Reitman arrived in Los Angeles to meet with Universal, they checked into the Beverly Hills Hotel and rehearsed their pitch. They needn't have bothered. When they arrived in Tanen's office, he was blunt with them. "Tanen said he hated the *Animal House* treatment," says Simmons. "He really thought it was just awful." But Mount

and Daniel had convinced their boss that the *Lampoon* was hot
with the audience they sought, so Tanen pinched his nose and
reluctantly agreed to make a deal to develop a script as long as
they promised to keep the budget under $2.5 million. Simmons
and Reitman immediately agreed. To them, that sounded like a
fortune.

Ramis, Kenney, and Miller split the contracted $30,000
writers' fee equally and got to work. Shortly after the deal was
signed, Mount visited the trio in New York, bringing them sand-
wiches from the Carnegie Deli to get off on a good foot. "They
had zero patience for bullshit," says Mount, who remembers
laughing through the entire meeting. "Chris said, 'My job is to
be the typist,' Doug said, 'My job is to make sure Matty Simmons gets murdered,' and Harold said, 'My job is to make sure
these two guys don't go to jail.'"

The studio gave the writers an office in its New York headquarters. Ramis described the Park Avenue base of operations as
predictably stodgy—full of old English antiques and stuffy hunt-
ing prints on the walls. "I remember Doug drawing little rats
on the paintings with a ballpoint pen that you wouldn't notice
at first look," said Ramis. "And I remember stuffing towels under
the door to keep the smoke in the room."

Ramis, Kenney, and Miller worked on the script eight hours
a day for three months. They would each write ten pages, then
swap and discuss what they'd done, and then swap again like a
collaborative daisy chain. Since they had no idea what a typical
Hollywood screenplay looked like, Reitman gave them a copy
of the script for *Butch Cassidy and the Sundance Kid* to use as a
blueprint. Within that structure, they crammed all of their most
extreme, debauched stories and set them in 1962 at a fictional
institution called Faber College, whose founding motto was

Knowledge Is Good. To them, the year the film took place was especially significant since they saw it as the last moment of idealism and innocence before John F. Kennedy's assassination would unlock the nation's darkest fears and unleash a new generation's revolutionary impulses.

When they completed the first draft of the script, the always-hustling Ramis, with a pregnant wife at home, accepted a job as the head writer on *SCTV*—a new television show from Second City's Toronto troupe that was attempting to draft on the success of *NBC's Saturday Night* with a sliver of its budget. The idea had begun as a defensive one. Second City simply didn't want to see any more of its homegrown stars poached by Lorne Michaels. While *SCTV* may have been less aggressive in its humor than his down-and-dirty New York show, it had a naïve brilliance to it. It was conceptually loony and affably dry. In other words, it felt . . . *Canadian.*

Rather than try to pretend to be something that it wasn't, it built its shoestring budget into its premise, which revolved around a third-rate TV station in a fictional town called Melonville. Just a half hour long, *SCTV* aired only once a month, and its irregularity and obscurity made it almost impossible to find on the dial. But somehow that also made it even more precious when you discovered it. "We tried not to think of ourselves as competitors to *Saturday Night Live* because we weren't," says Joe Flaherty, one of *SCTV*'s original cast members. "Theirs was an NBC network show with hundreds of stations; ours played on the Global Television Network. Well, they *called* it a network. They had four stations in Ontario." In addition to his head writer duties, Ramis also appeared on air in sketches with a rising stable of gifted improvisers that included, in addition to Flaherty, John Candy, Eugene Levy, Catherine O'Hara, Andrea

Martin, and Dave Thomas. "We thought, Well, we're doing it at a really cheesy Canadian television station, let's *be* a cheesy television station," said Ramis.

Ramis was stretched thin and wound tight. While working on the first thirteen episodes of *SCTV*, he would commute back and forth to New York to work on the multiple rounds of *Animal House* script revisions that Universal demanded during a particularly hellish period of development limbo. He, Kenney, and Miller were constantly barraged with nitpicking notes from the studio asking them to tone down the film's most offensive gags, including its most disgustingly viscous vomit jokes. "Thom Mount pretended to like what we were doing," says Reitman, "but Ned Tanen didn't even pretend. Every time he read it, he hated it more. He kept saying about the Deltas, '*These guys are the heroes?!*' "

Reitman had always hoped that he would be given the shot to direct *Animal House* when it was finally given a green light. After all, that was the basis of his original pact with Simmons. But Universal wasn't high on the idea of handing $2.5 million to the man whose sole calling card as an auteur was the $5,000 Canucksploitation flick *Cannibal Girls* (which came with the ever-classy tagline "These Girls Eat Men!"). "Universal didn't think my credits were highfalutin enough," says Reitman. "Of course, it broke my heart." Back in LA, Tanen had actually mocked up a list of a dozen more-established directors for his low-priority project, including John Schlesinger (*Midnight Cowboy*), Bob Rafelson (*Five Easy Pieces*), Mike Nichols (*The Graduate*), Alan J. Pakula (*Klute*), and George Roy Hill (*The Sting*). Not surprisingly, none of them was interested—if, in fact, Tanen's offers had even made it past their agents, which seems highly unlikely. Under the gun to get *Animal House* moving, Daniel struggled to come up with a candidate of his own. Someone young who got the *Lampoon* sensibility. Someone who also might say yes.

John Landis was a twenty-six-year-old high school dropout and movie brat who had basically grown up on Hollywood's back lots. He'd already been a mail boy at 20th Century Fox, a jobbing stuntman, and a blink-and-miss background actor. At twenty-one, he'd directed his first film—a ludicrous and lively low-budget comedy titled *Schlock* that's best remembered (if it's remembered at all) for being shot in twelve days for $60,000 and for featuring future Oscar-winning makeup effects maestro Rick Baker in a gorilla suit. As Universal was scrambling to find an *Animal House* director, Daniel's girlfriend, Katherine Wooten, was working as a script supervisor on Landis's second film, *The Kentucky Fried Movie.* Written and produced by David Zucker, Jim Abrahams, and Jerry Zucker (the "ZAZ" team that would go on to make *Airplane!* and the *Naked Gun* movies), *Kentucky Fried* was a loose string of buckshot, drive-by comedy skits that threw every absurd sight gag at the movie screen in the hope that a couple might stick: It had dwarves in clown costumes whipping topless women, a news anchor announcing in stentorian tones, "I'm not wearing any pants, film at eleven," and snippets of a movie-within-a-movie chopsocky epic called *A Fistful of Yen.*

"Katherine used to come home and say, 'You've got to meet this guy, John Landis,'" says Daniel. "So I went to his editing room and he showed me a twelve-minute reel of footage he'd made to help find more financing for the film. It was absolutely hilarious." Daniel handed Landis the *Animal House* script and told him to call him back and let him know what he thought.

"It was the funniest thing I've ever read and still is to this day," says Landis. "But it was also a *mess.*" Desperate to nail down his first Hollywood credit, Simmons agreed that Landis seemed like a close enough fit with the *Lampoon.* And Tanen, after some initial objections, shrugged and went along with the decision. "The fact that they hired this kid shows you how unimportant the studio thought this movie was," says Landis, who was thrilled to be offered a studio picture. The next day, Landis flew to New York to meet the writers.

Landis says that when he arrived at the *Lampoon* office, he walked into a wall of ice coming from Ramis and Kenney, who silently sat on the far end of the table sizing him up. Although Landis possessed a sharp, caffeinated sense of humor and wore a shaggy beard that at least made him *look* the part of a New Hollywood hipster, the writers allowed themselves to see only a fast-talking Tinseltown smoothie who'd just flown in from "The Coast." "Harold and Doug got possessive about the script," says Chris Miller. "They didn't want some jerk from Hollywood coming in and taking it away from us."

The young outsider wasn't shy about telling the writing team that large chunks of the script had to be scrapped. He told them that, as it was, there were no good guys in the story, just bad guys. There had to be some delineation between the Deltas and the Omegas—heroes versus villains, white hats versus black hats, slobs versus snobs. They couldn't all be thugs. And while a little gross-out humor was fine, the grossest of the chunk-blowing gags absolutely had to go. "He was an outsider and an obnoxious one," said Ramis. "John was really arrogant for his age and experience. He sort of referred to *Animal House* right away as 'my movie.' We'd been living with it for two years and we hated that. But he did seem to understand the material."

Eventually, the writers warmed up to Landis. But Ramis would be less understanding when it came time to cast the movie. From the earliest stages, they had imagined their circle of friends appearing in the main roles. John Belushi was obviously Bluto, the Deltas' most debauched slob, with a 0.0 grade point average. But they also saw Chevy Chase as the smooth lothario Otter, Dan Aykroyd as the chopper-riding motorhead D-Day, and the

Murrays as various other fraternity members. But Landis wasn't interested in making a *Saturday Night Live* movie. For his part, Ramis was hoping to play the part of Boon, the commitment-phobic smartass. Landis allowed him to audition for the part opposite Karen Allen, but he'd felt all along that Ramis was too old to play a college student. Instead, he gave the part to Peter Riegert, a stage actor who was dating Bette Midler at the time and was a mere three years younger than Ramis. The slight made Ramis fume.

Even though *Animal House* was a low-budget low priority at the studio, Universal was adamant that Landis cast *some* stars. He was told he had to sign up both Chase and Belushi. It wasn't explicitly stated as a deal breaker, but that's the way Landis interpreted it. He knew that he had to quickly think of a way to sabotage the studio's ultimatum. "I had to meet with Chevy," says Landis. "And I didn't want Chevy Chase. Not because I don't like Chevy Chase but because he was the star of *Saturday Night Live*. The first year, he'd always say, 'I'm Chevy Chase and you're not.' I thought whoever played Otter should be *Otter*. So what happened is Ivan and I had lunch with Chevy and he's desperately working Chevy to be in the movie. And I'm working desperately to have Chevy *not* to be in the movie, and Ivan was kicking me under the table really hard."

Landis's scheme went like this: The director knew that Chase was weighing another offer to star in the lightweight comic murder-mystery *Foul Play* with Goldie Hawn. He told Chase that if he was in *Animal House*, he'd just be part of an ensemble, but if he did *Foul Play*, he'd be the star of the film, like Cary Grant. Chase ended up choosing *Foul Play*. "I read *Animal House* and thought it was good," says Chase. "But I'd sort of already lived it. I hadn't lived Goldie Hawn." Ramis had a different theory as to why Chase passed on *Animal House*. Namely, that he was too competitive with Belushi and he didn't want to share the limelight or be upstaged by him. Either way, the studio was furious. Landis could not mess up his courtship of Belushi.

While *Animal House* was going through endless rounds of revisions, Belushi had flown down to Mexico to make his film debut in the Jack Nicholson–directed Western comedy, *Goin' South*. He'd only had a small part, but it had been an unhappy experience for him. Landis invited Belushi to his room at the Sherry-Netherland Hotel in New York and tried to sell him on *Animal House*. The director told him how playing the lovable glutton Bluto would essentially be like playing a cross between Harpo Marx and the Cookie Monster. Belushi's eyes lit up. Midway through Landis's sales pitch, the actor asked if he could use the phone in the next room and call room service. Landis figured, Why not? After all, Universal was picking up the tab. When Belushi returned, he seemed interested, but unwilling to commit. He told Landis that he would have to think about it and left. Five minutes later, there was a knock at Landis's door. It was room service with a heaving cart buckling under a Roman feast that included ten shrimp cocktails.

As Belushi waffled about whether to do the film, his old friend Doug Kenney stepped in to try to close the deal. In the end, Belushi would sign on to play Bluto for $35,000. Landis could breathe again. Not only because he'd secured the star whom Universal had demanded, but also because he no longer had to move on to his second choice for the part: the potbellied rock ham Meat Loaf. But he wasn't off the hook yet.

"We had Belushi, but Universal still wanted another star in the film," says Landis. "Now, I had been a flunky on the set of 1970's *Kelly's Heroes* in Yugoslavia. And Donald Sutherland and I had gotten very friendly. I used to babysit Kiefer. And when I was doing *Kentucky Fried Movie*, Donald was huge. And I asked him to be in it, and he was, as the clumsy waiter. So now comes *Animal House* and I called Donald and said, 'Look, we'll write you a part and you'll only have to be on the set for a day or two.'" Sutherland agreed to help Landis out. But since this wasn't some dinky, independently financed film, it was a *Universal* film, he asked for $50,000 for two days' work. He got it.

As for the other reprobates in the film, Landis could now cast whomever he wanted. The rest of the leads comprised young unknown stage actors and just plain young unknowns: Tom Hulce as freshman pledge Pinto, Stephen Furst as the "fat, drunk, and stupid" Flounder, Mark Metcalf as ROTC Nazi Doug Neidermeyer, Karen Allen as the put-upon Katy, Jamie Widdoes as chapter president Hoover, Tim Matheson as lady-killer Otter, Sarah Holcomb as the mayor's jailbait daughter, Clorette DePasto, Kevin Bacon as smarmy Omega Chip Diller, and Bruce McGill as grease monkey D-Day.

"I remember getting the script and reading it for the first time at the unemployment office on 90th and Broadway," recalls McGill. "It wasn't a cheerful place, but I was just laughing out loud. I thought to myself, *Can they really be making this movie?*"

Landis knew that a certain amount of rewriting would have to happen on the set, so he asked Ramis, Miller, and Kenney if they wanted to come along and play extras. Ramis was still smarting about being passed over for Boon. "I thought, Fuck that, I'm not hanging around to be an extra." Miller and Kenney jumped at the chance, with Miller playing a Delta named Hardbar, and Kenney as the fraternity's four-eyed pencil-necked geek weirdo, Stork, who delivers one of the script's most indelible lines: "What the hell are we supposed to do, ya moron?"

In October of 1977, the *Animal House* cast and crew arrived at the University of Oregon in Eugene. Landis had a thirty-day shooting schedule and a budget of $2.7 million. The producers,

Matty Simmons and Ivan Reitman, had a hard time finding a college that would allow them to shoot on its campus after they'd read the cavalcade of hard-R depravity in the script. But Oregon's dean jumped at the chance to host a Hollywood film crew. It just so happened that a decade earlier, he'd turned down another film looking for a location, and he was still kicking himself.

"I asked the dean if he wanted to read the script," says Reitman. "He said, 'Look, I'm the guy who said no to *The Graduate*. Obviously, I have no idea how to read a script, so why should I read yours? You can shoot here.'"

Kenney savored the adventure, driving cross-country from New York to Eugene in his Porsche. Deep down, he'd always harbored fantasies of being an actor. He'd even come up with a name for his movie-star alter ego: Charlton Hepburn. He'd had a bit part in a 1977 movie called *Between the Lines*, about the staff of an underground Boston newspaper. Says Reitman, "Doug loved the idea of dropping out of his life for a while and acting in a movie."

On set, Landis put both Kenney and Miller into service, asking Kenney to write a classroom-lecture scene for Sutherland near the beginning of the film. Kenney pounded out the actor's speech about John Milton (and the long-suffering Mrs. Milton) during lunch. Kenney had also suggested the writhing, epileptic toga-party dance called The Gator. When he and Miller weren't punching up dialogue on set or filling the background as glorified scenery, they were partying and smoking dope with the Deltas at the Rodeway Inn—the local motel where the cast was staying. They both thought that they could get used to the movie business.

McGill had hijacked a piano from the motel's lobby and stealthily wheeled it across the parking lot and into his room, which became a hub of after-hours indulgence. One night, the *Animal House* actors crashed a party at the Sigma Alpha Epsilon house on the Oregon campus and barely escaped with their lives. "They were all jocks, so I was a bit intimidated," recalls Jamie Widdoes, who played *Animal House*'s frat brother Hoover. "Some guy put his hand out for me to shake and said something and I popped his beer into his face like a fool. I ended up on the ground getting kicked. I was in the dentist's chair at 8 a.m. the next morning because I got my teeth knocked in." Adds McGill, "I got stomped bad. I got a black eye and I told Landis that I got it playing touch football. But he found out."

Although Landis was more or less the same age as his actors, he was a straight arrow who steered clear of drugs. "I was like the principal," he says. "If I walked in and they were smoking a joint, it got stashed right away." Ironically enough, the one person who rarely hung out in McGill's room was John Belushi. Due to his commitment to *Saturday Night*, he would work on the film from Monday through Wednesday, then head back to New York to rehearse and perform the show at 30 Rock. It was a grueling schedule, and Landis made sure that his star stayed away from trouble by renting him and his wife, Judy, a house close to the university instead of having them bunk at the Rodeway.

"Belushi would have been partying with us, I guarantee you," says Tim Matheson. "But they wanted to keep John away because they knew his tendencies." Landis insists that Belushi was clean throughout shooting (although he would be deep in the throes of cocaine addiction just a couple of years later when he reunited with Landis for *The Blues Brothers*). But one actor recalls Belushi's pulling out a vial of coke one night at a restaurant, taking a healthy bump in each nostril, then passing it around.

Landis says that the moment he knew that Belushi would become a movie star was when they were shooting the cafeteria scene in which Belushi slides his tray along the counter and binges on junk food. "I was behind the camera going, 'What is that? A hamburger? It looks good. I think we should eat the hamburger!' And Belushi could just do it so fast. Then, I'd go, 'Uh-oh, an éclair!' He truly was the Cookie Monster." The director also says that Kenney impressed him a lot as an actor, citing his famous parade scene at the end where Stork hijacks the local marching band and leads it into a dead-end alley.

When filming on *Animal House* wrapped, Landis returned to Los Angeles to edit it. There he was told by Sean Daniel and Thom Mount that not only had they been high on the dailies he'd been sending back from the set, but that all of the studio's young, fresh-out-of-college employees were begging to see them, too. After Landis cut together a rough version of the film, he extended an olive branch to Ramis and invited him to Screening Room 2 at Universal to see what he'd missed. According to a source close to the film, Ramis told Landis after it was over: "You fucked it up!" But Kenney and Miller thought differently. Kenney was convinced that not only was *Animal House* great, it would also be a box-office hit—even bigger than the top-grossing comedy to that point, *Blazing Saddles*. As for Miller: "I thought it would be a popular movie, but not that it would be *Gone with the Fuckin' Wind!*"

Still, the toughest audience had yet to see the finished film: Ned Tanen's heavyweight boss at the company, Lew Wasserman. Wasserman was sixty-five and a Hollywood titan of the old school. Four weeks before *Animal House* was released, the studio set up a sneak preview in Denver. Wasserman was in the audience. "The theater was jammed," recalls Reitman. "Somehow the word got out in the ether. From the first joke, when the mannequin gets thrown out of the Delta House window, the audience started bouncing. They just went nuts." Peter Riegert, who played

Boon, remembers Landis's calling him up after the screening and playing him a tape over the phone that sounded like a sonic boom. "I said, 'John, what is that?' And he said, 'That's the audience!' He'd taped the crowd's reaction as they were watching the movie." Says Landis, "After that, we went from being criminals to heroes."

National Lampoon's Animal House opened on July 28, 1978. It was the number-one movie in America for eight straight weeks. Roger Ebert gave the film four out of four stars, writing, "The movie is vulgar, raunchy, ribald, and occasionally scatological. It is also the funniest comedy since Mel Brooks made *The Producers*." By the end of its run, Landis's little movie that had cost less than $3 million would end up taking in more than $140 million, becoming the biggest comedy of all time. Kenney's prediction about knocking off *Blazing Saddles* had proved to be dead-on. Naturally, the muckety-mucks at Universal convinced themselves that they knew they'd been sitting on a hit all along.

Thom Mount says that in the giddy initial days and weeks after *Animal House*'s release, the studio realized that it had not only backed a winner, but had also found a sorely needed identity. "Paramount owned sophisticated movies, Fox owned romantic pictures, and Warner Bros. owned all of the action films. When the numbers for *Animal House* started coming in, I had the studio operators answer the phones by saying 'Comedy Central' instead of 'Universal.' We wanted to send a signal that we *owned* comedies."

By late October, when *Animal House* had already raked in more than $60 million, *National Lampoon* was comfortably profitable again for the first time since the crippling buyout deal. Matty Simmons would walk around the office at 635 Madison with a copy of *Variety* in his fist and a shit-eating grin on his face. Magazine sales were hitting an all-time high thanks to the success of *Animal House* (and the arrival of a new star writer, John Hughes). The film also goosed *Saturday Night Live*'s ratings, especially after a toga-clad John Belushi smirked on newsstands from the cover of *Newsweek*. The headline read "College Humor Comes Back." The accompanying article was a predictably hypey, star-is-born magazine profile about the white-hot twenty-nine-year-old actor whose barnyard charm had stolen the film. But it also broadened into something of a psychological snapshot of comedy's New Wave (which seemed especially *new* to the graying editorial board at *Newsweek*). Born in the pages of the *Lampoon*, bred on television with *Saturday Night Live*, the New Wave was now fully maturing on the big screen, poised to take over and transform Hollywood.

This new comedy revolution was a middle finger to the pious seriousness of the '60s, when college students could delude themselves into thinking they could stop the war just by growing their hair long. If you looked just beneath the surface of *Animal House*'s gross-out gags and food fights, you could see a serious statement being made. After all, here was a movie where the losers win, the winners lose, and the straight establishment (embodied by John Vernon's Nixonian Dean Wormer) is brought low by a bunch of immature miscreants out for a drunken good time. It would prove to be both a tidy metaphor and self-fulfilling prophecy for the people who'd made it.

They were outsiders who were on the verge of becoming insiders. The counterculture was becoming the culture.

5

Tinseltown Gold Rush

CLICHÉS BECOME CLICHÉS in large part because they contain more than a nugget of truth. As soon as it became clear that *Animal House* was not just a box office hit but a massive, industry-disrupting blockbuster, the old saying that "success has many fathers" couldn't have better described what was about to happen next. Everyone involved with the film began jockeying for credit: the young executives at Universal with their eyes on a corner office; the film's producers, Matty Simmons and Ivan Reitman; its director, John Landis; and its trio of *Lampoon*-affiliated writers—Doug Kenney, Harold Ramis, and Chris Miller. Had you spoken to any one of them in the late summer of 1978 when *Animal House* was firmly lodged atop the box office, you would have got an earful of self-congratulation and credit-grabbing. It was like an egocentric version of *Rashomon*: Everyone had a different, self-serving story about why they were responsible for the out-of-nowhere film's success. What had been a cordial and collaborative yearslong process turned into a predictable game of Hollywood self-puffery and chest-thumping.

Landis, who certainly reaped his fair share of the credit for *Animal House*'s success, recalls a conversation he had with Kenney shortly after the film came out. "Doug said, 'For a long time it was my movie, then it became Harold's and mine, and then Harold's and Chris's and mine. And then all of a sudden John Landis comes in and it's his movie. And then when it comes out, it's John Belushi's movie.'" Landis couldn't argue with Kenney's astute interpretation of events. Landis might have even felt the same way when Belushi appeared on the cover of *Newsweek*. But the subtext of what Kenney was saying was that on his next film, he intended to have more control. He wanted to make a Doug Kenney movie.

Though Kenney and the other screenwriters hadn't made much money for the *Animal House* script (they split $30,000 three ways, plus a few thousand extra here and there for each subsequent draft), they had been given five points on the back end to split. Typically, back-end points come in two varieties: gross points (which means the participant gets a cut of the movie's box office haul from the moment it opens) and net points (the participant's cut doesn't kick in until the movie recoups its production, marketing, and overhead costs). The writers had the far less favorable net points—about 1.6 of them each. That didn't sound like it would amount to much (if anything) before *Animal House* opened. But after the movie began making money hand over fist and the box-office receipts kept piling up, it turned into about $500,000 apiece. "Net points are kind of like monkey points; they're meaningless," says Miller. "But this movie was so cheap to make and made so much money, they couldn't hide it. There was no accounting creative enough to deprive us of our points. We got some very nice checks."

Landis had been paid $50,000 to develop the script and direct *Animal House*, which also may not sound like much, but he was a twenty-seven-year-old just happy to be making his first studio picture. In Hollywood, the saying goes: You don't get rich on your last movie, you get rich on the next one. As it was becoming clear that the film was headed to new, record-breaking heights, Ned Tanen gave Landis one net point as a gesture of goodwill (and no doubt an incentive for the now hot director to make his next movie at Universal). The majority of the profits, however, went to the studio, Simmons, and Reitman. While Simmons would end up making somewhere in the neighborhood of $12 million from *Animal House* (most of which went to refill the depleted *Lampoon* coffers), Reitman's cut would come to roughly $4 million.

Kenney remained fairly blasé about his windfall. After all, he was already a millionaire a couple of times over thanks to his well-timed cash-out from the *Lampoon.* "Doug's attitude about money was so cavalier," says Kenney's friend and eventual producing partner, Alan Greisman. "He once called me up and said, 'Hey, can you look in the back of your car; I think there might be a check from Universal for $45,000. And I went and looked in the backseat and there was a crumpled check for $45,000. He was doing that all the time."

If Kenney was nonplussed by his financial success on *Animal House*, Ramis was just the opposite. The thirty-three-year-old had a family at home and had been struggling and hustling for a decade since he'd first got to Second City. Now he could finally breathe easy for the first time in his life. "I literally took a copy of the newspaper review of *Animal House* to the bank to get the down payment on a house in Santa Monica," said Ramis. "I said to the loan officer, 'Look, I have a piece of this movie. I'm sure I'll be solvent.' That was my collateral. The guy laughed and gave me the loan right there."

Everyone involved with *Animal House* profited in one way or another. At Universal, Thom Mount and Sean Daniel both got promotions and would, in years to come, each take their turn running the studio in the post-Tanen era. John Landis signed a three-picture deal at Universal that would soon lead to *The Blues Brothers*. Matty Simmons got a development deal at the studio, too, and moved forward on a toothless *Animal House* spinoff show for ABC called *Delta House*. And John Belushi, who had now become the post-Chevy face of *SNL*, negotiated his own three-movie pact at Universal at ten times what he had been paid to pour mustard on himself as Bluto. He'd now be making $350,000 per picture. Unfortunately, the first fruit of his Universal deal would turn out to be pretty bruised and rotten—Steven Spielberg's colossal WWII comedy dud, *1941*.

If anyone felt shut out from all of the Monday-morning deal-making, it was Ivan Reitman. Sure, he'd made millions from *Animal House*, but he was beginning to feel as if everyone but him was getting the credit. "All of the smart Hollywood money was trying to grab all of us in different ways," says Reitman. "And I was sort of the unknown producer even though I put the whole thing together. Matty Simmons took a producing credit, John Landis was handed the funniest screenplay in a generation, and guys like Thom Mount and Sean Daniel, who were very important in getting the movie made, were also taking creative credit for it. It all sort of reduced how forefront I was in that group. I was sort of stuck outside. We were all suddenly very competitive with each other. We all had big egos." Reitman decided that the only way he would be taken seriously—or as seriously as he felt he ought to be taken—was to direct his own movie. Before *Animal House* had even been in theaters two weeks, Reitman was back in Canada shooting a low-budget summer-camp comedy called *Meatballs*, starring *SNL* new guy Bill Murray in his first lead.

It was one thing to be the director of a game-changing comedy such as *Animal House*, or even to be the studio that backed it. But by the late '70s, it was the creators, the comic minds, who were most in demand. There was a growing feeling that the sort of comedies that were considered sure-fire hits just a year or two earlier (Burt Reynolds in *Smokey and the Bandit*, George Burns in *Oh, God!*, Peter Sellers in the endless string of *Pink Panther* movies) were now, in the post–*Animal House*, post–*National Lampoon*, post-*SNL* world, as arthritic and unfunny as Henny Youngman working the Catskills. A generational fault line had opened up and swallowed yesterday's style of comedy. Soon, Steve Martin, Cheech and Chong, and Lorne Michaels's 30 Rock stable of cracked comic minds would replace them with their stoned observations, barbed satire, and absurd meta-shtick. Big-screen comedy was now a young person's game.

By 1979, 90 percent of movie ticket buyers would fall between the ages of twelve and thirty-nine. A premium was now being placed on those who could speak the new comedy language. It didn't matter if middle-aged suits such as Ned Tanen got it; it was enough to recognize that this was where the business was headed.

"I think the feeling in Hollywood was that we had introduced a new kind of comedy," said Ramis. "To us, it wasn't new because that's what we'd been doing at Second City and the *Lampoon*, but it was new to the movies."

Adds Sean Daniel, "After *Animal House*, everyone wanted to be in business with Doug and Harold. It was a total free-for-all."

The signs couldn't have been clearer if they were in flashing neon. It was time for Kenney to join Ramis and move to Los Angeles. He said goodbye to the *Lampoon* once and for all, hopped in his Porsche, and headed West to begin his new life as the Dream Factory's latest surefire star. The man who had built his career in large part by calling out phonies, was now headed to their mecca. Chris Miller, for reasons he still can't entirely explain, decided to stay behind in New York and kept writing filthy stories for the *Lampoon*. "I was not very quick on my feet," he says. "Doug and Harold immediately transplanted themselves to Hollywood. I didn't do that. I was more of a hippie than those guys. I thought we had a good thing going as outsiders and I wanted to preserve that. But Doug was excited about the move, and of course, he went out there and really got into cocaine. And that was all she wrote as far as Doug was concerned."

Kenney lived for a time at the shabby-chic Chateau Marmont, which is nestled into a hilly elbow of the Sunset Strip. Eventually, in an attempt to feel less transient and to put down some roots with Kathryn Walker (who was shuttling back and forth to New York to work on the stage), he took over the lease of the bachelor pad on Betty Lane in Coldwater Canyon where Chevy Chase had been living before he got married. When Walker was away, which was often, Kenney and Chase began to spend more and more time together. They would eventually become as close as brothers. While the two had plenty in common (sudden fame, smartass sarcasm, better-than-average backhands on the tennis court, and a need to always stay up later and rage a little harder than everyone else), each saw something in the other that they lacked: Chase wanted Kenney's Ivy League cachet and respectability; Kenney craved Chase's self-confidence and matinee-idol magnetism.

Kenney's new residence on Betty Lane quickly became the place to be—or at least the place to eventually *wind up* when everyplace else shut down. As he had back in New York, John Belushi would crash on Kenney's sofa whenever he was in town. Rock stars, *SNL* cast members, rising agents, and under-thirty industry players all found themselves pulled into Kenney's good-times orbit. One night, someone's car ended up in the swimming pool. It was a freewheeling social scene with a liberal open-door policy—all were welcome any time of day or night. And ever-present on the mantel was a sugar bowl full of Peru's finest marching powder supplied by the gracious host.

"We all grew up in the '60s with the idea that, Oh, this is harmless," says Kenney's friend Alan Greisman. "The worst that's going to happen is that you're going to wake up with a really bad hangover. Nobody accepted that cocaine was a harmful thing that could really kill you. I remember someone looking around the room at one of Doug's parties and saying, 'This is either the New Hollywood for the next decade or the Old Hollywood in six months.' It was a lot of sex, drugs, and rock 'n' roll. I don't remember ever having as much fun as we had back then."

One person who was curiously absent from Betty Lane was Harold Ramis, who had taken on a quickie assignment for Ivan Reitman doing a late-in-the-game rewrite of *Meatballs*. Everyone agreed that the original script for the movie was dumb, formulaic, and hopelessly past the point of salvation. In fact, Bill Murray had taken one look at it and passed on the role of the film's rebellious head counselor with a soft, chewy center, Tripper, even though he wasn't exactly being deluged with movie offers at the time. He said he'd rather sit around and play golf during his *SNL* summer hiatus. But when Reitman went back to the noncommittal star and told him that Ramis had agreed to polish the screenplay, Murray reluctantly agreed.

At least, Reitman *thought* he had agreed. The director began to panic when Murray (who still hadn't even signed a contract) didn't show up on the remote Ontario wilderness location until four days after shooting started. When he finally did arrive, Murray clutched a rolled-up copy of the revised script in his hand and told Reitman, "This is crap." In the margins, he'd written over and over again "S.O.T." It stood for "Same Old Thing." Rather than be embarrassed by serving up obvious, hackneyed bits that any stiff could deliver, Murray decided to rewrite his scenes himself. At night, he'd sit in his rental car and work until he fell asleep. For other scenes, he'd just ad-lib on the spot, as he did for the movie's climactic "It just doesn't matter" speech.

Reitman had been around the *Lampoon* long enough to know that he should just stand back and let the cameras keep rolling, capturing whatever inspired lunacy shot out of Murray's howitzer brain. *Meatballs* would end up becoming the sleeper hit of the summer in 1979. Made for just $1.6 million, the shaggy and endearing coming-of-age story made $43 million at the box office. Bill Murray had arrived as a movie star, and Reitman had finally got the attention and respect he'd been looking for—even if it came a little later than he would have liked. He was now a force in an industry that was being upturned so rapidly and unpredictably that even hustlers and hairdressers could become the new power brokers.

◆ ◆

From its earliest days, Hollywood has been portrayed as a promised land where anything is possible. It's a place where self-made dreamers can come and rewrite their pasts, turning them into origin stories that take on the power of myth. It's a town of endless reinvention. The earliest movie tycoons knew this better than anyone. Jack Warner was the streetwise son of a Polish cobbler who grew up in the rough, Mafia-controlled steel town of Youngstown, Ohio, before luckily falling into the nascent moving-pictures business and heading West. Louis B. Mayer was born in Minsk and grew up poor in New Brunswick, Canada, where he dropped out of school at the age of twelve; he would end up purchasing a small vaudeville theater in Massachusetts before expanding his way to California. Harry Cohn was the working-class son of Jewish immigrants, and he worked as a

New York streetcar conductor and sheet-music promoter before he would spin celluloid into gold.

Jon Peters was a man who saw his future in equally grandiose terms. He dreamed in CinemaScope. Born on the less glamorous side of the Hollywood Hills, in the San Fernando Valley town of Sherman Oaks, Peters was the son of a part-Cherokee former Marine who owned a truck-stop café. He died of a heart attack when Peters was ten. His mother was an Italian-American beauty whose family owned a hair salon where she sometimes worked. Short-tempered and quick to use his fists after his father's death, Peters left school behind in the seventh grade and was sent to juvenile hall by his mother after clashing with her second husband. Peters had become obsessed with the movies ever since he appeared as a child extra in the legendary parting of the Red Sea scene in Cecil B. DeMille's *The Ten Commandments*. Or so he claimed. He was so enthralled by the magic of cinema that he refused to wash his makeup off when he went home from the set at night. In his teens, his mother put him on a plane to New York with $120 in his pocket. There he found a job in a beauty salon dying the pubic hair of prostitutes.

After a failed marriage at sixteen, Peters returned to California and began working as a hairstylist. He would soon have his own chain of salons, where he charged $100 a pop to style the locks of fading and second-tier stars such as Jayne Mansfield, Sonja Henie, and Barbara Eden, and, soon enough, more promising ones such as Lesley Ann Warren, whom he would wind up marrying. For years, Peters claimed to be the inspiration for Warren Beatty's swinging, motorcycle-riding lothario stylist in *Shampoo*, but Beatty denies this. Driven by insatiable ambition, unrelenting chutzpah, and a dangerous air of macho swagger, Peters began dating Barbra Streisand after doing her hair for the 1974 comedy *For Pete's Sake*. His pickup line to the actress was as crass and bluntly to the point as nearly everything else that came out of his mouth. He told her that she had a great ass.

Peters and Streisand quickly moved in together and ended up buying a house in Malibu. Her inner circle of friends and handlers considered Peters a cocky and talentless wannabe, a thug who had parlayed his high-profile relationship with the A-list actress and singer into an entrée to the movie business. As her new manager, Peters was also making 15 percent of whatever Streisand earned. Streisand's friends thought that Peters exploited their romantic association and leveraged it into a role as the producer of her 1976 update of *A Star Is Born*, when, in truth, it had been Streisand's idea. The couple even flirted with the crazy idea of casting Peters as the male lead in the film. That production had been a notoriously tumultuous one, cycling through countless screenwriters and enduring on-set tirades by Peters. During one such flare-up, Peters was mouthing off to the film's line producer until the man couldn't take the abuse anymore and turned around and cold-cocked Peters. Crew members applauded. Afterward, that line producer never had a problem finding a job on a film again—Peters's enemies were only too happy to throw work his way. Peters's easily triggered jealousy concerning Streisand's costar, Kris Kristofferson, led to heated arguments on the set. At one point, after Peters yelled at Kristofferson, the actor fired back: "If I need any more shit from you, I'll squeeze your head."

Constantly underestimated and all-too-easily dismissed as a social-climbing dilettante, Peters may have gained admission to the film business through the side door of nepotism, but he quickly earned his keep once he was inside. Even his critics conceded that he had an innate street genius for marketing. *A Star Is Born* made $90 million at the box office, making it the biggest hit of Streisand's career at that point. The film's soundtrack, which Peters also produced, sold 8 million copies. It would no longer be possible to shrug Peters off as a '70s Sammy Glick, a gigolo hair-dresser acting above his station—not that people didn't try.

In 1977, Peters launched his own production company, the Jon Peters Organization (JPO). He took over a ground-floor suite on the Warner Bros. lot in Burbank and decked it out with mir-rored walls, rattan furniture, and palm-frond wallpaper inspired by the Beverly Hills Hotel. It looked more like a Rodeo Drive beauty salon than an office where actual work got done. JPO's first film would be the slick 1978 thriller *Eyes of Laura Mars* star-ring Faye Dunaway, who had recently won an Oscar for *Net-work*. He followed it up with *The Main Event*, an absurd (and absurdly bad) Streisand comedy about a perfume magnate turned boxing promoter that reteamed her with her *What's Up, Doc?* costar, Ryan O'Neal. Somehow the movie made $54 million. In April 1978, before *The Main Event* was released, Peters signed an exclusive three-year deal with the newly formed mini-studio Orion Pictures.

Orion was Hollywood's newest player. It had risen out of the ashes of United Artists, which had seen its five top executives simultaneously resign rather than answer to its bullying new cor-porate parent, Transamerica. United Artists had been a hot stu-dio in the '70s. Led on the creative side by Mike Medavoy, UA had a hands-off philosophy that attracted artistically ambitious directors, of which there were many in the post–*Easy Rider* era. It had been rewarded for that laissez-faire attitude with an im-pressive run of critical and box-office hits, including a string of Best Picture winners: *One Flew Over the Cuckoo's Nest, Rocky,* and *Annie Hall.* At Orion, Medavoy was essentially starting from scratch again. The studio quickly forged a joint partnership with Warner Bros. to have them market and distribute Orion's slate of movies. Then, to signal to the town that they were a major new force, Orion signed up a laundry list of established talent such as John Travolta, Burt Reynolds, and Jane Fonda to non-exclusive deals. As for his pact with Jon Peters, Medavoy admitted that he had an ulterior motive: "We made our producing deal with him at Orion primarily to get us instant access to his then-girlfriend, Barbra Streisand." Still, Medavoy conceded, "Jon seemed to have some kind of force field around him that sucked movie ideas and movie people in. He was a likable huckster who went on his instincts."

As a new shop, Orion was not only hungry for hits; it was starved for movies, period. In the summer of 1978, one of Peters's employees, a story editor and UCLA film school graduate named Donald MacDonald, attended a pre-release industry screening of *Animal House*. As a boss, Peters was especially dependent on his small staff of underlings to scout material and assess scripts for him because he simply lacked the concentration to read them himself. Peters preferred to have screenplays read aloud to him while he sat with his eyes closed imagining the movie to life in his mind. Words were so small; Jon Peters thought big.

On that summer evening, as the end credits rolled on *Animal House*, MacDonald rushed from his seat before the lights came up and hustled into the lobby to grab Harold Ramis and Doug Kenney before they left the theater. "He kind of intercepted us," said Ramis. "He literally snagged us walking out the door. He said Jon Peters would like to meet you guys and hear your ideas. It was very validating, obviously. Everyone was asking us, 'What do you want to do next?' Peters just happened to be the first one." Ramis knew that whatever he ended up doing next, he wanted to be the one to direct it. Part of him was still frustrated by how little say he'd had on *Animal House*, regardless of how successful it became. After years of work, John Landis just came in and took ownership of the movie and got his name above the title. Ramis wanted to make sure that that didn't happen again.

Ramis and Kenney met with Peters at his bungalow on the Warner Bros. lot. Peters's Ferrari was parked out front. Inside, the writers were greeted by a backslapping man in jeans and cowboy boots with longish hair and a neatly trimmed beard. He gave off the odd, dueling impressions of deferential humility and musky, alpha-male testosterone. After the introductions, Peters took his place behind his desk and sat down. He closed his eyes signaling that it was story time. Ramis and Kenney looked at each other curiously, thinking, Is this guy for real? Can this really be how it's done? Neither of them had been through this particular dog-and-pony show before. Kenney nodded to Ramis, urging him to go first. Ramis cleared his throat and launched into an idea for a dark comedy about the American Nazi Party marching in Skokie. It was based on actual events from the previous summer, which stirred national headlines due to the large number of Holocaust survivors who lived in the Illinois town. When he was done, he noticed that Peters's eyes were pressed tightly shut. He had a grin on his face.

It was now Kenney's turn to pitch. He began to describe a New Agey comedy adventure about an American hippie backpacking in the Tibetan Himalayas who got swept up fighting against a Chinese invasion with a bunch of Buddhist monks using magic and LSD. Kenney seemed to be making his pitch up more or less on the spot, mixing far-out druggie asides with plot points cribbed from the novel he never finished during his time at the *Lampoon, Teenage Commies from Outer Space*. Again, Peters continued to smile with his eyes closed.

Not sure whether to keep going or quit while they seemed to be ahead, Ramis launched into a third idea: a sort of Marxist revisionist Western about the class conflict between a heroic cowboy and his proletarian sidekick. Peters's smile morphed into an expression of utter bafflement. Said Ramis, "So I explained how when I would watch Westerns as a kid, I would think, Who's that Gabby Hayes character? Does he work for the other guy? Are they just friends? Why does he have a mule with all the pots and pans and the other guy just has a blanket? I wanted to look at that relationship. I called it *The Sidekick*."

Peters told Ramis and Kenney that he loved everything he'd heard. To them, it sounded like a Hollywood grease job which they weren't particularly buying. Still, Peters was serious enough that he wanted to take them to Mike Medavoy's office at Orion to see if the three parties could get a movie going together. Before the two writers shook hands and agreed, though, Ramis brought up one last bit of housekeeping that he wanted to address. Something Peters needed to know if they were going to move forward together. Ramis said that whatever idea they ended up doing, he wanted to direct it. Peters looked Ramis up and down, noticing his aviator glasses and safari jacket with lots of pockets, and said, "Why not? You look like a director."

Mike Medavoy was in a buyer's frame of mind by the time he met with Kenney and Ramis in the summer of 1978. At United Artists, he'd had his pick of prestige projects to choose from thanks to the studio's impressive track record. But Orion was a new company playing catch-up. By the end of its first year, the studio would race to put fifteen films into production. Still, it wouldn't have its first real hit until October 1979, when the Dudley Moore–Bo Derek sex comedy, *10*, raked in $74 million. Medavoy knew that the writers of *Animal House* could go to any of the deeper-pocketed majors, so he was thrilled that they were coming to him. Maybe that deal with Peters had been worth it after all.

When Peters arrived at Medavoy's office with Ramis and Kenney in tow, the writers were struck by a sense of déjà vu. Peters had been so high on their ideas that they assumed the meeting with Medavoy was just a formality before they walked out with a green-lighted movie. As they sat down, they realized that they were expected to wind up and start pitching again. "Harold spoke and Doug didn't really say a lot," recalls Medavoy. "Harold pitched his idea for a comedy about the Nazis marching in Skokie, and I thought, Oh, God, I don't think I find this as funny as you guys do." Ramis was taken aback.

"Jon Peters had led me to believe that Medavoy would do the Skokie idea," Ramis said. "But Medavoy argued that if they got one bomb threat on a theater it would shut the movie down. So he said come up with something else. And I'll never forget this; he said: 'Think urban and contemporary.'" Ramis and Kenney walked out of Medavoy's office feeling like they'd had the wind knocked out of them.

Two weeks later, they returned to Medavoy's office—this time without Peters—with an idea that Kenney had once heard Brian Doyle-Murray talking about. It had been tickling at the back of his brain ever since. A comedy at a country club based on all of the Murray boys' teenage memories as caddies outside Chicago. It hit all the same snobs-versus-slobs class-warfare notes that *Animal House* had. Doyle-Murray had even thought up a name for it: *Caddyshack*. Kenney knew that he probably shouldn't be pitching the idea without Doyle-Murray in the room. But he figured, Fuck it, Medavoy might not even bite anyway. . . .

An hour later, there was a surprise knock at the door of Brian Doyle-Murray's hotel room in LA. Doug Kenney and Harold Ramis barged in with the good news. "They told me that they had taken the liberty of pitching my idea," says Doyle-Murray. "Doug was going to produce it, Harold was going to direct it, and they wanted me to write it with them. I said, 'Fine, let's go to work!'"

Like The Dick Van Dyke Show

IT WAS NOW OFFICIAL: *Caddyshack* had been given the go-ahead by Orion.

Although Jon Peters hadn't been in the room when Harold Ramis and Doug Kenney pitched what Mike Medavoy said sounded like "the ultimate spring-break movie," the studio head brought him on as the film's executive producer. He considered it a show of good faith. A sort of finder's fee. Plus, it helped him justify some of the overhead costs of Peters's production deal at the studio. Later, Medavoy would sing a slightly different tune. "To my regret, I brought Peters in," Medavoy says. "I think it would have gone a lot smoother if I had put somebody in charge who was a little more responsible and not as crazy."

Peters wasn't exactly overburdened with "Go Pictures" at the time. The only project that he'd brought the studio so far was a not-terribly-promising little comedy starring teen heartthrob Robby Benson (and a monkey) called *Die Laughing*. When Thom Mount heard about the *Caddyshack* deal back at his office at Universal, he felt a little hurt that the boys whom he believed he'd backed so fiercely on *Animal House* hadn't come to him first. "I must say, I was totally jealous that we didn't have that movie for the studio."

Signing two-thirds of the screenwriting brain trust behind *Animal House* was a coup for the newly formed Orion. They had somehow snagged the hottest young writers in town. On paper, the partnership made more sense for Orion than it did for Ramis, Kenney, and Doyle-Murray. Ivan Reitman, for one, says he was mystified when he heard that they'd gone into business with someone like Peters. "I thought it was dumb," Reitman says. "I think Jon probably just convinced them that they were going to have more independence with him. That's a real writers' and directors' desire. I think he probably convinced Harold and Doug that they would be the bosses." It turns out that was *exactly* Peters's salespitch.

Peters told the boys that they would never have to deal directly with Medavoy or respond directly to Orion's meddling notes and controlling demands, because he'd be running interference. He was their protector, their pit bull. Peters told them, "I'll deal with them; you just make your movie." It's easy to understand how seductive that must have sounded to Kenney and Ramis. Both of them felt largely alienated from *Animal House* after John Landis came onboard. In his own crass, pugilistic way, Peters was the godfather they were looking for. He was as much of a Hollywood outsider as they were.

Still, even early on in their collaboration, Peters would prove to be hard to trust fully. On the surface, he painted himself as the *Caddyshack* writers' champion, willing to take on all corporate comers and smooth out any obstacles that lay in their way. Behind their backs, though, he could be manipulative and petty. Although Peters had told Ramis during their initial meeting that he "looked like a director" and wholeheartedly supported his ambition to be the one behind the camera, he tried to lowball Ramis on his directing fee. Later, Peters tasked one of his employees, Donald MacDonald, with drawing up a list of replacement directors in case he felt the sudden need, or just the vindictive whim, to take the film away from someone he'd sized up as weak. Ramis, of course, knew nothing of this.

With the ink dry on the Orion deal, it was finally time, in the words of Doyle-Murray, to get to work. As with *Animal House*, the three writers got together for marathon bull sessions in New York diners and bars, where they swapped stories about their youthful experiences as sub-minimum-wage service-industry slaves catering to hoity-toity snobs. Doyle-Murray would be an encyclopedia of stranger-than-fiction tales from his and his brothers' time as caddies at some of the finest country clubs on Chicago's North Shore—not only about the members but the eccentric wack jobs he'd worked side by side with. Both Ramis and Kenney were surprised to learn not only that the Murray boys had been caddies starting as early as age eleven, but their father had also clocked time lugging golf bags to earn money in his youth. He'd even once caddied for US Open amateur champion Chick Evans.

Kenney had his own deep well of stories. Over cocktails and more smokable refreshments, he unspooled countless anecdotes that his father had passed on to him about working as a tennis pro. Kenney himself had also worked in the pro shops of various bastions of blue-blood leisure entitlement, stringing tennis rackets and swallowing all of the clever, wiseass insults he wanted to fire back at the clubs' condescending members. This was his chance for revenge, albeit fifteen years late. He and Doyle-Murray both knew, deeply, the smoldering resentment, insecurity, and jealousy of growing up and feeling excluded—what it was like to have your nose pressed up against the glass, wondering what life was like on the other side.

"Brian and Doug both had lots of characters from their real-life experiences," said Ramis. "But I came to it as a total outsider.

I was a Jewish kid with no money who was standing outside the gates of the country club. No one I knew even played golf." Ramis would end up being Doyle-Murray and Kenney's sounding board, scribbling their wild stories down on yellow legal pads, juicing them with his own satirical topspin.

With reams of raw material assembled, the three writers were given a small, nondescript bungalow on the Warner Bros. lot in Burbank, directly behind Peters's office. When they came in each day, a towel would be stuffed under the door, a joint or three would be sparked up, and the script pounded out. "It was the three of us in a room every day for three months," said Ramis. "It was like *The Dick Van Dyke Show*: One types, one paces, and one lies on the sofa. We switched off, although I don't remember Brian typing very much." As the most grounded member of the group, Ramis said he was usually the one stuck behind the typewriter—the Rose Marie of the trio.

"I'd come in in the middle of their writing sessions and the room was just filled with smoke," says Trevor Albert, Jon Peters's young assistant at the time. "I couldn't believe they were smoking pot when they were working. I'd just left college and thought I was in the working world, and here these guys were getting high. They acted like college friends playing together. They were a bit like kids in a candy store. I thought, This is how I would like to work in the movie business."

Albert had been a film major at UC San Diego and was twenty-two when he was hired as Peters's assistant. Which essentially meant that he was a not-so-glorified errand boy. "I got the job on the promise that I would work on a movie, and I spent the first year taking Barbra Streisand's poodle to the dog groomer and driving Jon's kids to basketball games," he says. Any film-related task, no matter how menial, would have felt like a gift to him. He was making $100 a week, driving his own car to run Peters's

errands without even being reimbursed for gas. "Even though I
respected Barbra Streisand, I had no interest in the kind of mov
ies she was doing," he says. "But I was on a studio lot, and it was
a good way to begin my career despite Jon's sadistic management
skills." Albert recalls that the first time the *Caddyshack* writers
showed up at Warner Bros., he fetched their coffee. "I immediately thought I'd much rather be working for *these* guys. They
were smart and funny. I wasn't sure how smart or funny Jon Peters
was."

In addition to Trevor Albert and Donald MacDonald, the key
personnel at the Jon Peters Organization who would become
instrumental in the making of *Caddyshack* included an eager
young production executive named Rusty Lemorande, and Peters's top lieutenant and head of development, Mark Canton.
Canton was twenty-nine, ambitious, and a bit tightly wound,
with a frizzy nimbus of corkscrew curls on top of his head. He
had gotten his initial break working for Mike Medavoy during
his tenure at United Artists. Peters had met Canton when the
two were working on a never-made remake of the all-female
1939 MGM classic, *The Women*, for Barbra Streisand and Faye
Dunaway to star in. Peters eventually lured him away from Me
davoy to develop material for both him and his famous girlfriend. *Caddyshack* would end up becoming Canton's baptism
into the junior producer ranks.

The first draft of the *Caddyshack* script would wind up being
very different from the movie it eventually became. Set at an
upper-crust Illinois country club called Bushwood, the story revolved around a recent high school graduate named Danny
Noonan. Born on the wrong side of the tracks into a working-
class Irish-Catholic family with too many kids to count, Danny
is a good kid who spends his summer caddying for the stuffed
shirts at Bushwood while he figures out how he's going to pay

for college. He competes for a caddie scholarship—and for the love of an Irish club employee named Maggie O'Hooligan against a cocky fellow caddie named Tony D'Annunzio. Swirling around the love triangle, which is undoubtedly the main focus of the early script, are a bunch of young slacker caddies and some colorful club members making drive-by cameo appearances. "Doug always described it as a bildungsroman," said Ramis, "which is a fancy, Harvard way of saying a coming-of-age story. I always suspected that it would evolve more toward the adults, but it didn't start out that way."

The Danny Noonan character was based on Brian Doyle-Murray's oldest brother, Ed, who won the annual Chick Evans Caddie Scholarship to attend Northwestern University. It was one of the Murray family's proudest moments. The Evans scholarship was created to help outstanding caddies with financial need. When the writers were first hashing out the *Caddyshack* script, Kenney met with Ed Murray and interviewed him to help flesh out the Danny Noonan character. Doyle-Murray filled in the rest with his own personal observations gleaned from hauling clubs at $3.50 per eighteen holes. "A caddie comes into contact with different role models," said Doyle-Murray. "Doctors, lawyers, captains of industry, social climbers, horny young ladies, horny *old* ladies. It's its own subculture."

Initially, the *Caddyshack* script was basically about Danny Noonan's extraordinary education, his passage into adulthood. Less fleshed out were the adult characters who would do the educating. Among the still-evolving cast of Bushwood members were: the uptight WASP Judge Elihu Smails and his promiscuous niece, Lacey Underall (who's only seventeen in the early script); the obnoxious developer Al Czernak (described as "a stocky, balding cement block in a flaming leisure suit"; his name would later be changed to Czervik) and his Asian sidekick,

Yamamoto (later Wang); and Ty Webb ("a handsome, thirty-ish bachelor with clear eyes and an air of relaxed self-control," who, it must be said, wasn't a barrel of laughs by the time the first draft was completed). Doug Kenney had modeled Ty after himself—or how he liked to *imagine* himself: someone who sails through life without a care and a fondness for quoting Zen philosophers such as Basho, who famously *did not* say, "A flute with no holes is not a flute. A donut with no hole is a Danish."

When Kenney, Ramis, and Doyle-Murray were writing the character of Ty, they were tailoring the part specifically for Chevy Chase, as if it were a bespoke suit he could slide right into. Mike Medavoy had only green-lighted their pitch on the condition that they could deliver a star. And Chase, whose first post-*SNL* film, *Foul Play*, had just come out and been a hit in July, was definitely the kind of star Orion was looking to get into business with. Kenney and Ramis had even gone so far as dropping Chase's name as someone they had an in with during the *Caddyshack* pitch meeting. Still, if you squint hard enough, what leaps out most from the first draft of *Caddyshack* isn't the few memorable scenes that are already there (the Baby Ruth in the pool, Smails's Billy Baroo putter, the "Be the ball" and "Did someone step on a duck?" lines); it's the sheer number of ones that *aren't* there yet.

After three months, Ramis, Kenney, and Doyle-Murray handed in the first draft to an eager Jon Peters. He'd been talking up the project around town since day one, and he was itching to finally get a peek at what he'd been hyping. A typical Hollywood screenplay usually runs about 120 tightly formatted pages. Comedies tend to be even shorter. The first draft of the *Caddyshack* script was two hundred pages long. Peters was aghast. "It looked like the Bible," says Mark Canton. "I didn't know *what* it was."

Not once in those two hundred pages did the name Carl Spackler appear.

♦ ♦

As the holidays neared, the writers gave themselves a sorely needed vacation from working—and from Peters. *Animal House* was still in theaters chugging toward the $100 million mark at the box office. John Belushi and Dan Aykroyd's first Blues Brothers album, *Briefcase Full of Blues*, had just been released and would soon give Billy Joel the boot from the top spot on the Billboard 200. And *Saturday Night Live* had just kicked off its fourth season to record ratings. Seventeen million people were watching the show each week. The world, at least in terms of pop culture, was all of a sudden looking much more promising than it had just a couple of years earlier, largely due to the people who had worked in the hothouse of *National Lampoon*.

Feeling good about all he'd done so far on *Caddyshack*, Doug Kenney decided to return to New York and spend Christmas and New Year's with his long-distance girlfriend, Kathryn Walker. He wasn't the only one who was looking to spend the holidays with her. According to John Ptak, who was Kenney's agent then at the William Morris Agency, Christopher Walken was also taken with Walker at the time. Kenney wasn't sure how much had transpired between the two, but his jealousy (no doubt exacerbated by his increasing intake of drugs) led to a very strange evening at the Plaza around Christmastime, when Ptak, Kenney, Walker, and producer Alan Greisman met for drinks at the hotel's Palm Court.

Seemingly uninvited, Walken showed up and approached the table to join them. Curious looks were exchanged. Kenney became uneasy. He could sense *something*. Always a fool for the grand, scene-making gesture, Kenney decided that he had to prove his love to Walker and extinguish the threat of any rival.

"Like a rather wasted Lancelot, Doug started in around midnight about how he would do anything to prove his love for Kathryn," says Ptak. "So he ran out of the bar and into the center of 59th Street, where he stood firm, cars flying by, waving his arms about and letting everyone in the neighborhood know how he felt." Not sure that he'd made his point clearly enough, Kenney then lay down in the middle of the busy Manhattan street. Ptak and Greisman eventually pulled him off the asphalt and led him back into the bar. Angry and maybe a little scared by Kenney's display, Kathryn Walker left.

The eventful week was just getting started. Ptak had managed to finagle an invitation to Orion chairman Arthur Krim's star-studded annual New Year's Eve party. Ptak was staying in room 1009 at the Sherry-Netherland Hotel, tucked against the southeast corner of Central Park. Before heading over to Krim's party, the agent had some friends up to his room, including Kenney; Walker; Greisman; Lorimar development exec Sug Villa; Ptak's William Morris colleague Rick Nicita; and Rick's wife, casting director Wallis Nicita. At 10:15, they all left the room to swing by a party being thrown in the Universal suite upstairs by legendary film editor Verna Fields, whose guests included Roy Scheider and Oliver Stone. About an hour later, they returned to Ptak's room to get their coats and race over to Krim's party before the ball dropped. When the elevator doors opened on the tenth floor, the hallway was filled with thick black smoke. It was coming from Ptak's room.

Firemen blocked off the area outside the hotel and seemed to think that the blaze had started on a couch in the living room of Ptak's suite, most likely the result of a stray cigarette or joint. In the end, the fire in Room 1009 would cause more than $20,000 in property damage. Sometime shortly after 1 a.m., Ptak, Kenney, and the rest finally arrived at Krim's, looking shaken and slightly crispy. Some of the revelers there were curious about the blackened area around Kenney's nostrils. They were more used to seeing white there. Perhaps Doug had discovered an exotic new high they weren't yet familiar with.

After the chaos of the holidays that ushered in 1979, Doug Kenney returned to Los Angeles less relaxed than he'd hoped, but eager to get back to work. Shortly after *Animal House* opened, Matty Simmons rushed the spin-off TV series *Delta House* into production for ABC. Although Kenney was only minimally involved with it, he wanted everything that bore his name to be first rate—or, at the very least, not embarrassing. When *Delta House* debuted at 8 p.m. on January 19, it was obvious that it was nothing more than a shameless and feeble attempt to cash in on a hit movie. Though some of the film's cast returned for the series, the biggest stars (John Belushi, Donald Sutherland, Tim Matheson) were missing. So, too, were the film's signature moments of blackout drunkenness, pot smoking, and gratuitous nudity thanks to strict network standards and the show's odd, early-bird time slot. The only encouraging signs were the casting of a then-unknown Michelle Pfeiffer in the role of The Bombshell and the name of a recently hired *Lampoon* staffer in the show's writing credits: John Hughes. *Delta House* was unceremoniously canceled after thirteen weeks.

The show's flameout, though, didn't lessen Universal's desire to get moving on an *Animal House* sequel. While John Landis and the film's original trio of writers all had their hands full with other Hollywood projects, Matty Simmons was as determined as a junkyard dog with a bone. Chris Miller recalls an idea for a follow-up that he had knocked around with Ramis and Kenney. "The concept was, it was five years later, 1967," says Miller. "And all of the Deltas get together in San Francisco in the Haight for Pinto's wedding. Flounder is no longer called Flounder; he's called Pisces. We would do for the Summer of Love what we did for college and fraternities."

Kenney and Ramis already had enough to keep them busy with *Caddyshack*. Their new film wasn't just another writing job that would end when the script was completed; they were now also filmmakers—Kenney would be the producer, Ramis the director. It was a full-time commitment for at least the next year and a half. Still, they were intrigued by just how financially motivated Universal might be to get their hands on an *Animal House* sequel.

In the February 26, 1979 issue of *New York* magazine, Kenney cockily tested their market value through the press. In a brief news article titled "Frat Brats Stand Pat," Kenney says that he, Harold Ramis, and Chris Miller would be willing to work an *Animal House* sequel but only if they received significant raises: "Universal paid us $30,000 for the first script, which went through ten drafts," he said. "We made the studio an offer for this one, but it only came back with one third." According to the article, Kenney, Ramis, and Miller had requested $750,000. Kenney didn't confirm that number, but he didn't deny it either. "I won't say what the figure is, but we'd do it for less than a million with point equity. Still, it's not as much as we're worth."

While work on a second draft of the *Caddyshack* script began, Kenney found himself looking for a new home. Two of them, actually. He and Kathryn Walker had decided to look for a house together in the Hollywood Hills—somewhere that they could settle down and begin a grown-up life together. Kenney, who was revving fast on work, cocaine, and late nights, yearned for a sense of stability. He eventually purchased a home at 2761 Outpost Drive, just off Mulholland, near Runyon Canyon Park. The white stucco house sits atop a narrow, snaky road lined with eucalyptus trees and tucked-away houses. It was an adult purchase.

A place to put down roots. Tellingly, he left it almost completely unfurnished for the next year and a half—minimalism taken to the extreme. He would throw parties there where famous guests such as James Taylor and Joni Mitchell could find no place to sit. Kenney was good at impulse decisions, less so at follow-through.

The second home was a more professional and psychological one. Ever since Kenney had arrived on the West Coast, he had been adrift and unfocussed. He was the kind of person who walked around with a whirlwind of creative ideas in his head, but no outlet to channel them. His friend Lucy Fisher, who was still dating Kenney's best friend from Harvard, Peter Ivers, was now a successful movie studio executive. She and Ivers had been overjoyed when Kenney told them he was leaving the *Lampoon* and moving to LA. And they enjoyed seeing him once he was there. But they were aware that they were only spending time with daylight Doug. There was also an after-hours Doug who ran with a druggier crowd. "He had another life that we weren't aware of," says Fisher. "We just thought, Oh, he's being an asshole; he's doing too much coke."

Lucy Fisher had climbed up the studio ladder rapidly, which was especially impressive since the glass ceiling in Hollywood was still suffocatingly low for women in the late '70s. By the time Kenney arrived in LA, she had just moved from MGM to 20th Century Fox, where she was a VP whom the press had dubbed one of the town's new "baby moguls." Still flush with *Star Wars* riches, Fox was about to have an impressive year in 1979 with such films as *Norma Rae*, *Alien*, *Breaking Away*, and *All That Jazz*. Sensing that Kenney needed some discipline for all of his manic energy, Fisher encouraged him to set up a production company at her studio. She thought she could protect him there.

Kenney's agent, John Ptak, brokered a two-year deal that teamed Kenney with Alan Greisman and Michael Shamberg, two producers Kenney already knew socially. They weren't excessive partiers like so many of the other people he had met in LA; they were well-read intellectuals. Kenney's new partners had recently begun shooting a Nick Nolte–Sissy Spacek drama about Jack Kerouac and Neal Cassady called *Heart Beat*. The marriage wasn't particularly lucrative (according to the William Morris booking slip for the deal, the three split $117,000 annually, with more money to come with each green-lighted project), but it felt secure and safe. Plus, Kenney had always worked best when he had other people in the room to bounce his ideas off of, as he had at the *Lampoon* and on *Animal House*. When left alone with his own mad torrent of thoughts, as he was on Martha's Vineyard while writing *Teenage Commies from Outer Space*, it didn't go as well. He would become unmoored. Perhaps Greisman and Shamberg would be able to anchor Kenney. They might even persuade him to direct one of the films they developed. The new partners called their venture Three Wheel Productions. To celebrate, Kenney mocked up new company stationery whose logo showed a Tinseltown smoothie in gold chains leaning against a Jaguar sports car with the company's unofficial motto underneath: "See You in Court!"

Three Wheel Productions was given an office on the Fox lot just down the hallway from Lawrence Kasdan, Barry Levinson, and Mel Brooks, who was considered studio royalty at the time. "I remember one day bringing Doug to meet Mel Brooks," says Lucy Fisher. "Mel said, 'Oh, this is the new thing!' Like, I'm the King and now these guys might be the kings." Clearly, Brooks not only knew who Doug Kenney was; he was also aware that *Animal House* had just knocked Brooks's *Blazing Saddles* from the record books. One of the earliest projects that Kenney put into motion at Three Wheel was a comedy set at a swinging Club Med–style resort in the Caribbean titled *Club Sandwich*. The idea had been generated by Kenney's *Animal House* cowriter and old *Lampoon* friend, Chris Miller, who would be writing the screenplay with a former colleague of Harold Ramis's from *Playboy*, David Standish.

Michael Shamberg recalls marveling at Kenney's seemingly effortless ability to pull fully formed ideas out of the air. "It just came to him like jazz," he says. But Shamberg also could see that there was a dangerous side to Kenney, too. "I had people over at my apartment in West Hollywood one time, and Doug just laid out this serpentine line of coke on the table. They were doing just as much illicit substances after *SNL* shows as they were in Hollywood. I think every generation thinks they discovered drugs for the first time. But this drug was cocaine. And he was doing a lot of it."

Still, Shamberg insists that Kenney's coke habit never affected his work at Three Wheel. "He wasn't doing it at the office," he says. "Plus, Greisman and I were doing it occasionally too. So it wasn't like our hands were clean. It was just a drug to fuel his creativity. It was more in social situations, you know, Young Hollywood. For people of a certain generation out here it was very pervasive at the time. It wasn't like taking OxyContin where you just nod out. The thinking was, I'm going to get more done and be more creative. No one had died yet. And there was no one to say stop."

♦ ♦

By mid-May 1979, Kenney, Ramis, and Doyle-Murray had turned in their third draft of the *Caddyshack* script. It was certainly shorter—now a svelte 135 pages instead of a bloated two hundred—but even though the story was beginning to come into focus, it was still fuzzy around the edges. For example, there are several characters with speaking parts who would end up never appearing in the film at all. There's a scene between a pair of caddies named Feeb (who's described as "twitchy" and "with a hint of mental deficiency") and Injun Joe ("a big silent Indian of indeterminate age" and clearly a nod to the mute Native American character that Will Sampson played in *One Flew Over the Cuckoo's Nest*).

There's also Ray, "an old, professional caddie wearing a dirty golf cap with an emblem from the 1946 Buick Open," who has a conversation early on in the script with Goofy, "a gawky be-spectacled sixteen year old" caddie. Ray tells a truncated and less than memorable version of the infamous Dalai Lama story that would later be given to *Caddyshack*'s demented assistant greens-keeper, Carl Spackler, who is still nowhere to be found in the third draft:

> RAY
>
> I jumped a ship in Hong Kong and made my way to Tibet where I got on as a looper at this golf club up there in the Himalayan Mountains.
>
> GOOFY
>
> A looper?
>
> RAY
>
> A caddie—a jock! So I tell 'em I'm a pro, so who do they give me? The Dalai Lama himself—flowin' white robes and everything. So I give him his driver and he tees off—right into this glacier and his ball goes down this 10,000 foot crevice. And you know what the Dalai Lama says?
>
> GOOFY
>
> No.

RAY
'Shit.' Yeah—'Shit!' And you know
what else. I'm full of shit. Yeah.

The May 1979 script is just as undercooked in other sections. The seduction scene between Danny Noonan and Lacey Underall is, at this point, a trippy, psychedelic sequence where she gives him a hit of the drug MDA before they have sex, leading to a silly fantasia of hallucinations. The African-American Bushwood employee Smoke Porterhouse who power-sands the wax buildup off of Judge Smails's golf shoes has the less evocative name Westinghouse. There's a totally out-of-place and pointlessly lengthy action sequence in which three of the caddies attempt to steal a shipment of television sets at the harbor. And the Scottish greenskeeper, Sandy McFiddish (who's barely a walk-on cameo in the finished film), is the one who battles the nefarious Bushwood gopher. But it's not even a gopher. At this point, it's a mole.

Danny, Maggie, and Tony D'Annunzio are still the central characters in the film. Al Czervik's name is still Czernak. On the plus side, however, the caddies *do* bet on whether or not Spaulding will eat his own boogers ("Fifty dollars the Smails kid picks his nose"). A showering Mrs. Smails unwittingly asks Danny: "Will you loofah my stretchmarks?" The caddies break into an impromptu water ballet in the club's swimming pool. And the Baby Ruth "Doodie!" scene is still intact, which makes sense, since the incident was actually based on something that happened at Brian Doyle-Murray's Catholic high school. By the end, Ty Webb and Lacey Underall end up together. Danny wins enough money to go to college. And the last scene of the film has him saying goodbye to his family at the airport on his way to college . . . until he sees a gorgeous girl getting on an Air Jamaica flight with a golf bag, and he follows her instead.

It's a funny-enough script, but not *Caddyshack* funny. It's 50 percent of the way there at best. Ramis, Kenney, and Doyle-Murray knew it, too. But they weren't particularly concerned about it. All three of the writers planned to be on the set every day once they started shooting. And two of them—Ramis and Doyle-Murray—had years of improv training at Second City under their belts. If worse came to worst, they could always write and rewrite on the spot.

With shooting slated to start around Labor Day, it was time to forget about it and move on to the next obstacle: casting.

7

Finally, Some Respect

ALTHOUGH THE CREATIVE TEAM behind *Caddyshack* had already been working on the script for half a year, the project became official on June 25, 1979. That's the day when *Caddyshack* was first publicly announced in the industry trade paper *Variety*. If you read between the lines, there seemed to be something a bit calculated about the timing. Surely Jon Peters could have placed the item with the press sooner. But perhaps by waiting as long as he did, he was in some small way trying to steal some of the thunder surrounding another high-profile project that was about to start shooting on July 1—John Landis's *The Blues Brothers*.

As both films were being pushed through the Hollywood development pipeline, a friendly rivalry had begun to form. In the wake of *Animal House*, it suddenly felt as if the main players of that movie had split into two distinct camps: *Caddyshack* versus *The Blues Brothers*. John Landis, John Belushi, and the *Animal House* executive team at Universal (Thom Mount and Sean Daniel) were about to head to Chicago to tell the musical, mission-from-God odyssey of Joliet Jake and Elwood Blues, while Doug Kenney and Harold Ramis had their little class-warfare country club comedy. Both were tentatively slated to hit theaters sometime in the summer of 1980. As far as the *Caddyshack* team was concerned, though, they were the underdogs. It was a position that, frankly, they preferred. After all, Universal had opened its vault and given Landis a staggeringly large budget of $17 million (it would grow quite a bit larger), while Orion had tightly capped the *Caddyshack* budget at $6 million. Despite the film's enviable *Animal House* provenance and pedigree, Orion still very much considered *Caddyshack* a B movie.

Most big studio pictures are cast about three months ahead of shooting. And in June, Kenney reached out to his casting-director friend, Wallis Nicita, to see if she would be interested in coming on board and assembling the actors for his new film.

"I knew Doug socially very well because his girlfriend, Kathryn Walker, was a good friend of mine," says Nicita. "My then-husband, Rick Nicita, was her agent. We all socialized together." In fact, the Nicitas had been present during the infamous New Year's Eve inferno at the Sherry-Netherland in New York six months earlier. Nicita was five months pregnant when she began working on the film. She did it not only as a favor to Kenney but also because she'd read the script and thought it was hilarious, even if, Nicita says, "It wasn't Paddy Chayefsky and I wasn't thrilled about the way women were portrayed in it."

Nicita was given a vacant office on the Warner Bros. lot adjacent to Kenney, Ramis, and Doyle-Murray's writing bungalow. Thirty-two at the time, Nicita had made a name for herself by training under the best in her business, working in the office of Hollywood star makers Marion Dougherty and Juliet Taylor—two giants in the world of casting. In their own way, they had been as responsible as anyone for the rise of the New Hollywood in the late '60s and early '70s, redefining what movie stars could look like. Dougherty had more or less discovered Al Pacino, Dustin Hoffman, Gene Hackman, and Warren Beatty, plucking them out of New York's off-Broadway theaters and giving them their earliest flashes on celluloid. Taylor, her protégée, would cast more than thirty Woody Allen movies. Nicita was one of their most eagle-eyed disciples. She knew that a film like *Caddyshack* required fresh faces and out-of-the-box thinking, especially given its relatively small budget.

Nicita broke down the script, identified all the main parts, and sent it out to all of the top agents and managers in her bicoastal network and waited for submissions. She then culled the candidates down to just a handful for each role and set up meetings with the hopefuls. Thanks to Kenney and Ramis's recent triumph with *Animal House*, she had an added bit of leverage when it came to attracting the most in-demand actors. "Doug and Harold had a lot of clout at that moment," she says. "They were the darlings of the town. We had all come out from New York and it really felt a little like Camelot."

Both Ramis and Kenney were learning about the mysterious art of casting as they went. Neither had been through this Byzantine process before. With its intangible factors of charisma, chemistry, and box-office clout, it felt a bit like going on a series of blind dates. Still, Ramis knew that their top priority was pinning down the bankable A-list star that Orion had insisted upon from day one. "With any big movie, you need a million-dollar player, a headliner," said Ramis. They needed Chevy.

When Kenney approached his friend about being in *Caddyshack*, Chase told him that he was interested, but that there might be a scheduling problem. When *Caddyshack* was scheduled to begin shooting, he would probably still be working on his next movie, *Oh! Heavenly Dog*. The soft-boiled canine caper was an odd career choice for someone who was trying to establish himself as a serious actor (and who was well on his way after earning a Golden Globe nomination for *Foul Play*, which had made $45 million at the box office). Chase seemed to already know that his dog movie would most likely turn out to be unwatchable crap, but he was human. They'd hooked him with an insanely large paycheck.

Somewhat desperate, Kenney told Chase that they could probably shoot around him for the first two weeks if that's what it would take to get him to sign on. Plus, it wasn't like they were exactly paying him scale. It would be another fat payday for Chase. After working with a dog on a film that would, no doubt, *be* a dog, Chase liked the idea of spending some time on a movie set with friendly faces and kindred spirits who could make him laugh. Plus, he liked the idea of mocking the sport.

"I'd never gone for golf; I was more of a tennis player," says Chase. "My father told me to stay away from Republicans on golf courses, because they just wasted the day so they could stay away from their families. And I felt the same way. I mean, what the hell was that? Walking around like it was some kind of an aerobic sport!"

• •

Once Chase signed on, the *Caddyshack* team moved on to the next high-profile role to be filled: Al Czervik. For the flashy part of the film's superwealthy, insult-spewing bull in a china shop, Ramis had originally been thinking of reaching out to Don Rickles, who could turn anyone unlucky enough to fall into his trash-talking crosshairs into trembling, sobbing jelly. "He had the right obnoxiousness," said Ramis. But by the summer of 1979, Rodney Dangerfield was in the midst of an incredible run of volcanic guest appearances on *The Tonight Show*, often reducing Johnny Carson to a slumped, convulsive fool behind his desk, wiping tears from his eyes because he was laughing so hard. "He was just killing it every time he went on," said Ramis.

Dangerfield would bring his bug-eyed, collar-tugging, "No Respect" loser act to *The Tonight Show* thirty-six times. "I remember going in to see Doug and Harold when they were working on the script and saying, 'Dangerfield was on *The Tonight Show* last night and he was hysterical,'" says Nicita. "And I remember Doug saying, 'You know, I think he could do it.' The idea of Rodney rolling in there and doing his Rodney thing, they liked."

Dangerfield's renaissance during the '70s was one of those quirky show-business flukes. At the time, unconventional stand-ups such as Steve Martin, George Carlin, Richard Pryor, and Andy Kaufman were the new flavor—the ones who were connecting with baby boomers who'd grown sick of the safe-as-kittens, hardy-har-har Bob Hope comedy they'd been force-fed growing up. With his self-deprecating, quick-hit one-liners and sweaty, high-strung delivery, Dangerfield was reminiscent of that same bygone era that belonged to the Borscht Belt comedians who prowled the smoky stages of seedy third-rate rooms in Las Vegas and the Catskills. But Dangerfield's style was more subversive than he ever let on. He was an old-school comic slyly commenting on old-school comics, turning them upside down. That meta approach would resonate with young college students.

Born Jacob Cohen in Babylon, Long Island, Dangerfield was the son of a comic and juggler who used the stage name Phil Roy as he toured the vaudeville circuit. He abandoned the family when Dangerfield was just a child, leaving him to deliver groceries and sell ice cream on the beach to help out his single mother. The hard-luck tales in his act cut deeper than he'd ever acknowledge. Dangerfield began working as a comedian at seventeen under the name Jack Roy—a nod of respect to a father who didn't deserve any. Soon, he was performing onstage at Jewish resorts in upstate New York for twelve dollars a week. In 1951, after meeting his first wife, Joyce, he gave up show business and started a family, supporting them as an aluminum-siding sales-man. In the early '60s, he decided to give stand-up comedy one last stab and took on the name Rodney Dangerfield, thinking that if he failed again under a pseudonym the rejection might sting less. After booking a slot on *The Ed Sullivan Show* in 1967, Dangerfield was such a hit that he became a regular guest. The audience that had ignored him the first time around had caught up. He finally became a star at forty-four.

Kenney, Ramis, and Doyle-Murray knew all of this as honor-roll students of comedy. But acting on screen wasn't the same as getting up in front of a nightclub audience and doing twenty minutes of self-written material. Could he actually stand in front of a movie camera and do what came so naturally to him on Carson's stage? It was a little late to ask him, at fifty-seven, to learn such a daunting new skill. "Rodney was a complete crapshoot," says Trevor Albert. "No one knew what we were going to get." That would turn out to be a serious understatement when Peters invited Dangerfield to his office on the Warner lot for lunch.

"We brought him in and he comes to the studio in a big black limo," says Peters. "He comes into my office in this aqua-blue leisure suit and takes out a plastic bag and does two lines of coke on the table. He sniffs the coke, undoes his shirt, and says, '*Where's the pussy?*' " It was a hell of a first impression. Dangerfield would end up getting $35,000 for his role in *Caddyshack*. And though he would always graciously credit the film for launching his movie career, he would often do so while complaining that he actually lost $150,000 on the film, since he had to give up a month of headlining in Vegas to shoot it.

◆ ◆

Ted Knight had been nominated for six Emmys during his seven-season run on *The Mary Tyler Moore Show*. It's difficult to fathom how he only won twice. As Ted Baxter, the show's cluelessly pompous, word-mangling anchorman with a mane of impeccable silver hair, ice-blue eyes, and a chin seemingly carved from granite, Knight made egomania and stupidity oddly lovable from 1970 to 1977. The key to the character (aside from Knight's impeccable timing) had always been that beneath his confident gasbag veneer, Knight's Baxter was nothing more than a grown-up child—desperate for approval, easily wounded, and unwilling to come clean when he was wrong. It was that very complexity that made him the perfect candidate to play *Caddyshack*'s often-apoplectic presiding club majordomo, Judge Elihu Smails.

Tadeusz Wladyslaw Konopka was born to a Polish immigrant bartender and a housewife in Terryville, Connecticut, on December 7, 1923. On his eighteenth birthday, the Japanese attacked Pearl Harbor, so he dropped out of high school and enlisted in the Army. During WWII, he earned five Bronze Stars and was one of the first American soldiers to enter Berlin. After the war, he enrolled in a Hartford drama school and eventually landed jobs on the fringes of show business as a radio disc jockey, a ventriloquist, and a puppeteer. In the '50s, he moved to New York, where he studied at the American Theatre Wing. Throughout the decade and into the '60s, he was rarely out of work, whether on TV or in film, but fame eluded him (despite a small role in one of the greatest movies of all time, Alfred Hitchcock's *Psycho*). He was a working actor, but not a well-known one.

He officially renamed himself Ted Knight after arriving in LA in the late '50s—a name he'd once used hosting a kiddie show in Providence, Rhode Island. "When I was young, I was frequently cast in grade-B war movies as Nazis," Knight once said. "You know, the uber-lieutenant who had ways of making the underground heroine talk. Then the guerillas would attack the Gestapo headquarters and beat me to a Nordic pulp."

In the spring of 1970, at the late-in-the-game age of forty-seven, he auditioned for a new CBS ensemble comedy about a single working woman in a male-dominated profession. He was so desperate for a part on *The Mary Tyler Moore Show*, he came in to read for the role in clothes resembling those of a small-market newscaster's that he had purchased from a thrift store. As he tested for the show's producers, it was impossible to tell where Knight's insecurity began and Baxter's ended. He came back for three more auditions before he was given the role.

The irony is, Knight was so convincing as his dim-witted television alter ego that he lived in constant fear audiences believed he, too, was just an empty suit—that the two Teds were inseparable in the public's mind. When *The Mary Tyler Moore Show* finally ended, in 1977, Knight was so desperate to break out of his gilded cage of dopiness and land a starring role in a feature film that he probably would have paid Orion. What no one knew was that Knight had been diagnosed with cancer just two years before *Caddyshack*. He was convinced that working on a movie set would be the best medicine. "Ted was on my list of people who could do the part," says Nicita. "He was an iconic television comedy actor playing a straight-ass. He *was* this guy. It wasn't the most creative casting I've ever done." It's been rumored over the years that Jason Robards was also considered for the part of Judge Smails, but Nicita swats that notion away. "That would have been so tonally odd."

◆ ◆

As Nicita was casting *Caddyshack*, whenever she got close to zeroing in on the final two or three candidates for a particular part, she would put their head shots up on the wall of her office. It's an old trick she learned from her former boss. "That way you can physically see how their colors work with the other actors; it's like a painting in a way," she says. "It gives you a good map of how the movie's going to look." When it came time to cast the lead role (or at least what was considered the lead role at that point in the process) of Danny Noonan, she found herself staring at two photos: those of Michael O'Keefe and Mickey Rourke.

"Mickey made sense in a way because he was Irish," she says. He was also a little intense and Method-y for a giddily debauched country club comedy. "We were really leaning toward Mickey Rourke to play Danny," echoed Ramis. "He was great! He was young, he was cool, a very natural actor—not Hollywood at all. He seemed like a real person. Maybe *too real* for the movie. Michael O'Keefe seemed like a really good boy. Plus, he was a scratch golfer. Mickey Rourke was much more complicated."

O'Keefe was also someone that Orion was high on. The twenty-four-year-old actor had just wrapped another picture for the studio, *The Great Santini*, in which he played the sensitive son of a domineering, hard-ass Marine pilot played by Robert Duvall. The executives at Orion had been knocked out by O'Keefe's performance, especially in a scene in which Duvall bounces a basketball off of O'Keefe's forehead trying to make him either break down or fight back. He possessed a boyish vulnerability and sort of conflicted inner toughness. Orion knew that soon other studios would be after him. Why not grab him now before the secret got out? O'Keefe would ultimately earn a Best Supporting Actor Oscar nomination for *Santini* (and would lose to Timothy Hutton for *Ordinary People*).

O'Keefe, who had grown up in Larchmont, New York, began acting at fifteen when he appeared in a Colgate toothpaste commercial. He'd trained at the American Academy of Dramatic Arts in their teen program and had appeared on such TV shows as *M*A*S*H* and *The Waltons*. He made his feature film debut in 1978's *Gray Lady Down* opposite Charlton Heston. O'Keefe had been a hard-core *National Lampoon* fan as a teen, and had even gone to see Chase and Belushi in *Lemmings* when he was an undergrad at NYU. "The *Lampoon* totally shaped my sense of humor going back to the 'If you don't buy this magazine, we'll kill this dog' cover," he says. "During the audition process Doug Kenney and I sort of bonded. He had this combination of innocence and cynicism that somehow would move around within him depending on what internal winds were blowing. He was immediately like a big brother. He just engendered that kind of feeling in people. Doug wanted to be a rock star and he wanted to garner the attention of literary critics, and that's not so far from where my head was at back then."

During his first audition, O'Keefe lied to Ramis and told him that he'd been playing golf for years. "After I got the part, I thought, I'm in a lot of trouble now. I guess I have to get my shit together and get a golf swing." O'Keefe's father knew some of the members at the Winged Foot golf club in Westchester (O'Keefe had even caddied there as a teen) and pulled some strings to get his son some lessons with the club's pro, Tom Nieporte, who had won the Bob Hope Desert Classic in 1967. O'Keefe played golf every day for six weeks before the film started. When asked if he was aware that he had been competing against Rourke for the role of Danny Noonan, O'Keefe admits that he was.

"This was the early, young, hot, relaxed Mickey Rourke," he says. "He was as compelling as Marlon Brando in a way back then. I can see why they would have given him some serious consideration. But I'm a little more easy on the eyes than Mickey. Clearly, it would have been a much darker movie."

◆ ◆

Since the *Caddyshack* script had been largely cobbled together from the teenage recollections of Brian Doyle-Murray, he knew early on that he wanted to be more than just a writer on the film. With his years of Second City training and time on stage with the *National Lampoon Show* and skits on the *Radio Hour*, he was a more experienced actor than most of the stars they were casting in the film. So Doyle-Murray dug deep into his past and pulled out one of the most memorable oddballs he'd ever met in his years as a caddie to play in the film.

Doyle-Murray's *Caddyshack* character is Lou Loomis, the gruff, put-upon caddie master. The inspiration for the character was actually Lou Janis, the caddie master at the Indian Hill Club in Winnetka. Janis was a crusty golf course lifer with a fondness for drip-dry polyester clothing and who drove an old Ford Falcon. He would become a mentor of sorts for several of the Murray boys, giving them their first bitter taste of the working world. He was also a rabid gambler with a weakness for making insanely random wagers. Bill Murray, who also worked for Janis, would recall, "Louie was a gambler; he'd bet on anything—whether a member on the putting green would sink one or two of his three three-footer warm-up putts, whether or not a guy would pick up his tee after his opening drive, just about anything." Murray helped him pick which college football games to bet on. Janis also ran his own racket on the caddies, letting them charge food and refreshments against their earnings. He kept a running tally on a board outside his office in the caddie shack showing how much each kid owed him—a gag that ended up in the film.

Doyle-Murray had another reason to want to be on the *Caddyshack* set every day. He'd begun dating Sarah Holcomb—the young actress who would play Danny Noonan's Irish rose, Maggie O'Hooligan. The twenty-one-year-old actress from Weston, Connecticut, had made her feature film debut in *Animal House*, where she got to know Kenney. She had played Clorette, the underage daughter of Mayor Carmine DePasto, who goes to the Delta House toga party with Tom Hulce's Pinto and passes out, blackout-drunk. Although Ramis wasn't the one who cast her in that film, he thought she was so lovely in the movie that he wanted to work with her again. The only hitch was that they wanted Maggie to speak with a heavy Irish brogue. She had been written that way because all of the teenage girls who worked at Indian Hill during the Murray years had come over from Ireland on work visas. After she got the *Caddyshack* role, she and Doyle-Murray took a working vacation to Ireland as "research." "We were trying to be faithful to the Murrays' experiences, so I kind of stuck her with this awful Irish accent," said Ramis.

By the first week of August, most of the main roles in the film had been filled. But Orion was pressing for one more big-name star to join Chase, Dangerfield, and Knight. Golf loves a foursome. So Ramis, Kenney, and Doyle-Murray reached out to someone they'd always been able to rely on—even if no one else could: Bill Murray. *Meatballs* had hit theaters two months earlier and immediately established Murray as *SNL's* heir to Chase and Belushi—the next cast member most likely to make a successful jump from the small screen to the silver one. But Murray was already overextended. After the fourth season of *SNL* ended, on May 26, he flew out to Los Angeles and quickly began starring in a Hunter S. Thompson biopic for Universal called *Where the Buffalo Roam*.

The Thompson movie was loosely based on the gonzo journalist's 1977 *Rolling Stone* article, "The Banshee Screams for Buffalo Meat." And it had turned into a fully immersive, Method-acting experience for the *SNL* star. During filming, Thompson had moved into the guesthouse of Murray's rented home in North Hollywood. During one break in shooting, the two went to Thompson's ranch near Aspen, Colorado, and got into a heated argument after a long night of drinking about who was the better escape artist. Thompson then tied Murray to a chair and threw him into his swimming pool. Murray almost drowned before Thompson jumped in and rescued him at the last minute. As chaotic as his daredevil high jinks with the Good Doctor were, though, the production would end up being even more so. Murray would have only the smallest of windows between when *Buffalo* wrapped and when he was due back in New York to start the fifth season of *SNL*.

His older brother Brian assured him they'd somehow make it work, even if it was just for a week. What Doyle-Murray forgot to mention was that the character Murray would be playing didn't quite exist on the page yet. They'd figure that out, too. Next, was the question of Murray's salary. He was a star now— or at least well on his way to becoming one in the new Hollywood calculus. "I think I was kind of an afterthought," says Murray. "I got into the movie because of my brother Brian. I don't know how long they were at this thing. But between the time they started writing it and the time they started shooting it, I'd gone from being an unemployed actor to paying my rent and then being able to rent cars. Suddenly, I was on TV and then I was in the movies, and I had just done a movie that did surprisingly well. But I think the real reason why I got the job was because I was reasonably priced. I think they just wanted to toss me in because they could get me cheap."

Actually, it wouldn't be that cheap at all. On September 21, shortly after filming on *Caddyshack* began, *The Hollywood Reporter* ran an item about Murray's salary on the movie: "Could this be a typo by an eager press agent? For his starring role on *Caddyshack*, Bill Murray's salary will be $250,000 per week! If true,

Murray will be getting more per week than he gets for a whole year on *Saturday Night Live*." As far as the filmmakers were concerned that was now Orion's problem.

"With each new cast member that was hired, there was a sense of celebration around the office," says Jon Peters's underling Rusty Lemorande. "It was like, Hey, we got Ted Knight! Yay! Hey, we got Rodney Dangerfield! Hey, we got Bill Murray!" Now Ramis, Kenney, and Doyle-Murray just had to come up with some lines for their latest star . . . or not.

• •

Before Murray would end up joining the *Caddyshack* cast, there were smaller but still-vital roles that needed to be filled in the ensemble before shooting would begin in September. They were racing against the clock—and not just because the casting director, Wallis Nicita, was pregnant. On July 16, Nicita placed a casting notice in *Variety* seeking actors to play the following parts: "Lacey Underall, 17, slim, beautiful, long blonde hair, tan, athletic, sexy seductress; Tony D'Annunzio, 19, tough, streetwise, good-looking, well built, hip caddy, womanizer; Dr. Blaine Beeper, middle aged, attractive, rich, snobbish surgeon; Spaulding Smails, 17, overweight, aggressive, spoiled, obnoxious, arrogant . . . SAG talent send photos and resumes to Wally Nicita (c/o The Burbank Studios Producers Bldg. 5, 4000 Warner Blvd., Burbank 91522). No phone calls or deliveries."

Most of the remaining parts were hashed out in a series of seemingly endless casting sessions held in Nicita's small office on the Warner Bros. lot. "I got thousands of submissions," says Nicita. "Doug and Harold would come to the casting sessions, and I'd read with all of the actors. Doug and Harold were smoking weed all day. I mean, I don't think they were ripped all day long, but once in a while they would do that." There was one occasion, though, when Kenney decided that he would read with one of the hopefuls.

Although the part of the fast-and-loose seductress Lacey Underall was written as being seventeen years old, Cindy Morgan was twenty-four when she read for the part. Born Cynthia Ann Cichorski in Chicago, Morgan had been a communications major at Northern Illinois University and quickly began working her way up the small-market broadcast food chain until she made her way to the Windy City. "I was the morning-drive disc jockey at WLUP 97.9 FM in Chicago," Morgan says. "I had just come from doing the weather in Rockford. I was making $135 a week. They wouldn't let me do commercials, so I said, 'To heck with you guys, I'm going to LA.' They said I'd never get a job." But within a couple of months, Morgan was the new face of Irish Spring soap.

With ambitions of becoming an actress, Morgan began studying improv with Harvey Lembeck—an acting teacher who had worked with Robin Williams, Penny Marshall, and John Ritter. "I got the script for *Caddyshack* and thought, Well, this isn't me. Twelve years of Catholic school, I was far from Lacey Underall. But I thought, I'll give it a shot, I have nothing to lose." Jon Peters's assistant Trevor Albert remembers the day that Morgan came in. "She was running late and she was nervous as hell," he says. "But something special about her struck me." Morgan hadn't been their first choice. In fact, she hadn't even been on their radar. Nicita says that she was hoping to get Michelle Pfeiffer for Lacey, but the actress had been put off by the nudity required for the role. Peters, meanwhile, was thinking of another beauty whose hair he used to cut: Bo Derek. But no one else wanted her. This was right before she would become the biggest sex symbol on the planet with Blake Edwards's *10*.

Morgan admits that she was terrified when she went in to meet with Nicita for the potentially career-making part of the film's scene-stealing wanton sex kitten. But she told herself that whomever she was reading with—and hopefully it would be a guy—she had to make him sweat. When she walked into Nicita's office, Kenney volunteered to read with her. The scene she auditioned with was the one where she reads Danny Noonan's palm and slowly, teasingly licks it. Morgan went for it. When she was done, she saw a little trickle of sweat come down the side of Kenney's face. "That's when I knew I got the job," she says. She'd been in LA a mere eight months.

Scott Colomby, who had appeared on the sitcom *One Day at a Time* and who would end up dating Morgan after *Caddyshack* wrapped, was quickly hired to play Danny Noonan's Fonzie-like caddie adversary, Tony D'Annunzio. Hamilton Mitchell, a young, lanky aspiring LA actor came in and was so funny that they combined the roles of two caddies in the script and turned them into one for him named Motormouth. Dan Resin, a character actor best known for being the face of the toilet-freshening yachtsman the Ty-D-Bol Man, became the Porsche-driving Dr. Beeper. Veteran character actors Albert Salmi (*Gunsmoke*) and Elaine Aiken (*The Spook Who Sat by the Door*) were tapped to play Danny Noonan's contraceptive-averse Irish-Catholic parents. And a nineteen-year-old theater performer named Peter Berkrot was recommended for the role of Angie D'Annunzio (the caddie at the other end of Bill Murray's rusty pitchfork during the Dalai Lama speech) by *Animal House*'s Tom Hulce after they'd met at summer stock. "Wally Nicita called me and told me I was going to get $750 a week," says Berkrot. "I remember saying, 'I'll take it!' And she said, 'Of course, you will.'"

John Barmon, who had never acted before (or since), got the part of "hamburger . . . no, cheeseburger"–craving brat grandson

Spaulding Smails after his best friend's agent remembered her client's "fat friend." Lois Kibbee, a longtime star of the soap opera *The Edge of Night*, became Judge Smails's wife, who's described in the script as looking like a "Wagnerian dowager." Original Sha Na Na member (and future orthopedic surgeon to the LA Lakers) Scott Powell became a Bushwood club member named Gatsby. Jackie Davis, a jazz organist who played with Ella Fitzgerald and Sarah Vaughan, was cast as the golf-shoe-destroying Smoke Porterhouse (by now his name had been changed from "Westinghouse"). Dr. Dow, a soft-spoken philosophy professor at the University of Miami, became Al Czervik's Wang. And Minerva Scelza, the granddaughter of the film's Teamsters captain, was handed the role of pint size, gender-bending tomboy Joey D'Annunzio.

Real-life husband and wife Kenneth and Rebecca Burritt became Bushwood's elderly golfing couple, Mr. and Mrs. Havercamp ("That's a peach, hon!"). Violet Ramis, the two-year-old daughter of the director, played the youngest Noonan child, imprisoned in a playpen. And at the opposite end of the age spectrum was seventy-four-year-old Henry Wilcoxon as Bishop Pickering, who gets struck by lightning during the greatest round of his life (even though "the heavy stuff isn't gonna come down for quite a while"). Wilcoxon, who had been acting on screen since 1931, turned out to be the most delightful surprise to the other actors in the film. "I became very close to Henry and really miss him," says Bill Murray. "We didn't know who he was when we walked in the door. But he was one of the biggest deals in the world in the '30s. He was the Laurence Olivier of the time. He was the original Marc Antony with Claudette Colbert in *Cleopatra* and he's in *The Ten Commandments*. He was the one guy who I looked up to as an actor on the set."

Since Ramis would be making his directorial debut on the

film, he also wanted to fill out some of the more peripheral roles with friends—familiar and supportive faces that would make what was sure to be a stressful eleven weeks on set less isolating and lonely. Ann Ryerson, Ramis's old Second City troupe colleague from back in Chicago in the early '70s, played Grace, the female caddie whose Baby Ruth candy bar winds up in the Bushwood swimming pool, igniting the infamous "Doodie!" scene. And Brian McConnachie, a friend from the *Lampoon* days, along with his wife, Ann, played one the club's so-called Fun Couples. When Ramis called him up to ask if he'd be interested in a small role in *Caddyshack*, McConnachie was just wrapping up his first season as a writer on *Saturday Night Live*. He was waiting to hear if he would be invited back for a second. "I finally got the call to come back to *SNL* and then I got the call from Harold asking if Ann and I wanted to be in this movie," says McConnachie. "And I thought, This is the only time that this is ever going to happen to us. *SNL* will have to wait." He adds, "We were supposed to do a scene where we go skinny-dipping in one of the water hazards on the golf course. It was our first movie and we had a *nude scene*. Not bad."

With the cast coming together, what they now needed was a country club where they could be set loose.

8

Rolling Hills . . . and Action!

IN THE SUMMER OF 1979, while casting on *Caddyshack* was in full swing on the Warner Bros. lot, Harold Ramis began the needle-in-a-haystack process of finding a country club that would willingly swing its iron gates open to a Hollywood film crew. They knew it wouldn't be easy, since the climax of the movie hinged on a massive, fairway-annihilating explosion that would seem more fitting in *Apocalypse Now*. But it was nothing that a little old-school Hollywood deceit wouldn't be able to take care of. Both Ramis and Brian Doyle-Murray had always taken it as a given that they would find their Bushwood in their home state of Illinois, since the Indian Hill Club in Winnetka had been both the model and muse for their story from its inception. The studio had other ideas.

Orion was staring at an understocked cupboard of releases for the following summer, and if Mike Medavoy was going to get *Caddyshack* into theaters during that make-or-break season (as he desperately wanted to), *Caddyshack* would need to shoot in the fall—not exactly the ideal time to be making a sunny, short-sleeved golf comedy by Lake Michigan. Medavoy encouraged Ramis to look for a location in Southern California. That was a nonstarter for Ramis. Nervous enough already, the last thing he wanted on his first outing as a director was to have the studio swinging by and second-guessing every take and camera setup. It's hard to make a comedy when you're looking over your shoulder. The further they were from Hollywood, the more they would be able to make the movie *they* wanted to make. But it wasn't only a matter of self-protection. Being so close to the nosey suits would also cut in on the fun. The search refocused to Florida. The biggest problem there, however, would be finding a golf course without palm trees and flamingos. If they weren't going to shoot *Caddyshack* in the Midwest, they at least wanted it to *look* like the Midwest.

Rolling Hills would end up being an almost made-to-order compromise. Carved out of a 140-acre swamp in Davie, Florida, the eighteen-hole semi-private club seemed to be built with *Caddyshack*'s specific, idiosyncratic requirements in mind. Designed by renowned landscape architect William Mitchell in the late '60s, Rolling Hills (now Grande Oaks Golf Club) was dreamed up as an antidote to the rash of identical golf courses that had been sprouting up like toadstools across southern Florida at the time. Mitchell had become bored by all of the samey subtropical flora found in the area. Instead, he planted tall oaks and Australian pines.

"We kind of picked Rolling Hills by default," said Ramis. "We visited a lot of really nice country clubs and of course they didn't want us because what good country club wants to shut down for a movie and have trucks and hundreds of people trampling the golf course? But this place agreed to let us shut down four holes at a time and the players could play around us." As for the matter of the giant fireballs they were going to set off, Ramis told the Rolling Hills board not to worry, the script would be changing. That was a half-truth at best. Yes, the script would be changing, but not *that* part of it. What Ramis didn't notice when he was walking the course, making certain there were no palm trees, was that Rolling Hills was directly under the final-approach flight path to the nearby Fort Lauderdale-Hollywood International Airport and also that there was noisy condo construction going on nearby.

With their location locked in and their cast finally coming together, the producers recruited the last remaining members of their key crew. Ted Swanson had already been hired by Orion as *Caddyshack*'s production manager. Swanson's previous job had been working on a two-hour *Hawaii Five-O* movie in Singapore. Before that, his biggest credit was on 1976's Best Picture winner, *Rocky*, which he magically pulled off on a penny-pinching $1 million budget. Swanson was a pro, and a thrifty one at that. Since he was already based in Florida, he knew all of the local film and television crews and ended up hiring most of the below-the-line technicians who had been left hanging after Jerry Lewis's aborted comedy, *That's Life*, was shut down nearby. Lewis's financiers had simply run out of money just as cameras were to start rolling. Swanson would end up wearing two other hats on *Caddyshack*—as the film's number-crunching line producer and as an uncredited golfer in the Bushwood pro shop when Rodney Dangerfield comes charging in and asks if customers get a free bowl of soup with an especially ugly hat.

One of Swanson's most important hires on *Caddyshack* was Stan Jolley, the film's production designer. Responsible for the overall look of the movie, Jolley had to design all of the sets, turn a run-down maintenance shed into the film's caddie shack, and turn the main Rolling Hills clubhouse into an almost-exact replica of the one at Indian Hill back in Illinois. In the end, Rolling Hills would wind up essentially getting a free cosmetic facelift worth $175,000. Jolley, the son of Hollywood B-Western heavy I. Stanford Jolley, had got his start as a set designer at Warner

Bros. and 20th Century Fox in the early '50s before being hired away by Walt Disney to help draft the original sketches for Disneyland in Anaheim—something that particularly impressed the nostalgia-obsessed Kenney. In the '60s, he worked as an art director on such TV shows as *Mister Ed*, *Voyage to the Bottom of the Sea*, and *Get Smart* with its groovy opening-credits gauntlet of labyrinthine, 007-style doors.

The last piece of the puzzle, but the most important for an inexperienced director such as Ramis, was the film's cinematographer. At forty-nine, Stevan Larner was a good fifteen to twenty years older than most of the cast and crew on the set of *Caddyshack*. His most impressive credit was that he had been one of the directors of photography on Terrence Malick's 1973 outlaw road-movie masterpiece, *Badlands*. That, and the fact that he'd had a pre-Doors Jim Morrison as a student while teaching at UCLA film school. Michael O'Keefe had worked with Larner on 1978's *Gray Lady Down* and says, "He was an old pro who'd been around forever; he was going to make sure someone like Harold got all of the shots he needed, especially the ones he didn't *know* he needed." That was all well and good, but Kenney would later confess that the real reason they hired Larner was that he was a connoisseur of fine wines. He reasoned that Larner's highbrow tastes would give the film's look a touch of class. Specious logic, at best. But in Doug Kenney's mind, it somehow made perfect sense.

Though Kenney was the lead producer on the film, it was the first time he'd had any responsibilities on a movie set besides leading a marching band into a blind alley as he had on *Animal House*. Associate producer Donald MacDonald would end up becoming *Caddyshack*'s day-to-day problem solver, the person you went to not only when you had a question, but also needed an answer. When MacDonald had been hired by the Jon Peters

Organization, he was given the option of working on either *Caddyshack* or the Robby Benson monkey movie—which was, of course, no choice at all.

MacDonald took an immediate shine to Kenney and Ramis (after all, he was the one who collared them in Jon Peters's name after an early *Animal House* preview), and he seemed to go out of his way trying to protect them from his hard-charging, bombastic boss, who would mostly stay back in LA during the shoot. "Don was the only one at the company who had a real strong sense of story and a sense of film," says Peters's assistant Trevor Albert. "Everyone else was more of a hustler dealmaker. He was probably as important as anyone on *Caddyshack.*"

MacDonald and Albert joined Ramis and Kenney in Florida roughly eight weeks before shooting began on *Caddyshack*, supervising the construction of sets and juggling last-minute logistics. The first thing they did was set up a production office on the top floor of a low-rise, two-story brick motel adjacent to the Rolling Hills golf course, replete with rooms for editing, wardrobe, and makeup. The entire cast (except for Ted Knight, who was an early-to-bed-early-to-rise type and was given a rental home nearby) would live in the dormlike Rolling Hills lodge for the length of the shoot, turning the outdated digs into an unholy cross between a frat house, a love shack, and a twenty-four-hour drugstore. You could literally roll out of your bed (or someone else's) and be in the makeup chair within five minutes.

Rusty Lemorande was MacDonald's second in command on the set—the more senior Peters executive, Mark Canton, would come and go throughout filming. Relatively new to the nuts and bolts of on-location moviemaking, Lemorande looked around and became concerned by what he saw. "I was looking for all of the old mentors one would hire to assist an inexperienced director, and there were none," he says. "But I just kept my mouth shut because the crew had already been hired and there was no changing it. I mean, if you were building a house with a first-time contractor because you like him or he's a family member, you'd make sure that you had the best painters and the best carpenters just to be safe."

With a script that still wasn't finished as late as two weeks before filming started, a studio that was famous for its hands-off approach, a first-time director, and a less-than-detail-oriented first-time producer with a drug habit, what could possibly go wrong?

• •

Most of the *Caddyshack* ensemble arrived in Davie, Florida, over Labor Day weekend, 1979—a week before cameras were slated to roll. Chevy Chase was scheduled to head down several weeks later because he was still up in Canada rolling his eyes and biting his tongue through the making of *Oh! Heavenly Dog*. As for Murray, it was more or less accepted that he would simply show up when he showed up. No one had a clue when that might be. When Ted Knight first arrived at Rolling Hills, he took one look at the place (with its manicured fairways and buildings having been tarted up with a fresh coat of paint from Stan Jolley's crew) and exclaimed, "Gee, it's so pretty . . . too bad we have to destroy it." Rodney Dangerfield was less upbeat, calling Florida in late August "a sauna with gnats."

While the actors were settling in, the production brought in PGA Tour pro John Cusano to try to make the actors' collection of terrible golf swings look passable on film. "Aside from Michael O'Keefe and Bill Murray, they were all horrible," said Ramis. "Ted had no swing, Dr. Beeper had no swing, Chevy didn't have a real attractive swing. And Rodney, I don't even know if you'd call what he was doing 'golf' in the literal sense. He took one lesson and said, 'That's it!' and never went back."

▸ *The Harvard Lampoon*'s enormously successful 1966 *Playboy* parody

▾ Doug Kenney and Rob Hoffman with the debut issue of the *National Lampoon*, April 1970

▲ Members of Second City in 1969. From left to right: Brian
Doyle-Murray, David Blum, Harold Ramis, Jim Fisher, Roberta
Maguire, Nate Herman, and Judy Morgan

▾ Doug Kenney shows off his signature party trick at the
National Lampoon office.

• The *National Lampoon* staff gets serious in the early '70s. Co-founders Doug Kenney and Henry Beard (behind fake schnozzes): top row, third and fourth from left

• The *Lampoon*'s most famous cover: "If You Don't Buy This Magazine, We'll Kill This Dog," January 1973

• *New York* magazine anoints Chevy Chase as *Saturday Night*'s first breakout star, December 22, 1975.

‣ Former hairdresser
Jon Peters and his
famous girlfriend,
Barbra Streisand, in 1975

◂ Doug Kenney,
John Belushi, Chris Miller,
and Stephen Furst on the
set of *National Lampoon's
Animal House*

‣ The official theatrical
poster for *Caddyshack*—the
unhappy result of a fistfight
between Doug Kenney
and Orion executive Mike
Medavoy

SOME PEOPLE JUST DON'T BELONG.
19
Caddyshack
A Jon Peters Production
"CADDYSHACK"
CHEVY CHASE · RODNEY DANGERFIELD · TED KNIGHT
MICHAEL O'KEEFE and BILL MURRAY as Carl
Original Songs by KENNY LOGGINS · Music Composed by JOHNNY MANDEL
Written by BRIAN DOYLE-MURRAY & HAROLD RAMIS & DOUGLAS KENNEY
Executive Producer JON PETERS · Produced by DOUGLAS KENNEY · Directed by HAROLD RAMIS
R RESTRICTED
TECHNICOLOR®
SOUNDTRACK AVAILABLE ON COLUMBIA RECORDS & TAPES
ALL RIGHTS RESERVED
An ORION PICTURES Release
Thru WARNER BROS A Warner Communications Company

⏶ One big happy family? From left to right: Jon Peters, Chevy Chase, Ted Knight, and Rodney Dangerfield on the Davie, Florida, set of *Caddyshack*

⏷ Rodney Dangerfield doing one of his "bits"

⏶ Bill Murray amid battle of wits with the Bushwood gopher

⏷ Cindy Morgan leaves little to the imagination as the liberated libertine Lacey Underall.

‣ Bill Murray and Chevy Chase put aside their history of tension and "get weird."

‣ Michael O'Keefe and Sarah Holcomb as lovebirds, largely left on the cutting room floor: Danny Noonan and Maggie O'Hooligan

‣ *Caddyshack*'s climactic fireball, the result of some old-school Hollywood deception, was so gigantic that the nearby Fort Lauderdale–Hollywood International Airport received reports of a plane crash.

One of the last known photos taken of Doug Kenney: Hawaii, August 1980

When Peter Berkrot arrived to play wiseass caddie Angie D'Annunzio on the Friday of the long Labor Day weekend, he remembers heading up to the business office on the second floor of the Rolling Hills lodge to let them know he was there. He stepped off the elevator and bumped into Knight. Knight smiled and introduced himself. The *Mary Tyler Moore Show* star was there to pick up a plane ticket back to LA. After a few minutes of small talk with Berkrot, Knight turned around and said good-bye to the business-office staff with the booming farewell, "Have a nice hurricane, guys!" Berkrot thought that Knight's words were a bit cryptic. Maybe it was some sort of Old Hollywood saying to wish everyone good luck on the movie, like "Break a leg!" It wasn't. Berkrot quickly learned that a Category 5 storm was rampaging their way, swirling up from the Dominican Republic with winds of up to 175 miles per hour. Tens of thousands of people were evacuating from the Florida Keys.

Everyone taped up the windows in their rooms to prevent them from shattering, filled their bathtubs with water, and stocked up on batteries and booze. Lots and lots of booze. "We all went out to dinner that night, and that's when I fell in love with Doug Kenney," recalls Berkrot. "I was sitting right opposite from him and he was so good at making you feel like you were the only one there. Our table was next to a lobster tank and he said, 'In Korea, they have puppies in tanks.'" When they got back to the motel, some of them continued drinking and passing joints early into the next morning. "You couldn't find a more fun group to party with," says Ann Ryerson, who played Grace, one of the film's caddies.

Hurricane David would end up causing more than $1.5 billion in damage, but it had been downgraded to a Category 2 storm by the time it reached the Fort Lauderdale area. A few of the Rolling Hills sets were turned into kindling and the first floor of the motel had been flooded, leaving a plague of earthworms wriggling in the carpets of the ground-floor rooms. But all in all, they'd been spared David's wrath. The hurricane party, however, was a roaring success. It would keep rolling for the next three months. Occasionally, a movie would break out.

"It was 1979," said Ramis. "It was a pretty debauched country at the time. The cocaine business in South Florida was mammoth at the time and everyone was doing everything. I never judged it myself."

• •

Principal photography for *Caddyshack* began on the morning of Wednesday, September 5, 1979. Hurricane David had passed and was now running out of steam as it slowly made its way up the Eastern seaboard. It was a clear, sunny day in Davie, with temperatures that would reach a high of ninety-two degrees. For his first day on the job as a Hollywood director, Ramis showed up on set in a short-sleeved Lacoste shirt, tinted aviator glasses, and with little or no clue which way to point the camera. When first assistant director David Whorf asked about the initial setup, Ramis, feigning a confidence he didn't yet possess, suggested shooting in a direction that would have resulted in hours of resetting, repositioning, and equipment-lugging. He'd just learned his first lesson as a director: When asked a question you don't know the answer to, pretend to be collaborative, and respond: What do *you* think we should do? "They told me I had eleven weeks to shoot the film," said Ramis. "I had no idea what that meant because I'd never directed before. If they told me I had eight weeks, I would have done it in eight weeks. If they said fifteen, I would have done fifteen. I didn't know the difference."

The first day of shooting on any film is a time of frayed nerves and built-up anticipation. But by the first day on *Caddyshack*, the movie's script had been changed so many times (at least five) that it resembled a fruit salad—a sheaf of rainbow pages bound together by brass fasteners. Since each new round of revisions gets printed on its own distinct color of paper, the screenplay the actors were working with was like a sorbet of white, blue, pink, yellow, and green pages. The first major acting sequence that would appear in the finished film revolves around the early-morning chaos of the crowded Noonan household. The following scene, where Danny rides his ten-speed across the train tracks (metaphor alert!) and past rows of mansions on his way to Bushwood, was filmed back in Pasadena. But the first scene that Ramis would actually shoot in Florida was one that would never even make it onto the screen: An earlier—and Carl Spackler-free—version of the Dalai Lama scene.

The scene had been written as a brief exchange between an old caddie named Ray and Peter Berkrot's Angie D'Annunzio, with the part of Ray given to an inexperienced local actor. "If I remember correctly, he had some sort of disability," says Trevor Albert. "I don't know if he was a veteran or something. But I think the appeal was that he seemed off. The problem was he couldn't string two lines together. And that was such a brilliantly written speech, you didn't want to fuck it up." The local actor not only couldn't act; he ended up being more off-putting than funny. He seemed like a shell-shocked vet dealing with PTSD. You were laughing at the character, not with him—and then you felt horrible and guilty for laughing at him.

"The actor did a very poor job," said Ramis. "As we were filming it I was thinking, I'm going to get fired. This guy's horrible. They're going to see this back in LA and I'm going to get canned." When Ramis finally said cut, Brian Doyle-Murray walked over to the clearly rattled director and told him not to worry. Just move on to the next scene. When his brother Bill got there, they'd give the speech to him and reshoot it.

Later on that first day, Ramis filmed a comic fight scene

between two caddies in Lou Loomis's caddie shack, where a gumball machine gets knocked over and shatters, spilling its contents across the floor. Ramis shot the scene over and over again. With each minor tweak and inner deliberation, valuable time was running out. The scene wasn't nearly as important as the sweat he was pouring into it. A more experienced director would have simply said that's good enough and moved on to the next setup. Soon, the cast began to gently rib Ramis about how unseasoned he was. Says Michael O'Keefe, "The joke we'd always make is we'd come on the set and say, 'Harold, you're looking into the wrong end of the camera. That's actually the lens!' We were just giving him shit."

Ever the good sport, Ramis laughed along. "I was so nervous that when we sent our first dailies off to the lab to be processed I was afraid it would come back and there wouldn't be an image," he said. "Anything beyond that was gravy." Outwardly, Ramis was the picture of take-it-in-stride mellow composure. He'd later say that he had a mantra on the film that he kept repeating to himself in order to keep his sanity: "It's not my money." Sure, deep down, he knew he was an amateur slightly out of his depth. But that didn't mean he wanted everyone else on the set to think that, too.

Meanwhile, Donald MacDonald thought back to the list of directors that Peters had asked him to put together in case they needed to replace Ramis. He was praying that Peters had forgotten about it. Especially since he hadn't even shot his scenes with the actor who undoubtedly had the least experience and the most neuroses.

9

Rappin' Rodney

FROM THE BEGINNING, Rodney Dangerfield had always been the wild card. At fifty-seven, the stand-up comic looked at least ten years older, and had been performing on and off since 1940. He'd logged some hard miles on the road. Hollywood, with its cushy movie-star pampering, might as well have been Mars to him. In a long, itinerant career that took him from the small-time "Jewish Alps" resorts of the Catskills to the three-shows-a-night Naugahyde pseudo-glitz venues off of the Las Vegas strip to, finally, the rarefied high altitude of *The Tonight Show*, Dangerfield had never really entertained the idea of a career in film. Who would pay to look at a mug like his writ large on the silver screen?

In his four rocky decades in show business, Dangerfield had appeared in only one feature film—an obscure 1971 no-budget comedy called *The Projectionist*. In it, Dangerfield plays a tough-talking Brylcreemed cinema owner named Renaldi, who torments a daydreaming Walter Mitty–ish employee (Chuck McCann). The film opened and closed in New York and San Francisco without anyone's noticing, which suited Dangerfield just fine. Years later he would joke that the film was so bad "they showed it on an airplane and people were walking out of the theater."

But now that he was experiencing a miraculous late-career surge, maybe it was time to leverage his newfound popularity and see what this acting racket was all about. *Caddyshack* seemed like an ideal showcase, made to order for his unique brand of off-the-cuff patter. Not only did the filmmakers make their fandom flatteringly plain to him, they seemed to understand his limitations and weren't remotely put off by them. The character of Al Czervik, a superrich vulgarian blowhard condominium developer, didn't have a lot of lines in the first draft of the script. But, if anything, that made Dangerfield more confident about accepting the part. It was a juicy, glorified cameo. He didn't have to carry the movie; he could be carried by it, popping into the frame, dropping a couple of crass, rim-shot one-liners, and waltzing off as suddenly as he appeared. He thought, I can do this.

Dangerfield's first scene in *Caddyshack* comes midway through the first act, when he pulls up to Bushwood in a fire-engine-red Rolls Royce with custom CZERVIK Illinois plates and a horn that blares "We're in the Money." With his silent, Nikon-snapping stereotype sidekick Wang riding shotgun, he steps out of the convertible like a Tex Avery sight gag, wearing a white golf hat, red leisure slacks, a white belt fighting a losing battle with his gut, a lime-green shirt, and a rainbow cardigan sweater. He peels off a gaudy tip for the valet from an obscene knot of bills and instructs him to "park my car, get my bags, and gain some weight, will ya?" As the hard-charging bull walks into the Bushwood pro shop, Czervik turns to his pal and cracks, "I think this place is restricted, Wang, so don't tell 'em you're Jewish. Okay? Fine."

Ramis and his crew had spent the morning of Dangerfield's first day of work dressing the set. Brian Doyle-Murray had become a stickler on making every aspect of Bushwood—even a place as incidental and unimportant as the pro shop—look as authentic as possible. Each set was like a diorama replicating his youth, like his own personal Rosebud. For Dangerfield's first shot on the film, the comedian was supposed to wait behind a door until Ramis said "Action." Then he would barrel in to the pro shop with Wang as if he owned the joint, introduce himself, and rattle off all of the pricey equipment he wanted to buy (ten of this, twenty of this, "the whole schmear"). Finally, out of the corner of his eye he would spot a mannequin wearing an ugly, pastel-striped golf hat and say, "This is the worst-looking hat I ever saw." Meanwhile, just behind him, off to Dangerfield's right, Knight's Judge Smails, wearing the very hat, fumes a slow-burn for the ages. Dangerfield notices and says, "Oh, it looks good on you, though," as he turns his head and rolls his big bug eyes.

That's it.

On the first take, however, it didn't go quite as planned. Not even close. When Ramis rolled the camera, hit the clappers, and called "Action," Dangerfield just stood there like a redwood. Ramis got up from his chair and walked over to Rodney and asked if there was a problem. Was he ready to do the scene? "Sure," Dangerfield replied. Ramis returned to his chair, sat down, and again called "Action." Nothing. Ramis went back over to where Dangerfield was standing and said, "Rodney, when I call 'Action,' that's your cue to come in and do the scene."

"You mean, do my bit?"

"Yes, do your bit."

Ramis again went back to his chair and called "Action." Crickets. Ramis laughed incredulously, and said, "OK, Rodney, now do your bit!" Dangerfield barged into the room and nailed it, even shoehorning in a hilarious line that he improvised on the spot: "You buy a hat like this, I bet you get a free bowl of soup. . . ." From that point on, Ramis stopped saying "Action" before all of Rodney's scenes. He would just call out, "OK, Rodney, do your bit." Ramis had finally found someone with less experience than himself.

After the pro shop scene was done, Scott Colomby, who played Tony D'Annunzio, remembers Dangerfield sitting off to the side alone, stewing. He looked sweaty and haunted. When Colomby asked him what was wrong, Dangerfield said, "Nobody's laughing at me. I'm bombing out there!" Colomby assured him that he wasn't bombing at all; it was just that the crew wasn't *allowed* to laugh. They'd ruin the take. Dangerfield was so used to getting instant feedback from the two-drink-minimum crowds he held in the palm of his hand that he hadn't even considered that as a possibility. "He was very, very nervous," says Cindy Morgan. "I remember we had lunch together one day, just the two of us, and he was tugging at his collar just like he does in his act, saying, 'How am I doin'? How am I doin'?' And I said, 'Rodney, you're stealing it.' He wasn't getting that instant reaction and it was throwing him completely. Hearing people laugh was how he'd always gauged his timing. People who are funny are the most insecure people in the world."

Ramis began to set aside time on the nights before Dangerfield's scene to cater to his star's neuroses. Together, they'd comb over his lines trying to make them better, funnier. Dangerfield would later say that he'd stay up late every night coming up with twenty new jokes for the next day's scenes. Because of his own Second City training, Ramis welcomed Dangerfield's last-minute suggestions. His star may have seemed green in front of the camera, but he was a perfectionist. "Rodney needed every word, every syllable in place, every comma, every period," said Ramis.

"Rodney couldn't act," says Chevy Chase. "I remember we shot a master shot on the eighteenth green with five or six of us standing there, and you have to do your lines the same every time. And he had some joke he put in there and then when they did the close-up, he said something different. You can't do that! It has to cut together. He was not familiar with how movies are made."

While Ramis was shooting each day, his editor, William Carruth, was cutting together the film's dailies. Carruth was a third-generation editor who'd grown up on movie sets. He'd been a child actor in *The 5,000 Fingers of Dr. T* and *The Night of the Hunter*. His father, Richard, had been the music editor on *West Side Story* and Marilyn Monroe's *Gentlemen Prefer Blondes*. Carruth had got his start as an editor assisting the legendary Verna Fields on *Paper Moon* and *Jaws*. His first credit as a chief editor was on Peter Bogdanovich's 1976 comedy about the early days of Hollywood, *Nickelodeon*. Like Ramis, Kenney, and the rest of the film's young, laid-back crew, Carruth was a bit of a hippie maverick who wasn't immune to the joys of recreational marijuana use. He fit right into the rules-were-made-to-be-broken vibe on Ramis's set.

The *Caddyshack* production department had set up a small editing suite and screening room on the top floor of the motel next to Rolling Hills, where the celluloid that had already been processed hung like strands of spaghetti for Carruth to splice together. Dailies are the most obvious way to judge how well a movie shoot is going, but not an infallible one. They are simply the results of the previous day's footage that have come back from the processing lab. They're generally screened both on location by the director and his crew as well as back at the studio in LA, where nervous executives are trying to divine how things are coming along—or *not* coming along.

In Florida, gathering to watch dailies was like a nightly party. Ramis, with his relaxed, egalitarian attitude, welcomed pretty much anyone who wanted to sit in. "There was an openness to it," says Rusty Lemorande. "With Harold and Doug's personalities, anyone who was interested could come and watch. Nothing was hidden." And nothing was discouraged, either. The air in the screening room during dailies would get so hazy with pot smoke that some of the older crew members stopped attending. Everyone who stuck around would end up laughing their asses off, usually at Dangerfield's scenes. Every time he opened his mouth it was like a tommy-gun blast of outrageous, ad-libbed shtick. Shrapnel and spent shell casings seemed to fly from the screen. Three thousand miles away, both Jon Peters and Mike Medavoy, who rarely agreed about anything, told Ramis that he needed to give Dangerfield more scenes right away.

◆ ◆

Ramis and Kenney were still waiting on both Chevy Chase and Bill Murray, so it made sense to front-load the scenes with the young actors playing the slack-doofus caddies on the early part of the schedule. Joining them on the set was a new and not entirely welcome face. Despite Mike Medavoy's laissez-faire philosophy about policing his studio's filmmakers, the Orion head wasn't irresponsible. You don't just write $6 million checks without keeping some sort of eye on your investment. So the studio sent one of its veteran production managers down to Florida to see how things were going and report back.

George Justin was a no-nonsense sixty-three-year-old Hollywood lifer who'd served as a cameraman on Army training films during WWII. In his long and storied behind-the-scenes career, Justin had been a test director for George Cukor during the endless casting of *Gone With the Wind*. He'd been a production manager on classic films such as *On the Waterfront*, *A Face in the Crowd*, and *The Graduate*. And he had been the vice president of production management at Paramount during its heyday in the early and mid-'70s. He was the definition of a hard-bitten Tinseltown troubleshooter—a battle-ax who made sure that his films stayed on schedule and on budget.

It had quickly become clear to everyone that Ramis was a collaborative sort of director. If someone had an idea how to make a scene better, a suggestion that might make a mediocre joke funnier, or even an inspired notion for something that wasn't in the script, he wanted to hear it. It was the sort of "Yes, and . . ." thinking that had served him well back at Second City. During the filming of a sequence that would later be cut from the film, where a bunch of caddies arrive for work by bus at Bushwood, Jon Peters's executive in charge of production, Rusty Lemorande, had the idea of having them all try to push their way out of the bus door at the same time, causing a Three Stooges sort of bottleneck. Ramis liked the juvenile absurdity of the idea and shot the scene just as Lemorande had described it. "It was a total whim and Harold did it," says Lemorande. "That was the kind of process that happened on that film. Without that process, it wouldn't *be* that film."

George Justin, however, had overheard the conversation between Lemorande and Ramis—and he wasn't pleased. Soon, Lemorande found himself being chewed out by Justin. Lemorande was a lowly associate producer, and it wasn't his place to collaborate with the director as he had. It was simply unprofessional.

"Normally when you make a movie, once you lock the script, you shoot the script like the blueprint of a building," Lemorande says. "You don't start messing around with the blueprint. Well, we were messing with the blueprint all through shooting. If you had a good idea—or even a bad idea—you could bring it to Harold right on the set, and if he liked it, he'd use it. It was an open forum of ideas." Two days later, Justin was satisfied enough with what he'd seen and the pace of the film's progress that he went back to Los Angeles. Lemorande went back to offering more suggestions.

Like the rest of the cast, the young actors playing the caddies would see most of their scenes completely rewritten at the last minute or just scrapped all together. Most of them were so inexperienced they just assumed that this was how movies were made: You spend weeks learning the script and then it gets tossed out. "A lot of us caddies had much bigger parts in the script," says Ann Ryerson. "Especially Scott Colomby. I thought going in that the movie would be much more about the staff than those that they served. It shifted because Rodney was turning out to be so great. You have to follow the funny."

John Barmon, who played Ted Knight's spoiled louse grandson, Spaulding, recalls getting script revisions so frequently that they ran out of new colors for the pages. "I think after a while they just gave up on it," he says. But he and the other young novice actors were having too much fun to complain. "We had cars at our disposal and money in our pockets; we'd drive around Broward County and hit on local girls and bring them back to the set. Well, Scott Colomby didn't so much; he was dating Valerie Bertinelli at the time, and she came down." Barmon says that the Spaulding character was entirely a Doug Kenney creation. "Doug would kind of get upset with me when I didn't understand the lines he wrote for me," he says. "I had no idea what 'Ahoy Polloi' meant. He kept telling me, 'Spaulding wouldn't do that!' But Harold was the one who fed me one of my best lines. We were shooting the dinner dance scene, and he told me right before the camera started rolling to lean over and ask one of the diners, 'Are you going to eat your fat?' He loved to just set off these little unscripted firecrackers in every scene."

The caddies quickly discovered that Dangerfield, the very man who was in the process of elbowing them out of the movie, was more comfortable hanging out with them than his more age-appropriate costars. They had certain recreational habits in common.

"I'll tell you a story about Rodney," says Peter Berkrot, who played Angie D'Annunzio, one of the caddies. "I was on my way back from someone's room; it must have been around eleven at night. Back in 1979, there were basically only three kinds of pot. If you had enough money you got Thai stick, but we mostly got stuck with the stuff where you had to break it apart and clean out the seeds. And I had a tray with my weed walking through the lobby and saw Rodney and quickly went and hid my weed in my room. When I came back, he said, 'Was that weed? You don't have to hide that. I love weed. You know what I love more than weed? Coke.' I thought he was doing a bit, but we found out he wasn't. The only person who didn't take drugs on the movie was Ted Knight," he quipped.

Soon, Dangerfield was inviting the younger cast members back to his room to get stoned and listen to tapes of his stand-up act. "Rodney smoked more pot than anybody," says John Barmon. "He would get really stoned and walk around the halls of the hotel in his bathrobe with a towel wrapped around his neck and he'd see you and say, 'Hey, I want you to come listen to some of my set.' And you'd sit there in his room and he had one of those old cassette players and he'd be really interested in your reaction. I'm just some nineteen-year-old kid! He was so paranoid it wasn't funny. And then it would happen again the next night. And the next night. After about a week of this, you'd see him coming down the hall and you'd take off in another direction!"

Trevor Albert had the unenviable job of waking up the cast members each morning, making sure they got to the set for their call times. He quickly became the most unpopular man on campus. "It's not like everyone went back to their rooms after the day wrapped and practiced their lines," he says. "Well, they practiced lines, but a different kind." Albert says that the hardest person to rouse was Kenney, who raged harder than anyone. Being a producer didn't turn out to be the creatively fulfilling experience he'd hoped it would be.

"I had one experience with Doug hanging out in my room one night for about an hour," says Peter Berkrot. "I remember him taking out his Screen Actors Guild card. He said, 'I got this when I did *Animal House*. It's the most meaningful thing I own. It's the one thing I'm the most proud of.'"

There were days when Kenney was happily rewriting scenes on the fly with Brian Doyle-Murray or huddling behind the camera with Ramis, cracking up like schoolkids and discussing which particular take of a scene should be printed. But for the most part, he had frustratingly little to do. And he filled those long, idle stretches of downtime and boredom by taking on the role of the film's social director, driving around in a golf cart facetiously asking if he could get anyone a Fresca. When he didn't have a task to attend to, he'd just skulk off and indulge his coke habit—on the sly at first, then more openly. In fact, in one split-second shot in the film, you can see Kenney, playing one of Al Czervik's crass country club cronies, doing a line of coke in the background of a party scene. He wasn't trying to hide anything. Later, he would say, tongue only partially in cheek, "I discovered the only thing a producer has to do is stand in back of a gaffer with his hands in his pockets and find new ways to say no."

Not surprisingly, the easiest person to roust and escort to the set every morning was Ted Knight. He was in bed by eight every night and up at six. Perhaps due to his recent cancer diagnosis, Knight would become almost evangelical when it came to lecturing his costars about the benefits of healthy living, telling them that the Sweet'N Low they were using caused cancer in rats. He would constantly take fistfuls of vitamins and even brought his own juicer to Florida. "People like Doug were snorting coke and smoking out of bongs on the other side of the wall from where Ted was mixing his alfalfa-sprout smoothie," says Trevor Albert.

It wasn't just Knight's lifestyle that made him feel like a square peg. He'd simply learned a totally different process of acting. For a performer, film and television are related, but they can often seem like distant cousins. Acting on a drum-tight sitcom for seven years with its rat-a-tat daily work pace gave him both crack comic timing and a stubborn, marrow-deep commitment to sticking to what's written on the page. The script is sacred. In television, there's just no time to ad-lib. Knight learned his lines to the letter and expected the same from everyone else.

"Ted was from television, where everybody is prepared to do exactly what they have to do," says Rusty Lemorande. "Being on TV is like being a trapeze artist. You have to be prepared and work together—each one can make or break the other's performance. And that's not really how film works. His training was so different from everyone else on the movie."

Sharing scenes with Dangerfield would become especially maddening for Knight. He didn't sign on to play the straight man. And you could argue that that slow-burn frustration he felt in real life actually elevated his performance. Whether Al Czervik is heckling Judge Smails on the tee or mocking the size of his yacht, *The Flying Wasp*, the smoke that seems to be coming out of Knight's ears isn't just the illusion that comes from fantastic acting. It may not even be acting at all. On *The Mary Tyler Moore Show*, Knight got used to being the actor with the killer punchline. Now he was the playing the flustered foil to a jittery, wild-eyed lunatic saying whatever the hell he wanted. "Ted was trying to do his job and he's holding the script in his hand, and meanwhile Rodney is just running around saying whatever the heck popped into his head and Ted's trying to follow him. Ted was really angry," says Cindy Morgan.

Dangerfield's idea of a practical joke was inserting a line of dialogue that he knew would be way too dirty to make the final cut of the movie, but that he knew would get a laugh from the crew anyway. He was especially fond of blow-job jokes. Meanwhile, Knight's idea of a practical joke was having his name stenciled on the back of all of his costars' chairs so he could react in mock fury when they sat down to take a break. Those under thirty just rolled their eyes.

It wasn't just Dangerfield who felt Knight's wrath, though. John Barmon recalls shooting a scene in which Knight and Michael O'Keefe are having a conversation and Barmon's character, Spaulding, is in the background. Ramis thought the scene was a little too static, so he told Barmon to pick up a golf club and start swinging at a ball on the ground and missing it. Ramis told the young actor: "I need you to do something funny here." That's it. After each swing and miss, Barmon yelled, "Turds!" or "Double turds!" Ramis didn't mention any of this to Knight. "Ted saw the dailies and he was pissed," says Barmon. "Ted said to me, 'I understand you're a young actor coming up, but that's very unprofessional trying to upstage somebody.' I'd only been on the set for a week and Ted Knight was pissed at me! Harold liked to stir things up and see what would happen."

Ramis later admitted that he probably could have handled things differently with Knight, that he could have made a better attempt to bridge the generation gap, but ultimately he got precisely the performance he wanted out of him. "Look, Ted was a very traditional actor," said Ramis. "He'd learn the script and do it perfectly every time. But most of us had an improv background, so I felt comfortable letting actors ad-lib. The whole atmosphere down there was alien to him. Young people running around in South Florida being crazy. I tried to give Ted plenty of support and positive feedback, but he just thought everyone on the set was stoned all the time."

He wasn't far off. Especially by the time Chevy Chase showed up.

10

The Pizza Man

CHEVY CHASE COULDN'T WAIT to get to the set of *Caddyshack*. He'd spent the previous two months stuck in Montreal with the only-in-the-'70s triple threat of Omar Sharif, Jane Seymour, and the mangy mixed-breed daughter of the original Benji. To this day, Chase still has no idea why he agreed to do the film.

"I was just told by my agent to do something, *anything*," says Chase. "The whole time I was in Canada, I was thinking, I guess I've really moved on to greater things." In the back of his mind, he must have wondered: Is this why I left *Saturday Night Live*—to be in a crappy Benji movie? When the film wrapped, Chase couldn't get to Florida fast enough. It was time to have some fun again.

About a month into the *Caddyshack* shoot, Doug Kenney's agent, John Ptak, was hanging out in his client's motel room. Ptak had become Kenney's agent right after *Animal House* came out, but he was also more than that. He was a trusted friend who, as a UCLA film school graduate, could talk about movies on a level beyond wheeling and dealing, back-end points, and box office grosses. As the two were talking and laughing, there was a knock at the door. They asked who was there. The voice on the other side said, "Pizza man." When they opened the door, Chase walked in with a square-sided attaché case in his hand.

Ptak recalls that Chase looked more like a door-to-door sales-man than a pizza deliveryman in a sports coat and tie, both of which he immediately took off as he began to make a big pro-duction out of rolling up his sleeves and unlocking the case that he'd placed on the desk. Ptak was intrigued, but a smiling Kenney already seemed to have a good idea about its pharmaceutical contents. Chase opened it very slowly to drum up the suspense. It was empty. But then Chase reached into one of its dividers, grinned, and said, "I've got everything you need for every occasion."

By the fall of 1979, Chase's marriage to Jacqueline Carlin was in bitter pieces. Like Kenney, he was living the revved-up, hell-raising life of a man who'd fallen into fame rather early and un-expectedly and was now grappling with how to make sense of it. For him, reuniting with his partner in crime, Kenney, to make a lighthearted golf romp was just what the pizza man ordered. He could relax and cut loose. "It was pretty fucking nuts on that set," says Chase. "You're in Florida and the crew possessed what-ever you needed. It was the time when things were considered benign. John Belushi was still alive. And smoking pot had been going on forever."

Kenney and Chase's brotherly bond went beyond just the consumption of drugs, however. Kenney looked at Chevy and saw all the easy self-confidence he lacked. He'd been wildly praised and repeatedly rewarded ever since he graduated from Harvard and launched the *National Lampoon*. He'd managed to become a millionaire not just once, but twice. Yet he constantly seemed to question whether he truly deserved that success. Deep down, he felt like he was getting away with a fast one, and the fact that he was getting away with it so *easily* made him even more suspicious. He felt like an impostor. If Chase had those same doubts about himself, he never displayed them. That was what was so seductive about him. On the surface, at least, everything was a joke to him. "Being with Doug was like being with a girlfriend, but not gay," Chase says. "He was my best friend."

Kenney thought of Ty Webb as he did of Chevy—as the person he *wanted* to be. But as the character developed and took on new layers it became clear that Ty was the person that Chase already *was*. In Florida, the two friends would huddle and discuss how to play the character as Kenney brought Chase up to speed on how the shoot had been going. Chase thought it sounded like a mess. But as one of his generation's most natural improvisers, Chase was used to walking into a mess and spinning it into something immaculate and polished.

Kenney described the character of Ty Webb to Chase as being "*of* the establishment, but not *in* it." Even after a sixth revised draft of the script was completed in mid-October, Kenney was writing new lines for Chase on the spot and feeding him kernels of motivation before his scenes, such as the idea of quoting (or rather, misquoting) the seventeenth-century Japanese philosopher Basho. Like Ramis, Kenney had always been fascinated by Zen Buddhism and had read enough about the subject to offhandedly inject its esoteric teachings into the film, albeit with a comic twist. According to Bill Murray, it was Kenney's idea to have Chase make the mystical "Na-na-na-na-na" sound when he was putting.

"Doug had an idea for a putter with electromagnetic sensors that would signal you to putt when you'd reach alpha state," he said. When Chase was told to make a spiritual noise while he was sinking all of his trick shots on the green, he opted for something less Zen, channeling the signature bionic "Na-na-na-na-na" sound-effect from the TV show *The Six Million Dollar Man*. Chase's "Be the ball" speech was already in the script.

Chase came to the set every day ready to fool around in the hope of making something spontaneous and great. Having done two fairly conventional, just-hit-your-mark-and-say-your-lines studio jobs in a row, he felt like he was back in Studio 8H, or on stage with Belushi doing *Lemmings*. Each day, he would goose his dialogue (which was still a bit lifeless in the script) with wild riffs of improvisation that Ramis didn't just abide, but openly encouraged. "I called it guided improvisation, not just ad-libbing," said Ramis. "It was ad-libbing with a purpose. You could give Chevy an idea and he could just go."

Take the classic "Do you take drugs?" advice scene between Chase and Michael O'Keefe that appears early in the film. This is how the exchange appeared in the screenplay:

> **TY WEBB:**
> Danny, can I ask you a question-do you do drugs?
>
> **DANNY NOONAN:**
> No.
>
> **TY WEBB:**
> Good boy.

Now, here's how it appeared after Chase and O'Keefe put their "ad-libbing with a purpose" twist on it . . .

> **TY WEBB:**
> Do you take drugs, Danny?

DANNY NOONAN:

Every day.

TY WEBB:

Good . . . so what's the problem?

Like Dangerfield, Chase was bringing the *Caddyshack* script to life in real time. And even though his costar O'Keefe was less experienced and more classically trained, he returned every serve that Chase hit over the net. O'Keefe found it both liberating and slightly terrifying. "Harold gave Chevy carte blanche," he says. "We rehearsed it and sorted it out and Doug and Brian and Harold would sort of shape the premise and Chevy would just start spouting stuff. It was fun to try to match wits with those guys. I'm not in their league. I don't have the same skill sets they had. So with Chevy, I would just try to keep up. It was nerve-racking and challenging, but also exhilarating."

That spirit of on-the-fly abandon bled into nighttime acts of improvisation, too. Although they had little to do with the movie they were making, they informed the mad, anything-goes anarchy of the shoot. One night, as everyone was sitting around at the motel getting high, someone suggested that they hijack a few golf carts and race them on the golf course. Kenney had a better suggestion. Sure, they could race the carts, but what if they got a little bit more violent and creative about it. An hour later, a fleet of golf carts was chewing up and destroying the Rolling Hills fairways with a re-creation of the tank battle between George Patton and Erwin Rommel.

The weekend that Chase arrived, Jon Peters sent Mark Canton down to the set to check on the film's progress. Doug Kenney didn't have a problem with Canton, but his innate rebellious streak resented any sort of parental interference with his party. In a playfully passive-aggressive bit of authority-tweaking, he had the driver who was assigned to pick up Canton at the airport tell Canton that he was supposed to bring him directly to that evening's shooting location. The driver dropped the unwitting executive in the woods and left. After a very long fifteen minutes of standing in the pitch-dark in the middle of nowhere, another driver picked up Canton and told him he'd been had.

"When Mark finally showed up, he was great about it," says John Ptak. "He just laughed and said, 'You guys are great! Always funny! I'm a friend of comedy and love it!'" Canton knew that having a KICK ME sign put on his back and being hazed came with the assignment. And he knew the way into this crowd was to be a good sport and prove you could take it. He'd passed the test. Years later, when Canton became an executive at Warner Bros., he was so proud of having been the butt of a joke from the cool crowd that he put a sign on his office door reading: "Mark Canton: Friend of Comedy."

◆ ◆

For a few days in October, the *Caddyshack* cast and crew loaded up a convoy of grip trucks and headed to the nearby Plantation Country Club in Fort Lauderdale. As ideal as Rolling Hills was as a location, the one thing it lacked was a swimming pool. And Ramis had to shoot the Caddy Day sequence, including Lacey Underall's high dive and the infamous fecal Baby Ruth *Jaws* parody.

During the filming of the swimming pool sequences at Plantation, Rusty Lemorande had the idea of turning what had been written in the script as a throwaway synchronized-swimming routine with the Bushwood caddies into a full-fledged Esther Williams–style water ballet. Ramis loved the randomness of the suggestion and quickly thought how they could score it to "The Blue Danube" waltz. He told Lemorande that he'd do it only if Lemorande could procure a crane for the shot by the following day.

It was also at Plantation that Cindy Morgan was finally scheduled to shoot her first scene in the film. The script had her character, Lacey Underall, walking along the edge of the swimming pool in high heels and a revealing black bathing suit past a group of teenage male caddies, like Jayne Mansfield swishing and shimmying down the street in *The Girl Can't Help It*. The assorted pimple-faced pipsqueaks, mouth breathers, and droolers are so in lust for this goddess that they all suck in their guts and puff out their chests as she walks by. Lacey then slinks her way over to the high-dive board, kicks off her heels, climbs the ladder taking her sweet time, and executes a perfect swan dive into the pool. As movie entrances go, it's an unforgettably steamy one— part Coppertone ad and part kitten-with-a-whip striptease. The only problem was, Morgan was legally blind without her contacts and she was afraid of heights. Also, she could barely swim.

Morgan was already insecure about her status on the film. During the casting process, she'd been given the role of Lacey only to have it taken away because it had been promised to Brian Doyle-Murray's girlfriend, Sarah Holcomb. Then she had the role again and didn't again until finally she did. This went on for about a week, until Holcomb decided that she would rather play Danny's Irish girlfriend, Maggie. "I remember getting ready to do the dive scene in the bathroom, saying, 'I can't do this, I can't see, I can't dive. I'm not Lacey; I can't do this.'"

Morgan had to do the scene basically sightless. It would have been too dangerous to dive from that height with rock-hard 1979 contact lenses. "They would have gone right through your eyes," she says. "So I went up to the diving board looking like I meant it and I did the best that I could, but they ended up cutting to a stunt diver." Morgan never left the diving board. She just walked up to the edge and turned right around.

After the day wrapped, the producers took the cast out to dinner. There were maybe twenty or thirty people there. All through the meal, Doug Kenney kept needling Morgan for not having done the high dive. She couldn't tell if he was joking or genuinely upset. She knew that Lacey wouldn't have let it bother her, but it was making her feel self-conscious. Then, midway through the meal, some new actor came in and sat at the other end of the table. She couldn't place him, nor was she particularly trying to. When dinner ended, everyone went back to the Rolling Hills lodge. Morgan was tired after a long, stressful day and retired to her room. Then, she says, "there was a knock at my door. I opened it and it was that new actor from the end of the table. He said, 'Do you want to get out of here?' And I said, 'Yeah.' I woke up the next morning on a nude beach in Jupiter, Florida. And that's how I met Bill Murray. . . ."

11

Total Consciousness

LIKE ALL STORIES worth telling, this one begins with a stolen VW bug. Well, not stolen, exactly. Bill Murray had recently finished shooting his Hunter Thompson movie, *Where the Buffalo Roam*, in Los Angeles. He was tired and restless and felt the need to get off the grid. He knew that he had to report for duty on the Florida set of *Caddyshack* soon (although he'd purposely left his arrival date vague), and he also knew that his *Saturday Night Live* boss, Lorne Michaels, had a car in LA that he'd been talking about shipping to New York. Murray thought he'd save him the headache. He told Michaels that he would drive his Volkswagen Super Beetle to Manhattan when he came back for the show's new season in the fall. It seemed so sensible. Problem was, Murray didn't bother telling his boss about certain detours he'd planned on taking.

"Occasionally, I would hear from Bill on the road," Michaels said later. "He'd be in Florida, and I'd say, 'But Bill—is Florida on the way?' Or a week later, he'd be in Aspen and I'd say, 'But Bill. . . .' It took all summer to get the Beetle, but Bill had installed a stereo."

By the time Murray steered Michaels's VW through the gates of Rolling Hills in October of 1979, about midway through production, Ramis had already been worrying for days. Where was Bill? Had anyone heard from Bill? It was simply the cost of doing business with such a magnificent flake. Ramis had known that this was a possibility going in. Murray brought an exciting air of imminent mischief wherever he went, regardless of whenever he arrived. He was a once-in-a-generation kind of talent to whom the rules simply didn't seem to apply. Whenever he was onstage or in front of a camera, he didn't know how to *not* be interesting. But still, where the hell was he?

After parking Michaels's car, Murray spotted a *Caddyshack* production assistant sitting in a golf cart and asked if he could get a lift to the set. A few minutes later, the crew noticed something coming around a bunker. Ramis could finally breathe. As the golf cart pulled up with his MIA star, Murray leaned out of the shotgun side and announced, "Which way to the youth hostel?" Ramis and Murray hugged and slapped each other on the back. He was excited to catch up with his brother Brian and Doug Kenney. But that would have to wait. Ramis had Murray for only six short days.

Before Murray even arrived in Davie, there had been buzz around the set about what to expect from the mercurial comedian. Murray was known for his short, unpredictable fuse and stormy moods. "Any problems I've had with Bill over the years have nothing to do with the quality of his work," said Ramis. "He's just a moody guy, and sometimes it's difficult to work around those moods." Back at 30 Rock, Dan Aykroyd had even come up with a name for Bill's rages: The Murricane.

For proof of just how violent The Murricane could be, all you had to do was flash back to February 18, 1978. Lorne Michaels had invited Chevy Chase to return and guest-host *Saturday Night Live*, the show he had turned his back on just two years earlier. Chase had just wrapped his first big Hollywood film, *Foul Play*, during which he'd briefly fallen for his costar, Goldie Hawn. Chase was nervous about returning to his old stomping grounds, but also completely oblivious to all of the ill will that had built up against him since he'd left. He didn't know if he'd be treated as a traitor or hailed as a conquering hero.

As the week's writing and rehearsal periods went on, Chase began to throw his weight around behind the scenes, wielding his fame like a cudgel and big-footing other performers. Tensions had been simmering just under the surface all week. All of the unsaid feelings and unfinished business finally came to a head right before the dress rehearsal on Saturday. Chase was sitting in the office of writers Al Franken and Tom Davis when Murray stormed in and confronted him about all of the ugly stories he'd heard about Chase. He told Murray to get lost.

After dress, Murray picked up where he left off, only this time hitting Chase well below the belt. Gossip had begun to spread that Chase and his wife at the time were having marital difficulties. While sitting in adjacent makeup chairs, Murray reportedly said to Chase, "Go fuck your wife . . . she needs it!" Chase responded with an insult about Murray's acne-scarred face, saying that it looked like Neil Armstrong landed on it. Finally, five minutes before airtime, Murray called Chase out of John Belushi's dressing room for what has become an infamous backstage brawl. Chase would later say that he suspected it was Belushi who had put Murray up to it, whispering poison in his ear. Either way, Murray was ready to escalate from verbal blows to physical ones.

Animal House director John Landis was backstage that night visiting Dan Aykroyd when he heard the fight break out. "I heard this tremendous noise and I looked down the hall and there was this crowd of people holding them back from one another. They had just come to blows and they were being pulled apart. As Chevy was screaming obscenities at him, Bill pointed his finger at Chevy and said, '*Medium talent!*' I had never seen Bill Murray before, but to come up with an insult like 'Medium talent' in the heat of anger . . . I was impressed. I was like, *Who is that guy?!*"

The fight didn't last long. Belushi and Brian Doyle-Murray broke it up quickly, absorbing some body blows themselves. Still, the altercation was more symbolic than anything else. Murray would later say, "It was really a Hollywood fight. A 'Don't touch my face!' kind of thing . . . a kind of non-event. It was just the significance of it. It was an Oedipal thing, a rupture. Because we all felt mad he had left us, and somehow I was anointed avenging angel who had to speak for everyone."

Now, on the set of *Caddyshack*, Murray and Chase were going to have to either get along or keep their distance. It would be the first time that they would be in close proximity to each other since that fateful evening at Studio 8H. The fight wasn't known by everyone on the set. Jon Peters says that he had no idea about the pair's history of bad blood when he cast them in the film. But there were enough people in the overlapping worlds of *SNL* and *Caddyshack* that everyone was soon brought up to speed and sat back waiting for the potential second round of fireworks. "I was never told that they shouldn't be on the set at the same time," says Mark Canton. "But I think they *chose* not to be on the set at the same time. They were not the best of friends. Everyone seemed to know it."

The walking-on-eggshells atmosphere around the two was fragile enough that Brian McConnachie, who had known them both back at the *Lampoon* and also had a small role in the film, recalls being in his room at the Rolling Hills motel talking to Murray one night when Chevy walked by. McConnachie didn't know whether to stay or go or hide the cutlery. "I felt like I was caught cheating with one of them." But in the end, all of the anticipation of WWIII ended up being for naught. "To me it was all hearsay and rumor," said Ramis. "They were determined to get along from the beginning. As soon as Bill arrived, it wasn't like they *embraced* each other, but they were respectful and co-operative." According to several people on the set, it probably helped that, unlike so many others on *Caddyshack*, Murray wasn't a coke user, and thus less likely to fly off the handle at the slightest paranoia-produced provocation. Another reason that Murray may have been a Boy Scout is that he was working for Kenney, Ramis, and his older brother—three people he'd always looked up to.

Murray's first scene to be shot was the Dalai Lama monologue that had been abandoned after the inexperienced, slightly-off local actor who was first hired to deliver it whiffed. Back then, Murray's character, Carl Spackler, was a blink-and-you'll-miss-him footnote in the script. They needed to create the character out of whole cloth on the spot. That might have intimidated most actors, walking into a situation where almost nothing is defined. Not Murray. That was the stage on which he thrived. Murray had had a chance to let Carl marinate in his head during his cross-country trip in Lorne's VW. So when he arrived, he arrived fully committed to a handful of half-baked ideas. None of which he shared with Ramis before the cameras rolled.

Ramis had left large gaps throughout the shooting script for Murray to fill in later with the insane passages of spontaneous genius that he seemed to pull out of the ether. Ramis had envisioned the Carl character as a whacked-out contemporary Harpo Marx, popping up here and there to do silent bits of bizarre slapstick (according to Ramis, he saw Dangerfield as Groucho and Chevy as Chico). As they prepared to shoot the Dalai Lama scene, the crew set up outside the red, barnlike caddie shack. Murray and his costar in the scene, Peter Berkrot, were introduced, but

Murray was already in character with a funny, thousand-yard stare in his eyes. He was working without a script—and without a net. "I remember Bill was standing there with this scythe, like Death," says Berkrot. "A huge rusty scythe. And he points it at me and I said, 'Absolutely not! Are you crazy?' I was terrified because this thing was really nasty-looking. It looked like it would have taken off my head by accident. So Bill goes, OK, and picks up a pitchfork. And that's what he held at my neck during the whole scene. It was sharp."

Murray had already been told the basic premise of the Dalai Lama scene. Before they shot it, Ramis handed him the script pages of the original speech, more as a springboard than something to stick to. Murray took a few minutes to read it, then he nodded. He was ready to go. When Ramis called "Action," Murray stuck out his jaw and curled his lower lip in a strange way that Ramis had seen many times before over the years. *Murray was going to play Carl as the Honker.*

Ramis was laughing even before a twisted line came out of Murray's twisted mouth.

> **CARL SPACKLER:**
> So I jump ship in Hong Kong and I
> make my way over to Tibet. And I get
> on as a looper at a course over there
> in the Himalayas.
>
> **ANGIE D'ANNUNZIO**
> A looper?
>
> **CARL SPACKLER**
> A looper. You know, a caddie. Looper.
> Jock. So I tell them I'm a pro jock
> and who do you think they give me?
> The Dalai Lama himself. The twelfth

son of the Lama. The flowing robes,
the grace, bald . . . striking. So
I'm on the first tee with him, I give
him the driver, he hauls off and
whacks one . . . Big hitter, the
Lama. Long. Into a 10,000 foot crevice
right at the base of this glacier.
You know what the Lama says?

                ANGIE D'ANNUNZIO
No.

                CARL SPACKLER
Gunga galunga . . . Gunga Lagunga. So
we finish eighteen and he's gonna
stiff me. And I say, 'Lama, hey, how
about a little something, you know, for
the effort, you know.' And he says,
'Oh, there won't be any money, but when
you die, on your deathbed, you will
receive total consciousness.' . . . So
I got that going for me . . . which
is nice.

The miracle of the Dalai Lama scene on screen is that it feels completely tossed off and spontaneous. But Berkrot says they shot it for seven hours. During each take, Murray would toss in new things trying to keep it fresh and unpredictable. And each time, he would press the rusty tines of his pitchfork a little harder on Berkrot's neck. "I remember at one point, I said to him, 'Can you take it easy with the pitchfork? It really hurts.' And he said, 'Quit whining, Berkrot!' He was totally in character between takes."

Trevor Albert remembers watching the scene being shot and thinking that Murray was going to murder this poor kid. "I remember watching that pitchfork go into his skin and there was this feeling of, One slip too much and he could stab him because Bill was so intense about it and so in that moment. He's like a wild animal and you don't know what he's going to do. I'd never seen anyone with that sort of unpredictable power. He made me nervous. That's part of the thrill of his performance."

When Ramis finally called "Cut and print!" he couldn't have been happier. Murray had been worth waiting for all along. He knew that he and Kenney and Doyle-Murray would have to figure out a lot more places to squeeze Carl into the story. "The Dalai Lama thing was really a fun one to do," says Murray. "I took it and ran away with it. But the basic premise where I jumped a ship in Hong Kong and looped for the Dalai Lama, that was all Brian's. Given that setup, anyone with any chops at all could make it good. I guess they thought it was funny because they started saying, Why not just have this guy all over the place?"

• •

Ad-libbing wasn't invented on *Caddyshack*. It's been an integral part of the filmmaking process since the birth of cinema. Some of the most memorable movie lines during the past fifty years have been the result of on-the-fly moments of inspiration. Robert De Niro's "You talkin' to me?" scene in *Taxi Driver*, Clemenza's "Leave the gun, take the cannoli" line from *The Godfather*, Roy Scheider's deadpan "You're gonna need a bigger boat" button from *Jaws*, even John Belushi's zit-popping spray of mashed potatoes in *Animal House*—they were all spontaneous moments of magic. They're proof of film as a living, breathing medium.

"We always trusted improvisation," said Ramis. "It never felt like we were ad-libbing and winging it. It's an actual technique and a method that allows you to create material instantly. It's not grabbed out of thin air."

For some actors, that sort of freedom can be paralyzing. For others, like Bill Murray, it's liberating. Murray's longest scene in *Caddyshack* was his famous "Cinderella Story" monologue. And it's a scene for which no lines were ever actually written. It sprung sui generis from Murray's head. "All it said in the script is: Carl is outside of the clubhouse practicing his golf swing, cutting the tops off flowers with a grass whip," said Ramis.

Actually, this is how it appeared in the shooting script on the day in October, 1979, when it was filmed:

> SCENE 244: EXT. CLUBHOUSE (SAME DAY—LATE AFTERNOON) The sky is beginning to darken. CARL, THE GREENSKEEPER, is absently lopping the heads off bedded tulips as he practices his golf swing with a grass whip.

That was all Murray was given. Before rolling the camera, Ramis huddled with Murray and gave the actor some motivation. "When I used to jog during a brief period of physical fitness in my life, I would encourage myself by pretending I was the announcer at the Olympics," said Ramis. "Like, they're coming into the stadium, Ramis is in the lead! So I said to Bill, 'Did you ever do imaginary golf commentary in your head?' And he said, 'Yeah, yeah, yeah, don't say anymore. I got it!'"

Murray's only request before Ramis yelled "Action" was to have the flowers changed from tulips to mums. In the scene, Carl stands outside of the clubhouse dressed in a grass-stained shirt buttoned up to his Adam's apple, his camo hat, tan workpants, and big clunky unlaced boots. An insert shot of the sky reveals ominous storm clouds gathering. Carl chokes up on the grass whip like a golf club, steps up to the flower bed, waggles his hips, and then . . .

CARL SPACKLER
What an incredible Cinderella story.
This unknown, comes outta nowhere to
lead the pack at Augusta. He's at the
final hole. He's about 455 yards
away, he's gonna hit about a two
iron, I think . . . *(Carl reels back
and swats the head off of a mum.
Petals fly like confetti)* Boy, he got
all of that. The crowd is standing on
its feet here at Augusta. The normally
reserved Augusta crowd is going
wild . . . *(he pauses as he notices
some golfers coming)* for this young
Cinderella who's come out of nowhere.
He's got about 350 yards left. He's
going to hit about a five iron, it
looks like, don't you think? *(Carl
pulls the grass whip back to demolish
the next mum)* He's got a beautiful
backswing . . . That's . . . Oh! He
got all of that one! He's gotta be
pleased with that. The crowd is just
on its feet here. He's a Cinderella
boy, tears in his eyes, I guess, as he
lines up this last shot. And he's got
about 195 yards left, and he's got a,
it looks like he's got about an eight
iron. This crowd has gone deadly
silent. Cinderella story, out of
nowhere, former greenskeeper, now about
to become the Masters champion. *(Carl
reels back one last time and, Swat!,
blasts the third mum to smithereens)*
It looks like a mirac . . . It's in
the hole! *IT'S IN THE HOLE!!!*

Murray says that he did the entire sequence in one unbroken
take. "I was good back in those days," he says. "I could do some-

thing when they turned the camera on. I was wired into what I was talking about. Improvising about golf was easy for me. And it was fun. It wasn't difficult to come up with stuff. And there was a great crowd of people there to entertain. If you made Doug or Brian or Harold laugh, you sort of earned your keep. You made your bones."

Just as Carl watches his third shot at Augusta go in the hole, his reverie is broken by Henry Wilcoxon's Bishop, eager to get in a quick nine holes before the storm rolls in. He deputizes Carl as his caddie. As the Bishop hits one miraculous shot after another, buffeted by hurricane winds and rain coming in sideways, he asks Carl's advice about whether he should keep playing. Carl responds, "I'd keep playing, I don't think the heavy stuff's gonna come down for quite a while." When the Bishop misses a putt and looks to the heavens and exclaims, "Rat farts!", the music playing underneath it is from *The Ten Commandments*—an insider's nod to one of Wilcoxon's iconic early films.

The sequence with Wilcoxon required Murray and the seventy four year old actor to stand under whirlybird rain towers for hours—an endurance test for an actor half Wilcoxon's age. "I loved the guy," says Murray. "During our breaks, I would ask him for advice and he told me about a book he read that influenced him. It's called *The Art of Dramatic Writing*. I still reread that book all the time to get what I need. It talks about premise, and how everything just has to jive with the premise. It's quite uncomfortable to be under a rain machine. We'd get drenched and his coat would end up weighing forty pounds. But he was a great pro and nailed everything he did. Those are the guys you meet that make a difference."

For the great British star of the London stage and Cecil B. DeMille's Hollywood epics, *Caddyshack* would be his final major film role. Wilcoxon died in 1984 at the age of seventy-eight.

◆ ◆

Since Bill Murray's time in Florida was so limited, Ramis worked him hard, brainstorming situations for Carl and shooting them with little or no preparation. They could worry about finding a place for them in the film later. "Everything we shot with Bill in the movie was just him riffing," said Ramis. "We just described the physical action and he made up the lines. He'd done so much improv at the *Lampoon*, he could just go. He would just turn up and do weird stuff. That's how he worked."

Murray was due back in New York for the beginning of the fifth season of *SNL* on October 13, 1979. Ramis and his fellow writers scrambled for more impromptu Carl moments. Kenney thought up a raunchy sight gag (it's actually Carl's introduction in the film) in which he's standing in a sweat-stained gray T-shirt and a camouflage hat behind a hedge leering at a foursome of older-women golfers and seems to be masturbating until it's revealed that he's actually working the plunger on a ball washer. As Carl quietly moans and vigorously tugs the pump handle, Murray uncorks a pervy string of ad-libs: "You wore green so you could hide from me. . . . You're a tramp." Ramis nearly ruined the take because he was laughing so hard off camera.

Then there was the matter of the smattering of Carl's scenes with a golf-course-destroying gopher. At that point, the gopher was far less important to the film than he would eventually become in postproduction. Most of Murray's gopher scenes were little inserts of him setting up explosives, fashioning clay bombs, and trying to flush the varmint out of his network of underground tunnels with a hose. In fact, Ramis shot only one scene of Murray with a gopher puppet—back then it was nothing more than a mangy, matted, chinchilla-looking sock puppet that Trevor Albert wore on his hand and pushed up through a hole in the ground. It looked as crude and primitive as a kid's stuffed animal.

The gopher scenes were random and disjointed, but the crew rushed to nail down as many of them as they could before Murray had to leave. "We had Bill talking about the gopher," says Rusty Lemorande. "We had Bill dragging the fire hose around the course; we had Bill turning on the hose and having the water rush up through all the greens. But that was the extent to which the gopher was referenced. It was all the effect. There was no sign of the cause."

When he was shooting the gopher scenes, Murray didn't understand how they would all be pieced together in the finished film. But that wasn't his problem. Plus, he was having a blast shooting them. "It was the time when people were making movies like *The Deer Hunter* and *Apocalypse Now*," says Murray. "And that was my Vietnam movie. The ridiculously inappropriate firepower I used to kill a small rodent. And a guy who was taking it all personally and it didn't have anything to do with him. Carving those clay bombs of the rabbit and the squirrel, that stuff, you're just amusing yourself. And if I'm making myself laugh and making these guys laugh, then it's funny."

Ramis worked Murray around the clock and to the point of exhaustion during his contracted six days in Florida. Murray never complained even though he was spent.

Recalls Cindy Morgan, "There was one day, you could hear on the walkie-talkies, 'Where's Bill?' . . . 'He's sleeping in a sand trap!' . . . 'What do you mean he's sleeping in a sand trap?!'"

◆ ◆

Cindy Morgan's initiation on the set of *Caddyshack* was a brutal one. She had been petrified while shooting her first scene as Lacey Underall on the high-dive board. She'd been endlessly baited by Kenney afterward for not nailing it. And she'd woken up the following day on a nude beach in Jupiter, Florida, with Bill Murray after an evening of sandy abandon. It had certainly been an eventful beginning. The second scene she would shoot was even more so, and would end up becoming her absolute low point on the film. In the script, Morgan's Lacey has a love scene with Michael O'Keefe's Danny in Judge Smails's bedroom. Morgan knew that nudity was required—and she insists that she was OK with it. She just never thought she'd end up feeling so exploited by the way it all unfolded.

Jon Peters always expected that *Caddyshack*'s target audience would be men between the ages of eighteen and twenty-five. It was the same rich demographic vein that had been mined to turn *Animal House* into the biggest comedy of all time. And the hope all along—ever since he had first approached Kenney and Ramis about partnering up—was that that same pay dirt would be struck twice. Peters thought it was absolutely essential to have an R rating and to give those male moviegoers some gratuitous "tits and ass." The problem was, Peters had a surprise in store. Knowing that his movie's big nude scene was coming up on the schedule, he invited a photographer from *Playboy* to visit the set and shoot some candid skin pictures for Hef's magazine. No one had bothered to mention this to Morgan until she was about to film the scene. "I got a call from Peters and he says, 'We're sending *Playboy*.' I said, 'Thank you, that's a big compliment, but I can't do it.' And he goes, 'What do you mean you can't do it?!' And I said, 'I'm the Irish Spring girl and I feel it's a conflict.' And he goes, 'You don't understand, you're doing it!' "

Morgan says that she was fine with appearing topless in the scene, but being naked for a few fleeting seconds on film was an entirely different matter from having topless pictures in a magazine where they would be forever frozen in time under some teenage boy's mattress. "She didn't want to do it," said Ramis. "And I'm the good guy. I said, 'I don't want you to do anything you're not comfortable with.' So Jon's surrogate on the set, Don MacDonald, ran for the telephone. And he came back and said, 'Jon wants to talk to you.' Jon said, 'She won't do the nude scene?' And I said, 'Well, no, is it that important? She's not comfortable.' And Jon said, 'Put her on the phone; let me talk to her for a sec.' When she got off, she said, 'I'll do it.' I asked, 'What did he say?' And she said, 'He told me if I didn't do it, I'd never work again.' Jon's Old Hollywood."

Morgan did the scene in the end, but without the *Playboy* photographer present. "I don't have a problem with nudity," Morgan says, "I have a problem with bullies." For his part, Peters doesn't even try to deny his position. "She was definitely pressured to do the nude scene by me," he says. "The producer side of me was like, How can we not have a nude scene? I wanted her to get naked, absolutely." Morgan says that Peters told her that if she did not allow the *Playboy* photographer on set, he would take away her billing on the film, her billboards, and her paid ads—all of which he eventually followed through on. Peters even "forgot" to invite her to the film's New York premiere when it opened the following summer. Morgan was so shaken by Peters's coercion that she called her agent back in LA to complain. "He said, 'Honey, you're not some doe-eyed girl from the Midwest. Handle it.'"

After Morgan agreed to go through with the scene, she sat down with Ramis, and they worked out some ground rules. He had to clear the set of all but the most essential crew: Ramis, Michael O'Keefe, the cinematographer, and the focus-puller. That's it. John Barmon, who played Spaulding, remembers trying to sneak onto the set that day to get a look at Morgan in the flesh, but was stopped at the door. In solidarity with his costar,

O'Keefe suggested that everyone else in the room take their shirts off, too, to make the still-rattled Morgan more comfortable. They did.

When Cindy Morgan returned to Los Angeles after the film wrapped, the first thing she did was fire her agent.

◆ ◆

When Ty Webb and Lacey Underall have their first moment of meet-cute flirtation at the Bushwood dinner dance, there was more than just blazing sexual tension between the characters. Behind the scenes, Chevy Chase and Cindy Morgan had developed a rocky relationship that burned hot one minute and cold the next. In their introduction, when Ty asks Lacey what brings her to "this nape of the woods," she says that her father wanted to broaden her. When asked what she does for fun, she says that she enjoys "skinny skiing" and "going to bullfights on acid." It seems as if the unflappable Ty may have met his match. In an early draft of the screenplay the relationship between the two is less comical. They also end up together—two damaged souls who couldn't be less right for each other, which somehow makes them perfect for each other.

That early script changed, of course. Many times. In a movie full of men acting like boys, Lacey is the lone take-charge woman—aggressive and progressive in a way that none of the male characters are. In fact, Kenney had gotten Warner Bros. to screen *To Have and Have Not* for Morgan so she could study Lauren Bacall sparring with Humphrey Bogart for pointers. Putting aside the fact that Morgan is often parading around Bushwood clearly without a bra, in skintight tennis clothes, she's the movie's idea of a liberated female who knows what she wants and how to get it. And she wants Ty Webb, at least for the moment. "After what I'd been through with the pool scene and the blowup with Jon Peters over the nude scene and the *Playboy* photographer,

I had gotten a lot more confident and a lot tougher," says Morgan. "I felt like I wasn't just playing Lacey; I had *become* Lacey."

A few scenes after they meet at the dance, Lacey pulls up at Ty's home in a yellow Mercedes. The place looks like a cross between a disheveled space-age bachelor pad and a Benihana, right down to the gong doorbell. As Lacey wanders around his unkempt living room, she finds an uncashed check for $70,000 (Ramis's inside joke aimed at Kenney's habit of obliviously leaving five- and six-figure checks lying around like forgotten laundry tickets). Lacey then sits down next to Ty at his organ, does a tequila shot with him (yes, it was real tequila), and asks him to sing her a love song. The majority of this was not in the script. Ramis was dead reckoning at this point in the shoot. But right before the scene, the two actors got into an argument sparked by a condescending joke about Morgan's lack of acting experience. It got heated. And ugly. "Chevy's prickly," admitted Ramis. "He's difficult, and not always great to women."

Though both actors prefer not to pick at long-forgotten psychological scabs, insults were exchanged. "Chevy said something and I didn't like it, so he walked," says Morgan. "He wasn't going to shoot with me. Harold came up and said to apologize, and I said, '*You* apologize.' So after a forty-five-minute standoff with Harold running back and forth between us, Harold came back and said, 'OK, I'm going to shoot two masters,'" meaning he was going to cheat and make it look like his two bickering stars were in the same shot together when they couldn't even stand to be in the same room. Eventually, the storm passed. But Morgan is convinced that the lingering anger helped juice their scenes with a feisty, anything-can-happen electricity.

Before Morgan sat down next to Chase at the organ, Ramis whispered into her ear, "Tell him to sing you a love song." It was just another of the director's last-minute firecrackers designed to keep everyone on their toes. So Morgan did just that in what she thought was a rehearsal take. She didn't know the camera was rolling. Chase made up his love song's lyrics on the spot: "I was born to love you/I was born to lick your face/I was born to rub you/But you were born to rub me first." If you look closely at Morgan during the scene, you can see the exact moment when she realizes that the camera is rolling for real. She sort of sobers up, snaps to attention, and goes with it, adding her own un-scripted grace note. "I played along," she says. "I wasn't going down without a fight. I had a big wad of gum in my mouth and I blew a bubble in his face. And that was the scene."

Although Ramis wasn't happy with all of the time that had been wasted by Morgan and Chase's spat, he decided to exploit their animosity when it came time to capture the moment when Ty gives Lacey an oil massage. He and Kenney both suggested that Chase might want to think about clumsily spilling a little too much oil on her back. It would be funny, they promised, egging him on. Chase, already on thin ice with Morgan, figured why not. "That scene was all Doug and Harold," says Chase. "I was trying to convince her, as I was with girls at that time in my life, that sleeping with me was the right thing to do. And they said to maybe spill a little too much baby oil. I went a little over the top."

At the exact moment that a shocked Morgan realizes that she's been completely doused, she cranes her neck back and says, "You're crazy!" It was her genuine unscripted reaction in the moment. "That was an entire bottle of baby oil," she says. "I had no idea it was coming, and it was all in my hair so you knew we weren't going to get a second shot at it. I was half mad and half laughing, which pretty much describes all of our scenes together. It wasn't always tense between us. You can see scenes in the film where he's feeding me lines and helping me. But during the mas-sage, let me tell you, love and hate are a lot closer than you think."

In virtually every single moment on-screen between Chase and Morgan, there's a battle of the sexes going on off-screen. You're witnessing a man using every trick he can think up to get the upper hand on a woman, and a woman trying to hold her ground and give it right back. You can see competitiveness and cooperation, fits of anger and brief flashes of respect, passion, and dispassion. It's all right there in the baby-oil scene. What you don't see during that particular moment is what was happening right on the other side of the wall on the set while they were shooting it: Doug Kenney slumped in a chair sound asleep, still hungover from partying the night before.

◆ ◆

During the second half of production on *Caddyshack*, both *Variety* and *The Hollywood Reporter* sent reporters down to Davie, Florida, to check in on the progress of the film. These sorts of set visits by entertainment journalists tend to be pretty rigged affairs. They're like UN weapons inspections. Anything negative or incriminating is hidden, and everyone is on his or her best behavior for a day or two. Tough questions and investigative sniffing were the last things on these reporters' minds. Back in the late '70s, the trades were still essentially house organs for the major studios, glorified press agents. Had their eyes been open, they might have noticed quite a bit—rampant drug use, acrimony among the film's stars, a first-time director who had tossed his script in the trash long ago.

The Hollywood Reporter item would come out first. Jon Peters, who back then never missed an opportunity to hype himself in the press, flew out for the set visit to glad-hand the visiting journalist. Peters boasts about how in sync he is with Ramis, Kenney, and Doyle-Murray, talking about how they all "clicked" because none of them know the words "It can't be done." Ramis is quoted saying that he resisted the temptation to come in "over-prepared"—a whopper of an understatement. And Kenney jokes about how unnecessary he is as a producer. The reporter swallows all of the self-promoting and self-deprecating platitudes without an ounce of skepticism, ending his toothless article with the following: "Hopefully, it will possess some of that *Animal House* audience rapport and gold. If it doesn't, it won't be because Peters, Ramis or Kenney haven't given it a good shot, mixed with energy, imagination and daring. And those are qualities which helped build this business in the first place." Oh, brother.

Variety, meanwhile, digs a little deeper in its report into the nuts and bolts of the production, talking about the heavy rains that have slowed production, how much money the film is pouring into the Florida economy, and how Kenney, despite the failure of the recent *Animal House* spin-off show, *Delta House*, can envision a *Caddyshack* TV series. The story casts a slightly ominous eye toward the competition that *Caddyshack* will face at the box office from *The Blues Brothers*, Steve Martin's *The Jerk*, and *Airplane!* It also alludes to the film's big finale, still yet to be shot, for which Ramis will blow up the golf course. Apparently, the lockjawed board members at Rolling Hills had let their *Variety* subscriptions lapse. Because they were still under the impression that the fiery, pyrotechnical orgy of destruction had been cut from the script. As free PR goes, the one-two punch from the *Reporter* and *Variety* was a bonanza. Or, at least, hadn't been harmful. Plus, with the reporters now gone, the party was free to continue. All contraband could be safely taken out of hiding.

Pool or the Pond

ON MOST MOVIE SETS, the open consumption of hard drugs such as cocaine would be prevented by layers of responsible and experienced middle-aged producers and representatives from the studio on the set. But the fact that Doug Kenney *was* the producer turned those normal checks and balances into a joke. That, combined with Jon Peters's only-occasional presence in Florida, and Orion's hands-off, go-make-your-movie-without-studio-interference ethos, made *Caddyshack* a perfect storm. Or, in this case, a perfect blizzard.

Before he would find himself on the business end of a rusty pitchfork courtesy of Bill Murray in the film's Dalai Lama scene, Peter Berkrot was a nineteen-year-old wannabe theater actor from Queens. He wasn't sheltered, exactly, but he certainly had never been exposed to the sort of Hollywood decadence he was about to discover in Florida. "I had never seen cocaine before I got to the set of *Caddyshack*," he says. Although he stuck mostly to drinking and smoking pot, Berkrot says that the sight of coke was hard to ignore at the motel where the cast was staying. As the shoot went on, coke use on the film would escalate. Recreational use that started by the gram turned into binges indulged by the ounce. It seemed to be the fuel that kept the film running.

Hamilton Mitchell, who played Motormouth, one of the film's caddies, says that he was initially shocked to see that cocaine use on the set of *Caddyshack* was so brazen and public. And because of the shoot's Florida location, the coke that was being delivered was of the highest quality. "I would never recommend drugs to anyone," says Mitchell. "But this was *really* good cocaine. Pure, like they had just beaten it out of a leaf in Colombia and somebody had carried the leaf to us and turned it into powder in front of us just so we knew how pure it was."

Michael O'Keefe calls his eleven weeks in Florida "a permanent party." "Cocaine was everywhere," he says. "It was driving everyone. People would come into your dressing room with salt shakers and it would be lunch and someone would say, 'Do you want to do a line?' 'Yeah, sure!' It was no big deal. This was the '70s. No one thought anything was wrong about it. Those of us that did it got sucked into the whole bacchanalian rave of it, and believe me when I tell you we went as mad as any of the ancient Greeks."

Chevy Chase, who has talked openly in the past about his own addiction and recovery, said that cocaine just always seemed to materialize on the set of *Caddyshack*. "At the time we didn't know it was addictive. We just knew that we had money to spend and it was a great high," Chase said later. "It always seemed that I could drink more and do more drugs than anybody else and still appear straight. . . . At that time, I was taking it and I didn't feel that *I* had a problem. By the time you think you have a problem, you're half dead."

Brian McConnachie remembers how nervous certain people would get when their dealers didn't arrive on time. And Cindy Morgan recalls one afternoon when she saw Doug Kenney running down the hallway of the motel yelling, "The eagle has landed; the eagle has landed! Get your per diems in cash, the dealer's here!"

"Nobody was trying to rip off the studio and get high," says O'Keefe. "People were trying to make a good movie, and that was just the culture at the time. And Ted Knight was *not* into it. That was not fun for him. If the call to show up on set was for 7 a.m., Ted was there at 6:45. And he would just seethe all day long."

The surge in cocaine use had begun in the music business in the early '70s. Back then, label A&R reps would wear little coke spoons around their necks, always ready to dig into a vial and share it with a potential client like a post-Woodstock sort of handshake. From there, it spread into the film business. With the rise of the New Hollywood generation in the wake of *Easy Rider*, studios were being inundated with younger and younger baby-boomer executives whose cachet hinged on seeming as hip as the filmmakers they were trying to get into business with. Soon, cocaine would become prevalent on movie sets, at Malibu and Laurel Canyon parties, and in the editing suites where impossible deadlines seemed significantly less impossible after a couple of reenergizing bumps. *Caddyshack* was hardly an anomaly.

By the late '70s, a gram of cocaine could cost as much as $100, with a bulk discount when purchased by the ounce (twenty-eight grams). And those were LA prices. In Florida, where coke was cheaper due to its abundance, it seemed like a going-out-of-business sale. By the time *Caddyshack* started production, it had already become what was known in Hollywood circles as a "coke film." Martin Scorsese, who grappled with cocaine addiction while making 1977's *New York, New York* and 1978's *The Last Waltz*, was merely one of the more high-profile abusers until the drug nearly derailed both his career and his life. Meanwhile, over at *Saturday Night Live*, drugs weren't just informing the show's topical humor; they were also ever-present backstage. Coke use got so bad at 30 Rock that Lorne Michaels reportedly posted a sentry outside of the elevators on the seventeenth floor to act as a lookout for curious law enforcement types. Cocaine simply seemed to be an accessory to show business wealth and fame.

After the *Animal House* gang split off to make *Caddyshack* and *The Blues Brothers*, there wasn't just a sense of competition about which comedy would end up performing better at the box office in the summer of 1980. There was also an almost-perverse one-upmanship about which production was more wired. "*Caddyshack* and *Blues Brothers* were like two separate camps tattle-taling on the other," says Brian McConnachie. "One would say, 'They're using more cocaine than we are!'"

John Landis, who was in Chicago directing John Belushi and Dan Aykroyd in *The Blues Brothers*, had noticed a stark change in Belushi since *Animal House*. He'd become a junkie. The director insists that during *Animal House*, Belushi was totally clean. But when he arrived in Chicago just two years later, things had changed drastically. It was almost as if the more famous Belushi got, the larger his appetites became, the more coke he needed to function.

"On *Blues Brothers*, John got very addicted to cocaine," Landis says. "It was terrible." The delays caused by Belushi's binges, unexplained absences, and downward spiral into drug addiction would help send Landis's budget on the film soaring from $17.5 million to $27 million.

As tales of hard partying and rumors of drug use on the set of *Caddyshack* began to filter back to Los Angeles, they ended up making their way over the transom into Mike Medavoy's office at Orion. It was nearing the end of the shoot, but the executive was worried that "recreation money" was being siphoned from the budget.

"Listen, anyone would have been concerned about it," says Medavoy. "And I think anybody would have wanted to do something about it." Medavoy picked up the phone and called Jon Peters. It was time for a come-to-Jesus talk. "We got a call from Mike Medavoy," says Peters. "He said, 'I got a problem.' I was like, 'Now what?' He said, 'I hear there's drugs on the set.' And we all started pissing our pants. He wasn't wrong. It was a huge party, but we worked."

Peters called down to Florida and said that he was coming right away. "It turns out there was some concern from the studio," said Ramis. "Someone in the accounting department leaked that everyone on *Caddyshack* was taking their per diems in cash, which is . . . *unusual*. So I think Medavoy called Jon Peters and said, 'What is going on down there?' And Jon said, 'Fuck off! Who are you to tell them what to do?' Jon defended everybody. And no one got arrested or anything. It never got in the way of work . . . I don't think. What got in the way of work was the way we worked."

When Peters arrived on the set, he called a meeting with Ramis and Kenney. He laid into them about the pace of shooting, the loose atmosphere, and the lack of professionalism, not to mention the drug chatter that had made its way back to Medavoy. In a sense, Peters was merely the messenger, but to Kenney he looked a lot like the enemy. Never one to bend to authority when it was easier to snap, Kenney began arguing with Peters, reportedly saying, "What I think is if you come back here again, you'd better come back with a different attitude or not come back at all." If Kenney was in a calmer, less paranoid state of mind and had paused to really give Peters a full hearing, he might have learned that Peters had been backing them against Orion for some time. Any freedom they'd enjoyed from the studio during the shoot was because of Peters and his acting as the firewall. But few Hollywood figures have ever presented a more convenient target than Jon Peters. It was much easier for Kenney to feel under siege and paint him as a spineless Tinseltown stooge. But sometimes people are more complex than a *National Lampoon* cartoon.

When things finally cooled off, Peters pulled Ramis aside and told him that he had one other thing he wanted to talk to him about. He'd been looking at the dailies back in LA and was knocked out by what both Chevy Chase and Bill Murray were doing on camera. He didn't understand why they didn't have a scene together. It seemed so obvious. "We had two of the biggest stars in the world of comedy, and they didn't talk to each other," says Peters.

That was going to have to change fast.

◆ ◆

Unfortunately, Bill Murray was already back in New York.

"My part just kept growing like a mushroom," says Murray. "I'd go back to New York and work on *SNL*, and they'd call me up and ask if I wanted to come back down and do some more. And I thought, Hey, go to Florida in the winter, that doesn't sound too bad. So I'd turn around and go back, and there'd be another scene for me to do. They just kept adding more and more to the part and then they said, 'We'd love to have a scene between you and Chevy.'"

Murray was happy that everyone had been so pleased with what he'd done during his whirlwind week in Florida that they wanted to beef up his role even more, but he hadn't signed up for doing a scene with Chase, which was, of course, fraught with hostility and history. With Lorne Michaels's blessing, Murray got a few days off from the show to fly back down. When he arrived, he wasn't particularly shocked to learn that nothing had been written yet for him and Chevy. That seemed to be standard operating procedure on the film. Once again, they'd have to wing it.

During lunch, Ramis, Kenney, and Doyle-Murray, along with Murray and Chase, sat down to brainstorm not only what might happen in a scene between Carl Spackler and Ty Webb, but *why* it would happen in the broader context of the story, and *where* it might fit into the film that they'd already shot. In the end, they shrugged and decided that it didn't really have to make sense in the larger framework of the narrative. The film was so slapdash already, what difference would one more random encounter make? "It has nothing to do with the movie," said Ramis, "but actually, no scene has anything to do with the movie."

Says Murray, "Basically they asked me if I wanted to do a scene with Chevy. And I was like, well, we had to try to figure out how these two people would collide. And part of it was dictated by the fact that it was an extra scene that wasn't written in the shooting schedule and it had to be accommodated. They didn't really have much of an idea." Adds Chase, "We decided that I would be playing night golf and the premise was going to be 'Do you mind if I play through?' after I hit a ball into Carl's shack and it landed on his special grass you could play on and also smoke. Bill was very careful with that character, and he set up the shack. I remember he filled the wall above the couch with *Hustler* magazine centerfolds."

The X-rated pinups weren't Murray's only contribution to the decor of Carl's shack. He also thought that he might repurpose a ripped-out car seat with a blanket over it as a ratty couch and use an old wooden wire spool as a coffee table. Skid row chic. By the time lunch was over, the five writers had worked out the beats of the scene, but hadn't bothered to write anything down. This would be pure improv. They were given a premise; the rest was up to them.

"We shot it that same night," says Chase. "And the idea was that when I came into Carl's shack, it looked like I had an ax in my hand and I'm going to kill him. You just see the shadow; it doesn't look like a golf club. So he sees me and goes, 'Oh, hi, Ty!' "

Says Murray, "Chevy came in sideways, hitting a golf ball. And then we just sort of did a take and we said, 'OK, we got that.' And then it was like, let's take it again. And we kept building it a little bit at a time. We didn't do many takes. Just two or three. And I'd never really done anything with Chevy. We'd always had sort of a . . . *funny* relationship. But it was like, 'OK, I liked that when you did that. Let's just keep going.' And we kept going and it was funny because Ty Webb's not far from who Chevy is. So he was pretty comfortable in his space. And I was comfortable as Carl. So he could be free to laugh at me. And if Ty laughed, Carl thought it meant, 'Hey, he's my friend!' It's a really fun, self-aware example of whatever the heck Harold maintains the movie is about—status."

"Bill is aggressive; he likes to push you in a scene," says Chase. "Carl started going with the pot and the wine and we had to put my ball on that little square of grass and he started talking about chinch bugs. It just came from him. He was fucking hilarious. I had to do whatever I could to keep from laughing. And I tried to get him to laugh, so when he asked if I had a swimming pool, I said, 'A pool and a pond, the pond would be good for you.' That's all winging it. As I said it, I could see Bill give a little look like he might crack, but he didn't. He's too professional. The scene really defined our characters. Carl clearly wanted more than he had in life and was happy to see me because

I had a pool and a big house. And I clearly wanted *less* of him. Harold had to stop me and Billy at some point, because we could have gone on all night."

Chase and Murray shot one other scene together that never made it into the film. Ty and Michael O'Keefe's Danny Noonan are playing golf, and Carl pulls up on a huge riding lawnmower and gives Ty a mush-mouthed tutorial about his backswing, hitting a few balls belonging to some other golfers playing behind them. As the furious golfers come running toward them, Carl and Ty speed off on the mower (Chase narrowly escaped getting shredded by the mower's blades when Murray floored it a little too hard). It's easy to see why the scene didn't make the cut. It's not very good. Certainly not a fraction as inspired as the pool-or-the-pond scene, where you can see two men rooting up years of bruised egos and wounded pride. It isn't just two *SNL* stars ad-libbing about grass you can smoke, chinch bugs, and "getting weird"; they're exorcising years of perceived slights. It's a therapy session disguised as a two-handed comedy jag. This one, four-minute moment would finally be the thing to thaw the off-screen iciness between them.

"We got over everything," says Chase. "The tension was short-lived. I have nothing but admiration and affection for Bill. He still can be a surly character, to say the least. But ultimately, he's a good guy. Even though I'm the number one star in the movie under the title, I'll always think of *Caddyshack* as Billy's movie."

13

The Dynamite Caper

AFTER TWO MONTHS of hard partying and filming on the fly at Rolling Hills, the time to say goodbye to their home away from home was fast approaching. In a couple of days, the cast and crew would load up and head due south on I-95 to Key Biscayne, near Miami, where they would shoot the final unshot pages in the script—the yacht club scenes, including the stunt-heavy water sequences in which Rodney Dangerfield's gaudy cabin cruiser, *Seafood*, turns Ted Knight's *The Flying Wasp* into driftwood. Some were sad to leave the nonstop bender behind; others couldn't pack up and get the hell out of the dorm of debauchery soon enough. Before they left, though, there was still one last scene to get in the can, and it would require stealth, diversions, outright lies, and wanton mayhem and destruction.

By that point in the production, almost every page of the *Caddyshack* script had been tweaked, revised, or simply ignored and thrown into the garbage. One of the few scenes that never changed at all was the one that the governing board at Rolling Hills was under the impression would be changed first—the climactic explosion at the end of the film that accidentally sinks Danny's putt and unsuccessfully attempts to send Carl's nemesis to gopher heaven, all scored to the "1812 Overture." In what can only be described as a classic feat of old-fashioned, bareknuckle Hollywood producing, Jon Peters hatched a brilliantly devious campaign of subterfuge.

Rigging and setting off the film's big explosion wasn't cheap. By some accounts, the pyrotechnics alone would end up adding as much as $150,000 to the film's budget. Others say the number was much lower. Either way, it could only be done once. There were no second takes or do-overs. The crew had constructed a fake elevated green off to the side of the Rolling Hills course, which would act as ground zero. Several of the club's stately oaks were wired to blow. A giant fuel truck was backed up onto the course. "I've got pictures of that truck pumping gasoline *directly* into the ground," says Cindy Morgan.

While preparation for the big bang was underway, including the hiring of dozens of extras, Peters says, he extended an invitation to the Rolling Hills VIPs. He asked them if they would be so good as to accompany him for dinner and a scenic boat ride. It was his way of saying thank you for all of their hospitality and cooperation. "Jon was going to take these guys for a ride and by the time they got back, it would just be too late to do anything. What balls!" says Michael O'Keefe.

As soon as Peters and his party passed through the gates of Rolling Hills, Ramis sprung into action. All of the principal cast and extras were gathered around. Ramis held up a megaphone and announced, "We only have one chance to get this right." He made sure that everyone knew where he or she should be looking when the blast went off. "Harold was anxious that no one get hurt," says Trevor Albert. "Whenever there's a stunt of any sort, if you're a responsible human being it flashes through your head: I hope we've done everything we can to make sure this goes right. With all of the unpredictable stuff that had gone on on the movie and the total lack of discipline, I was just like, I hope this goes well. There's no improvisation in *this*."

There are several separate explosions as Danny's ball hangs on the lip of the cup and Carl plunges the detonator. Ramis said that he made sure to set up multiple cameras so that his one-shot deal was covered by every possible angle as an insurance policy. "The reactions when that thing went off were absolutely genuine because no one knew what to expect," says Peter Berkrot. "We were expecting fireworks and we got Guadalcanal. You could feel the heat and the shock waves of hot air. You couldn't fake the response."

While Peters and his hoodwinked guests were finishing up their meal, they caught a news report on the restaurant's television. It said that there had been a huge explosion at Rolling Hills. It's easy to picture jaws dropping into laps, forks clanking on bone-china plates, monocles plopping into bowls of lobster bisque. The magnitude of the blast had been so severe and the fireballs and curling plumes of thick black smoke so extreme that an incoming commercial pilot radioed into the control tower at the Fort Lauderdale airport reporting a plane crash. Peters did his best to calm down his guests. Still, when the *Caddyshack* crew left Rolling Hills the next morning, some said it had the charged air of a bunch of gangsters making a quick getaway, fleeing the scene of the crime one step ahead of the authorities. Surprisingly, the damage to the course itself was minor. Some downed tree limbs, a couple of craters in the grass that needed to be filled in and resodded. Still, no one expected to be invited back to Rolling Hills anytime soon.

In the early drafts of the script, the film ends right after the explosion with Danny at the airport, supposedly headed off to college but distracted at the last minute by a babe headed to Jamaica who makes him change his plans. He follows his bliss instead of the responsible path he's supposed to take. Life lessons are learned, etc. There was also supposed to be a brief *Casablanca*-like scene in which Ty and Lacey walk off into the sunset with Chase saying: "Should we get together? We couldn't respect each other less." Ramis ended up going with something far more arbitrary. A bug-eyed Dangerfield looks at the camera and barks the one-liner: "Hey, everybody, we're all going to get laid!"

Why?

At that point, the question had become: Why not?

"It was a totally improvised line that I can't even believe I left in the movie," said Ramis. "It makes absolutely no sense, which at that point was pretty much par for the course."

◆ ◆

Located thirty-eight miles south of Fort Lauderdale, Biscayne Bay is a horseshoe-shaped lagoon nestled just below Miami on the Atlantic coast of Florida. The *Caddyshack* crew arrived there at the beginning of November to film what would end up being the most ambitious stunt scenes in the movie. The production designer Stan Jolley repurposed a slightly-down-on-its-heels waterfront restaurant called The Rusty Pelican to stand in for the ritzy site of Judge Smails's yacht christening. Along with the Caddy Day pool scenes that were shot at Fort Lauderdale's Plantation Club and the snooty "Dance of the living dead" party scenes shot at the Boca Raton Hotel and Club, it would be the film's most important location after Rolling Hills. Ramis would shoot there for only four days, but constructing a collapsing hydraulic dock and bringing in stunt water-skiers from Busch Gardens added an extra week of work.

The christening of Judge Smails's sloop before its maiden voyage was in the first drafts of the *Caddyshack* script and appears in the finished film with only some minor tweaks. For example, Judge Smails's "dinghy" is called *The Bluebird* instead of

The Flying Wasp and Al Czervik's enormous cabin cruiser is called *Thunderball II* instead of *Seafood*. There's also no mention of the helter-skelter maritime stuntwork or Smails's Thurston Howell III–style dedication to his new craft:

```
           JUDGE SMAILS
  I've got a little poem that I'd like
  to read in honor of this occasion, if
  I may? Spaulding, get your foot off
  the boat!
    It's easy to grin/ When your ship
  comes in/ And you've got the stock
  market beat./ But the man worthwhile/
  Is the man who can smile/ When his
  shorts aren't too tight in the seat.
```

Both Ramis and Kenney would later admit that the carefully choreographed chaos at Biscayne Bay was among the most anxiety-ridden moments of the shoot. But in the end, it would go off without a hitch. Ironically, the final day on set would be one of the few that actually traveled from script to celluloid without some last-minute overhaul. Now, on November 19, eleven weeks after cameras started rolling, *Caddyshack* had finally wrapped. The first-time director and novice producer were proud of how little they'd compromised so far. It was time to celebrate.

At the wrap party, Ramis could finally stop worrying for the first time in three months—at least until they got back to LA to start editing. During their time in Florida, he'd been too busy and had been saddled with too many tiny responsibilities to join the nightly pageant of drug-fueled hedonism. So at the wrap party, he made up for lost time, getting so wasted that he had to be literally carried back to his hotel room.

"We had wrap parties every night on that movie," says Cindy Morgan. "But the mother of all wrap parties was that last night.

Everybody was there. Doug was sitting next to me and he goes, 'I want you to look around this room and tell me: Who do you respect the most?' I said, "Me." He went crazy. 'What do you mean you?!' And I just felt like after everything I had been through, I didn't break under the pressure. I'd been bullied and threatened. I did what I had to do and I was proud. I think he just thought I was being arrogant. But I meant it. I couldn't wait to get the hell out of there."

During the last few weeks of filming, Kenney had grown especially close to Trevor Albert, who had begun the film as Peters's assistant and ended it as Ramis's assistant. Now that the movie was over, Albert wasn't sure where that left him. All he knew was that he didn't want to go back to driving Peters's kids around and taking Barbra Streisand's dog to the groomer.

"Of everybody there, it was Doug and Harold that I wanted to work with again despite the chaos," says Albert. "I told Doug that I didn't want to go back to working for Jon and he said, 'Why don't you come be my assistant now?'"

At the wrap party, Kenney was full of naïve optimism and not just because he was stoned out of his gourd. He and Ramis wouldn't know what they had until they got into the editing room back in LA, but he felt the same confidence he'd always had at the end of big projects, and those had always turned out to be charmed. Why should this time be any different? This Hollywood thing seemed so easy. You write a movie with your friends, you fly off with someone else's money and have a blast, and then people kiss your ass and throw money at you when it's a hit. That night, Kenney walked around the party, thanking everyone and predicting that *Caddyshack* would not only be a huge box-office success; it would be even bigger than *Animal House*.

It was the last time he'd ever feel that bullish about anything.

14

The Unkindest Cut

IN DECEMBER OF 1979, Harold Ramis and Doug Kenney returned to Los Angeles to begin the arduous process of editing *Caddyshack*. It was a task that neither of them had ever undertaken, never mind remotely understood. Editing may be the least glamorous part of an otherwise glamorous art form. But it's arguably the most important to its outcome. It's where you *find* the film.

To those who don't splice film for a living, editing can seem as mysterious as alchemy—a cross between hard science and ethereal sorcery, where celluloid is either transformed into gold or into just a pile of flammable confetti. In his classic 1979 Hollywood memoir, *When the Shooting Stops . . . The Cutting Begins*, veteran Hollywood editor Ralph Rosenblum (*Annie Hall*) writes, " 'Don't worry, we'll fix it in the cutting room,' is a prayer that's been uttered in every language, on every location, in every country where films have been made. . . . The cutting room becomes the last-stand corral for everyone's hopes that the unrealized dreams, the dead moments, the inevitable blah sequences from weeks of shooting will finally be brought to life."

There was a lot of "Don't worry, we'll fix it in the cutting room" prayers on the set of *Caddyshack*. From looking at the dailies, anyone could tell that Ramis's tendency to crumple up the blueprint and embrace improvisation had produced a handful of scenes that were way funnier than they ever were on the page. But by tossing out the skeleton that a script provides, he would end up making things a million times more complicated for himself when it was time to cut it all together. It would be like trying to put together a jigsaw puzzle that's missing half of its pieces.

"For better or worse, Harold had no experience as a director," says Trevor Albert. "So the script wasn't a bible to him at all. Someone who was more seasoned might think: I need these guideposts along the way to make sure the whole thing holds together. Harold didn't feel that way. The whole premise of improv is you're creating it on its feet, but that isn't how editing works. I'd studied enough about how movies got made to look at how the script was changing and think, Jesus, this is insane! There's no way this is going to end well."

The work began in a small suite of three connecting offices in the editorial building on the Warner Bros. lot. Along with the editor Bill Carruth, the original team consisted of two assistant editors, Robert Barrere and Rachel Igel, as well as Albert, who served as an apprentice. With Brian Doyle-Murray mostly back in New York, now working as a writer on *SNL*, Ramis and Kenney were in the editing room virtually every day for ten to twelve hours, dutifully overseeing the grueling shovel-and-spade work and smoking pot. More than one person who was there compared the *Caddyshack* editing headquarters to working inside of a bong. As they did while writing the original treatment of the film, they would begin each day by sealing the gaps around the door with gaffer's tape to keep the funky fog inside.

"They were really fun guys," says Rachel Igel, a nonsmoker who had just returned from London where she'd been working for the staid BBC. "I lived in England through most of the '70s, so I missed all of the popular culture like *Saturday Night Live*. Their brand of humor was completely new to me. Harold was incredibly nice and easy to be around, and Doug I really liked, but he was a little crazy. You go from working for a magazine like the *National Lampoon* to coming to Hollywood and suddenly having a lot of money, a lot of women, and a lot of drugs—I think he was just overwhelmed."

The first hurdle in editing a movie is assembling a so-called rough cut, which is like a slab of raw marble yet to be chiseled. Then the director has a certain number of weeks to cobble together his or her initial pass at the film. Rough cuts obviously run longer than what eventually ends up in theaters. Still, even by that standard, the first assemblage of *Caddyshack* made *Lawrence of Arabia* look like a movie trailer. It was four and a half hours long. In the meantime, as Carruth, Ramis, and Kenney tried to make sense out of their highlight reel of hilarious ad-libbed odds and ends, the stench of weed coming out of their office was so powerful, the other editors in the building complained. They weren't lectured or warned; they were simply moved to an office in Jon Peters's bungalow.

"It was such a different time," says Igel. "The kind of thing that people did normally back then would be impossible today. You'd get fired. But back then, it was like, 'Oh, these guys must be geniuses. Let's let them do what they want and see what we get.' In Hollywood, when a movie makes a lot of money, on the next one they think these people must know something, so they give them a pretty wide berth."

That wide berth gave them the latitude to feel as if they could leave in a raunchier version of Bill Murray's ball-washer masturbation gag that stretched on for thirty minutes—self-indulgent even for a roomful of stoners. Ramis and Kenney were either so in love with their material or so zonked that everything they'd filmed in Florida seemed indispensable. When Peters finally got his first look at Ramis's cut after a couple of weeks, he was stunned. "We didn't have a movie," says Peters. "We had a bunch of scenes that didn't play together."

The original narrative through line of *Caddyshack*—the love triangle between Danny, Maggie, and Tony—turned out to be a snooze. It just wasn't working. At least compared with Rodney Dangerfield's in-your-face one-liners and Bill Murray's bonkers monologues. "The story that was there to congeal everything together didn't work," says Rusty Lemorande. "The story of Danny needing the scholarship but he may have impregnated a girl and that meant he would have to marry her as a good Catholic boy and give up his college dreams, the actress who played his girlfriend [Sarah Holcomb] did it with an Irish accent that was not particularly workable. All of those scenes played flat and dull. And through the process of editing, those scenes started ending up on the cutting room floor. That first cut was a true disaster."

Ramis and Kenney didn't have enough experience to know how to fix what they were looking at. Peters was freaking out, throwing fits at top volume. And Carruth didn't know whom he was supposed to be taking his marching orders from. "He listened to everything we said, which was a mistake," said Ramis. Something had to be done quickly. Something drastic.

The only good news was that no one from Orion, especially Mike Medavoy, had been in the room during that calamitous first screening. Orion was still in the dark. For now, the notoriously hands-off studio would remain hands off. But even its patience would end up having limits.

◆ ◆

While Ramis was scrambling to put together his first bloated cut of *Caddyshack*, Kenney left the Warner lot early one night to attend the premiere of 1941. The WWII comedy was Steven Spielberg's shoot-the-works, spare-no-expense follow-up to *Jaws* and *Close Encounters of the Third Kind*. He'd become Hollywood's newest Boy Midas. And for some bizarre reason, he'd chosen to spend that creative capital on a shrill, laughless comedy about the Japanese invading Los Angeles, starring Tim Matheson, Treat Williams, and John Belushi in his first big-screen role since *Animal House*. The early buzz on the film was deadly. In a town where schadenfreude is the emotional default setting, the knives were out for Spielberg's folly.

Kenney hadn't seen Belushi in a while. Both had been wrapped up with the endless demands of newly minted fame, but he was eager to see his old friend notch another triumph. But as the audience squirmed in silence, it was clear that it was not to be. It was a film with too many characters, too many gags that were designed to be fizzy but turned out to be flat, too much . . . *everything*. In one of his typical displays of sick gallows humor, Michael O'Donoghue had buttons printed up for the occasion that read: "John Belushi: Born 1949, Died 1941."

After the premiere was over, Kenney ran into his old *Lampoon* boss, Matty Simmons, in the lobby. They were both trying to tiptoe out of the theater as quickly as possible so that they wouldn't run into anyone connected with the movie and have to put on a happy face and spin congratulatory lies. According to Simmons, Kenney pulled him aside and said, "We gotta talk about this turkey." Simmons replied, "Hey, at least it's not *our* turkey."

As December was drawing to a close, Peters wasn't sure how much longer he would be able to hold Medavoy off. The executive was eager to see his studio's hot new comedy from the geniuses behind *Animal House*. Peters was stalling for time until he could figure out how to save the film. He believed that the best thing to do would be to edit around the funniest scenes. In other words, keep the name-brand stars such as Dangerfield, Knight, Chase, and Murray and lose the no-name caddies and their storyline.

Said Ramis, "When the movie started to transition from the caddies' story to this kind of madcap Marx brothers movie, it became a free-for-all. Rodney had funny things, and Chevy had funny things, and Ted had funny things, and Bill had funny things, but they didn't necessarily add up to anything." It wasn't a movie; it was a scattershot Greatest Hits compilation.

Ramis seemed to accept that he was out of his depth and that some sort of triage needed to be done. But Kenney dug in his heels and insisted that they could fix it if they were left on their own. The last thing he wanted was to hand over control to someone like Peters. What did he know about comedy? It was a fight that, deep down, Kenney would soon realize that he couldn't win. The film was about to slip through his fingers, sending him into a tailspin of black moods and self-destructive behavior. How had it come to this, he asked his friends? This time, *he* was supposed to be the one in charge.

"Jon Peters and Mike Medavoy were kind of Doug's bosses," says assistant editor Rachel Igel. "And I know that he felt the film was being taken away from him. I don't know if that's true, but I think he felt that way. He was used to working in a situation where he could do whatever he wanted. At the *Lampoon*, he had creative freedom. And nobody has that on a movie, even if you're Martin Scorsese."

During those initial disastrous days in the editing room, Sean Kelly, Kenney's old pal from the *Lampoon*, ran into Doug and Harold at a bar in LA. Kelly had come out to Hollywood for a few days trying to sell a movie, as so many staffers at the magazine had in the heady gold-rush days after the success of *Animal*

House. "They walked in and they were in a state of misery that was astonishing," he recalls. Kelly asked them what was the matter. They had just seen the first cut of *Caddyshack*.

"They said it was horrible; they couldn't believe that this had happened to them. Everything about it seemed to be sophomoric and didn't work and the jokes weren't timed. I think Doug realized it was the first time he'd been a part of something that he thought wasn't great. He was like, 'Oh, my God, I guess I'm out of gas.' They were really kicking themselves."

On Peters's orders, Rusty Lemorande put together a list of experienced editors who might be able to come in and play the role of white knight on the film. They screened what they had for a number of candidates. One of them sat down with Peters, Lemorande, and Mark Canton after watching the mess of a film and bluntly told them that he would fix it if they gave him six weeks and $200,000. "That was a *huge* amount of money back then," says Lemorande. "And he made it clear that he wasn't going to be showing it to us piecemeal as a work in progress. It was a take it or leave it proposition." When he left, the three looked at each other and said, *Is it really that bad?!*

Knowing that there was no way they could go back to Orion and ask for that kind of money (certainly not without showing them the fiasco they had on their hands), Lemorande proposed another idea. Before joining the Jon Peters Organization, he had worked at CAA, one of Hollywood's biggest and most high-powered talent agencies. His boss there had represented *Breakfast at Tiffany's* director Blake Edwards. Lemorande had got to know Edwards's longtime editor, Ralph Winters. Maybe he'd be willing to take a turn with the scissors? At seventy, Winters might not *get* Caddyshack, but he might just be able to save it.

Winters was a disciplined, seasoned pro whose credits reached back to early '40s. He'd earned six Oscar nominations for editing and won twice, for 1950's *King Solomon's Mines* and 1959's *Ben-Hur*. He wasn't as square as his résumé and driver's license suggested. He'd worked on a number of Peter Sellers comedies, including *The Pink Panther* and *The Party*. He had the delicately trained eye of an artisan—he could look at that slab of marble and see what shape it should take. Even though Winters was well past retirement age, he had other jobs lined up. But he agreed to come in at nights and free of charge as a favor and make some suggestions. "Ralph only worked on a couple of reels of the film, but the improvement was gigantic," says Lemorande. "It showed us what editing could do. He was our savior."

After a week or so, Winters had to stop moonlighting on *Caddyshack* to start another job, but he suggested another editor who he thought would be able to pick up where he left off. David Bretherton had won an Oscar for 1972's *Cabaret*, and seemed like an even better fit than Winters since he'd recently worked on *Silver Streak*, another improv-heavy comedy starring Richard Pryor and Gene Wilder. Plus, he was a decade and a half younger than Winters. At fifty-five, he was inching closer to their target audience, albeit in baby steps. Bretherton looked at the film and told Peters, Ramis, and Kenney that the footage that they had was salvageable. He reassured Ramis that he didn't screw it all up. It just needed to be finessed.

The good news was, the film might be saved after all. The bad news was, Jon Peters was getting more actively involved, meaning that there wasn't much need for Kenney to be around anymore. "I don't think Doug and Jon Peters were necessarily the greatest combination in the world," says Mark Canton. "But that's not that unusual with movies. Different producers have the material first, then the financiers and the studio get involved, and everybody thinks they know better. That's the toughest part of this business—it's a team sport." Adds Trevor Albert more bluntly, "It's hard for me to imagine that Doug and Harold really respected anything that came out of Jon Peters's mouth creatively."

As Kenney was losing his grip on his own picture, he began spending more time back at his production company, Three Wheel, on the Fox lot. While he'd been on location in Florida, his producing partners, Alan Greisman and Michael Shamberg, had put a number of movies into active development, including a comedy about a milquetoast with telekinetic powers that would reteam Kenney with his pal Chevy Chase, titled *Modern Problems*. Both Greisman and Shamberg were relieved to have their third wheel back. "Doug's mind worked at an amazing capacity," says Greisman. "Having him around just kicked things into a different gear. He was a whirlwind. At that time we had *Modern Problems* going with Chevy, Chris Miller's Club Med comedy, and a project that Jules Pfeiffer was working on about a young city mayor that was inspired by Dennis Kucinich. We thought, OK, great, we have a project for every wheel now." As happy as Kenney was to be busy and feel wanted, the escalating amount of cocaine he was taking only amped up his insecurity and paranoia. He wasn't about to let go of *Caddyshack* without a fight.

15

Enter the Gopher

BACK IN THE CUTTING ROOM, *Caddyshack* was beginning to come together thanks to new editor David Bretherton's judicious scalpel. It was now a long way from the four-and-a-half-hour whale it started as. But it was still far from being tight, or even releasable. As Peters started to become more and more hands-on, he was freer and freer with his suggestions on how to make *Caddyshack* work. Ramis felt steamrolled, but he was in no position to fight back. With the teenage Danny-Maggie-Tony love triangle now basically chopped out, they needed to find some sort of connective string to hang all of their gemlike comedy beads on. Peters came up with what sounded like an insane idea.

While they were in Florida, Ramis had shot several scenes of Bill Murray plotting against his nemesis, the golf-course-destroying gopher. But there was hardly any film that showed the actual gopher other than the one scene in which a crude sock puppet (on the hand of Trevor Albert) pops out of a hole and steals Rodney Dangerfield's golf ball ("Hey, that kangaroo stole my ball!"). According to Ramis, Peters said, "What if we made the gopher the thing that tied the film together?" Kenney and Ramis thought Peters was kidding at first. Peters was the kind of person who floated a lot of dumb ideas before landing on a good one. But he wasn't joking. Kenney's heart sank, the metallic taste of anger rising in the back of his mouth. Their satire about class warfare was about to be hijacked by a goofy anthropomorphic rodent.

Ramis tasked Rusty Lemorande with finding a real, live gopher. Everyone agreed that the puppet they had was simply too cheap and crappy-looking to work. They asked animal trainers about using groundhogs, woodchucks, beavers, and squirrels. They were told no dice across the board. If the gopher was going to be a bigger part of the movie now, their threadbare puppet wasn't going to cut it. This being years before computer-generated effects would become commonplace, they were beginning to realize that they were going to have to hire a special-effects company to create an animatronic gopher. And that meant they would have to go ask Orion for more money. It was time to stop stonewalling and make the studio their partner in solving the problem. Jon Peters swallowed hard and went to go see Mike Medavoy.

It wasn't just a matter of begging for gopher money; there were also a number of smaller special-effects shots that still needed to be completed, such as the point-of-view crosshairs insert when Rodney Dangerfield looks through his high-tech, radar-equipped putter and the lightning that strikes the Bishop while he's playing the round of his life. Peters was going to need $500,000 all in. He knew Medavoy wouldn't cough it up easily. Then again, he prided himself on being a natural-born hustler. Even when you saw through his bullshit, it was hard to say no to him.

"The way he explained it was 'It's gonna be really funny! It's gonna be really funny!' Typical salesman," says Medavoy. "I was like, 'OK, tell me *how* it's going to be funny.' And he said, 'I don't know, but it's gonna be really funny! Trust me!' And in Hollywood, 'Trust me' means 'I'm about to fuck you.'"

Before cutting Peters a check for half a million dollars, Medavoy said that he needed to see how desperate the situation actually was. Peters set up a screening for him on the Warner Bros. lot. "At that point, you could tell it was funny," says Trevor Albert. "But the characters were sort of all over the place. I think it was hard to figure out what the fuck it was." When the lights came up inside the theater two hours later, Medavoy grimly told Peters that he had his money. He looked like he needed a drink. Now they just had to find someone who could bring their gopher to life.

By 1980, John Dykstra had become a special-effects legend. He'd been mentored in the late '60s and early '70s by f/x wizard Douglas Trumbull on such films as *Silent Running*, and he had gone on to become an integral early part of the pioneering effects company Industrial Light & Magic. Dykstra had won an Oscar at ILM for his work on *Star Wars* (he was the brain behind George Lucas's gee-whiz lightsabers and X-wing tie-fighter battles), but he clashed with Lucas and split off to form his own effects house, Apogee. The Van Nuys–based company had been hip-deep in work on *Star Trek: The Motion Picture* when Peters, who had already been turned down by The Henson Company, called. Dykstra agreed to look at *Caddyshack* to see if he could come up with a solution.

"They were using this really rudimentary sock puppet thing for the gopher at the time," says Dykstra. "None of these guys knew anything about animatronics. It was a real seat-of-your-pants movie. For us, it was a pretty small assignment."

Rusty Lemorande tells a slightly different story. According to him, Dykstra didn't actually create *Caddyshack*'s gopher from scratch. Lemorande, a former puppeteer, says that during postproduction, as soon as it became clear that they would need a new-and-improved gopher (something with more polish and personality than a hand puppet), he reached out to a friend of a friend named Jeff Burke, who worked at Walt Disney's Imagineering department building animatronic creatures for the studio's theme parks. Burke said he would build their gopher on his off hours as long as Lemorande didn't tell anyone, otherwise he'd be fired. He asked for $5,000. When Burke was finished with the assignment, Lemorande went to his house and handed him five grand in exchange for the gopher, as if it were some sort of film noir kidnap exchange. According to Lemorande, Dykstra then added the ability for the gopher to move its ears, dance, and cough smoke from its mouth with a range of expressions using hydraulics. "They wanted a cute character," says Dykstra, "but to be honest, gophers aren't very cute. He ended up looking more like a chipmunk." The dolphin-like sounds the gopher makes were recycled from the 1960s TV show *Flipper*.

What both parties agree on is that Dykstra and his team at Apogee created the gopher's world—a network of underground tunnels that the animal would move through as it was toying with Bill Murray's psychotic assistant greenskeeper. Dykstra and his team (including puppeteer Joe Garlington, who actually manned the gopher) created their subterranean sets on a flatbed trailer covered with dirt and contoured sod and brought it out to a golf course in Encino to shoot the gopher sequences. They shot scenes on the course's practice green, where they created vinyl-tube "runnels" in the ground showing the gopher's burrowing wake of destruction. They also finished all of the film's other effects sequences as part of a carefully negotiated and tightly budgeted overall package deal. Ramis, who was still mired in the editing room, would occasionally stop by to supervise, but according to Dykstra, the day-to-day work was overseen by Peters's lieutenant, Donald MacDonald. "We had a great time," says Dykstra. "There was a lot of 'Wait a minute, what if we did this?!' Just a bunch of crazy ideas. There were no limitations. We were just trying stuff."

Now Peters and Ramis just had to figure out which music their new hydraulically boogying gopher would dance to.

• •

One day while Ramis and Kenney were in the editing room, Peters popped his head in and asked if they had given any thought to who they wanted to do the movie's music. Ramis and Kenney had been so consumed by soul-crushing gopher issues and the intensive slicing and dicing they'd been doing that they just looked at one another vacantly and shrugged. Finally, Ramis offered, "How about Pink Floyd?" Needless to say, the band took a hard pass. Instead, Peters reached out to a friend who had recently collaborated with Barbra Streisand on the song "I Believe in Love" for *A Star Is Born*—Kenny Loggins.

Loggins had started his career writing songs in the early '70s for those SoCal purveyors of mellow folk rock, the Nitty Gritty Dirt Band, before branching off to form the hugely successful yacht-rock duo Loggins and Messina with Jim Messina, formerly of Poco and Buffalo Springfield. The two parted in 1976 to pursue solo careers. "I Believe in Love" was one of the songs on Loggins's first go-it-alone album and became a hit thanks to Streisand's interpretation in *A Star Is Born*. That was the beginning and end of Loggins's history with Peters. "Jon and I were in two different worlds," he says. "He was a Hollywood high roller and I was much more of a bumpkin who made it overnight in rock 'n' roll."

Loggins recalls getting a call one day from his A&R rep at Columbia Records, who asked him what he thought about doing songs for movies—still a fairly new concept in 1979. The next thing he knew he was driving down from Santa Barbara to Peters's palatial home in Malibu. Peters asked Loggins if he was free to take a look at his latest movie and see if he had any song ideas.

"I went to Warner Bros. to watch a rough cut of *Caddyshack,* and before it started, Jon said, 'I'm going to have this gopher come out of his hole and do a little dance at the beginning.' And I said, 'That's the stupidest thing I've ever heard!'" Stupid or not, Loggins remembers laughing his ass off while watching the movie with a notebook on his lap to scribble ideas in.

"I ended up writing four pieces of music for the movie," says Loggins. "But the main one was 'I'm Alright,' which just came to me from watching the opening scene of Danny on his bicycle. I'd never written a song specifically for a movie before, but I found it to be really easy because the emotional situation was handed to you on a platter. You didn't have to come up with something out of the blue like you usually do as a songwriter. The temp music they put behind Danny was Bob Dylan's 'Gotta Serve Somebody,' and what I got from that was they were telling me that they wanted to present him as a rebel caught in this country club environment where he had to suppress that. I felt like the song should have a fuck-all-you-people quality to it."

Loggins says "I'm Alright" poured out of him in a few hours at his kitchen table in Santa Barbara the same evening that he saw the unfinished film. Then he went into the studio and cut the song, using the movie's opening-scene golf course sprinklers as percussion. When he brought the demo home, he listened to it and just started cracking up.

"I knew I fucking had one in the bag," Loggins says. "That doesn't happen often enough. I just listened to it and thought, This is a smash!" Peters agreed. He then tapped veteran composer Johnny Mandel (*M*A*S*H*, *The Last Detail*) to fill out the rest of the light, jazzy score for the film.

With John Dykstra finishing up work on the gopher scenes and the music now in capable hands, Ramis and Kenney finally had some time to catch their breath and take stock. The movie was coming together. It may not have been the movie that either of them had originally had in mind, but it was nonetheless inching toward the finish line. Ramis was supervising the sound mixing in anticipation of testing the film with preview audiences. Each day was filled with dozens of minor technical decisions, and Kenney was feeling more and more like an uninvited crasher at his own party.

"Doug would come into my office with questions about technical things and he seemed really sad," says Rusty Lemorande. "I think he just wanted to have something to do. He felt that the whole thing was a ship that was moving off that he thought he'd be on and he wasn't."

Michael O'Keefe says that during postproduction he was called back to reshoot a scene between him and Sarah Holcomb to fill in a narrative gap in the edit. It was the scene when Maggie finds out that she's not pregnant and does a celebratory dance in her nightgown on the golf course. O'Keefe was working on another movie at the time, and his hair had been cut short for it. So they slapped a preposterously cheesy-looking wig on him and stuffed it under a baseball cap. There had been some debate about whether to even bother with reshooting the scene. Lemorande remembers advising Peters that they should just drop it altogether. Peters agreed. But Kenney insisted that it stay in. Sensitive to how estranged Kenney was feeling, Peters let him have his way even though he was the one who ultimately had final cut on the film. He just wanted to keep the peace.

On April 25, 1980, Bill Murray's Hunter Thompson movie,

Where the Buffalo Roam, opened in 464 theaters. It was the first film of his to come out in the wake of *Meatballs,* and although it was being distributed by Universal, Orion was tracking it closely. After all, if Murray managed to score his second hit in a row, that would only mean good things for *Caddyshack*. The critics savaged it. In what was one of the more upbeat reviews (two out of four stars), Roger Ebert wrote, "This is the kind of bad movie that's almost worth seeing." Universal quickly yanked it from theaters after it limped its way to $6 million at the box office. Thompson himself would subsequently disown the picture. Soon, there were to be even more bad omens.

On May 24, the fifth season of *Saturday Night Live* came to a close. By that time, both John Belushi and Dan Aykroyd had left the show to pursue movie careers. During the run of the season, Lorne Michaels seemed to be doing everything he could to help *Caddyshack* out—Chevy Chase, Ted Knight, and Rodney Dangerfield had all guest-hosted. The season finale, hosted by Buck Henry, would turn out to be the end of another five-year era like the one at *National Lampoon* after Kenney and Henry Beard cashed out. The remaining Not Ready for Prime Time Players, including Bill Murray, would not be coming back. And Michaels, the creative spirit and protean spark behind the enterprise from the very beginning, was unceremoniously let go by NBC. He would not step foot in Studio 8H again for another five years.

A week later, the *Caddyshack* team got some distressing news of its own. In March, President Carter had announced that the United States would officially boycott the 1980 Summer Olympics in Moscow after the Soviet Union ignored his ultimatum to withdraw its troops from Afghanistan. Now, in the aftermath of that announcement, the studios were furiously jockeying and reshuffling the release dates of their summer films to fill in the yawning gap on the calendar they'd left open for the Games (when their audiences would have been at home, glued to their TV sets). On June 5, *The Hollywood Reporter* announced that Orion would be pushing *Caddyshack*'s release up from August 8 to July 25. Ramis and Kenney now had two fewer weeks to put the finishing touches on the film.

As Kenney was feeling more and more alienated from *Caddyshack*, he looked for areas where his input might be welcomed. One of those areas was the film's poster. Without his knowledge, Orion's marketing team had put together the preliminary one-sheet for the movie. Along with its trailer, this would be the first—and perhaps most indelible—impression that potential audiences would get of the film. It had to strike the perfect tone if *Caddyshack* was going to have a strong opening weekend in what was a very busy summer. Orion had spent a lot of money hiring some of the biggest-name poster artists to mock up their ideas. When Ramis and Kenney saw them, they hated every single one. The image that the studio was pushing the hardest was designed to resemble a Norman Rockwell painting, like *The Saturday Evening Post*'s version of *Caddyshack*, with all of the characters from the film lined up in front of Bushwood. "Doug got all fired up," said Ramis. "He'd been up all night and he didn't look good and he was really itching for a fight."

According to Ramis, Kenney stormed into Peters's office, and what had started as a verbal tirade turned physical. "They started wrestling," said Ramis. "No punches were thrown, it was inept wrestling, but finally Jon calmed him down and said, 'Come on, let's go see Mike Medavoy, and we'll talk about it.' So we go to see Medavoy and Doug starts in on him. And Medavoy says, 'You don't want to discuss this; you want to *fight*.' And Doug says, 'Yeah!' And *they* started wrestling." Says Medavoy, "It wasn't a fight I was relishing. I thought the whole thing was too stupid for words."

In the end, Peters suggested that Kenney, Ramis, and Brian Doyle-Murray create their own poster. He gave them the various sketches that Orion had commissioned and some scissors. The three of them then sat on the floor of Rusty Lemorande's office as if they were kids on a rainy-afternoon playdate and pasted them together like a ransom note. Peters then brought it to Medavoy's office and told him this was the poster they'd be using. Kenney had won a small victory, but his contempt for the studio, for Peters, for the gopher, and for allowing himself to ever be put into such a helpless position was reaching its limit.

◆ ◆

In June, Chris Miller flew to Los Angeles to meet with Doug Kenney, Alan Greisman, and Michael Shamberg at Three Wheel Productions about the Club Med comedy he was writing for them with his partner, David Standish. *Club Sandwich* was the first screenplay that Miller had worked on since cowriting *Animal House* with Kenney, and he was excited to catch up with his old friend and see how life as a Tinseltown celebrity was going. Miller and Standish were supposed to meet the producing trio and get their notes for the next round of revisions on the script. But after two weeks, Miller still hadn't heard from Kenney. He was impossible to track down. They finally arranged for a 9 a.m. meeting at the Three Wheel office at Fox on Miller's last day in town.

When Miller showed up, Greisman and Shamberg were there, but Kenney was not. They waited . . . and waited. Finally, Kenney barreled in looking disheveled and acting contrite. He said he had overslept. As they started talking about the script, Kenney seemed distracted. Then, Miller says, "this greasy motherfucker showed up, and he was Doug's coke dealer. It turned out that Doug had been up all night doing coke and that's why he was late. The guy and Doug disappeared into one of the offices and when they came out Doug was a *lot* happier. Then Doug proceeded to lay a rail of coke along his arm from his elbow down to his hand and snorted it in one go. Standish and I, our jaws dropped. I'd never seen anyone do so much coke in a single snort. It was remarkable. But I also thought: Doug, is this you? What's going on? It was almost like Hollywood had destroyed Doug in some way. At the time, someone asked me what Doug was like and I said he was like a broken mirror. All the shards were brilliant, but they made more sense together. He was talking a mile a minute, and sometimes he'd be funny, but he was incoherent. I was shocked."

Rumors about Kenney's unslakable coke habit were starting to filter back to his old *Lampoon* friends in New York. But they brushed it off as Doug being Doug. After all, this was the same guy who just up and left the *Lampoon* to live in a tepee on Martha's Vineyard to write an aborted novel and who left uncashed six-figure checks lying around. It was just another fleeting phase he'd pass through on the way to his next success. Then his old *Lampoon* pal Sean Kelly heard a story that made him suspect that Kenney might be going through something more serious and troubling.

"Someone told me that Doug would spend his late nights driving his Porsche fast on Mulholland Drive with the headlights off. I thought maybe it's a myth that he's spreading about himself or it may be true, but it's not a good a sign. That's a death wish."

Judgment Day

MOST FILM EDITORS WILL TELL YOU that comedies are especially tough to cut. Not just because timing, with jokes, is absolutely critical down to the millisecond, but also because after watching the same gag over and over again—maybe hundreds of times—it's impossible to know what you're looking at anymore. Is it still funny? Was it *ever* funny? Test screenings provide an essential second opinion. A sort of appeals court. No filmmaker likes to subject his or her art to the fickle whims of ordinary folks pulled off the street. But a roomful of strangers with no skin in the game will let you know pretty quickly whether you're sitting on a triumph or a train wreck.

On *Caddyshack*, there were three previews: one on the Warner Bros. lot in Burbank, a second in Phoenix, and a third in San Diego. Assistant editor Rachel Igel remembers watching one of the previews play out from behind the glass partition of the projectionist booth and thinking it went well—certainly better than she had expected after so much chaos and cannabis in the editing room, not to mention that whole last-minute gopher drama. But Rusty Lemorande remembers everyone being a bit deflated: "I think we felt we had a stronger film than the reaction cards indicated," he says.

Harold Ramis and Jon Peters were equally split. The only thing they seemed to agree on was that the Baby Ruth "Doodie!" joke brought the house down. After six months of postproduction, Ramis had survived his first directing experience—barely. Part of him was excited; another part felt beaten down and resigned. "It just wasn't *Animal House*," he admitted. "*Animal House* was very tight. We gave John Landis a very tight script and he shot it almost word for word with very little improv. And *Caddyshack* was the opposite. It was more like, Let's be funny and see what happens today. I wasn't the practiced filmmaker that Landis was. He grew up with a camera making little movies. I never made a little movie. *Caddyshack* was the first thing I ever shot. So it didn't quite hang together. It was my $6 million scholarship to film school."

For his part, the unsinkable Peters recalls, "When I saw the gopher in, I felt like it was going to be a giant hit!" Either way, the film was not reedited in any significant way after those three previews. Certainly nothing compared with the drastic series of face-lifts it had already weathered.

While *Caddyshack* was going through its final sound and effects mixing stages, John Belushi and Dan Aykroyd's *The Blues Brothers* hit theaters, on June 20. In its own way their film had gone through a similarly tortured evolution, plagued by out-of-control budget overruns triggered by director John Landis's overreaching ambition and Belushi's snowballing drug habit. The two films were like a pair of high-speed locomotives on parallel tracks that both derailed before reaching the station. The critics were unkind to *The Blues Brothers*, but it would still end up making $57 million at the box office—just over double its final budget. There was another comedy that summer, though, that would catch everyone by surprise—especially Doug Kenney.

In early July, just a few weeks before *Caddyshack* would open,

Kenney and his best friend from Harvard, Peter Ivers, decided to check out the competition an absurd, gag-a-minute satire of Hollywood disaster movies called *Airplane!* It was the kind of cheeky, sophomoric sendup that the early *Lampoon* might have conceived. When the lights came up at the end of the film, Kenney was probably the only person in the theater who wasn't laughing. He felt like he'd been gutted. Recalls Ivers's girlfriend at the time, Lucy Fisher, "I remember Doug saying after he saw *Airplane!*, 'This is going to be what's popular now and I'm not going to be.' He just didn't think *Caddyshack* was good enough." They had beat Kenney at the game he had once mastered: The Art of Parody. *Airplane!* would end up making $83 million on a budget of less than $4 million. It would be the comedy hit of the summer.

After surviving his wrestling match over the posters for *Caddyshack*, Mike Medavoy had no reason to include Kenney in the movie's still-evolving marketing campaign. Still, he gave him a small budget to go off and write and record some radio and TV spots for the film. Kenney, Ramis, and Doyle Murray asked their old pal from Second City and *The National Lampoon Show*, Joe Flaherty, if he wanted to pitch in. The four met several times for boozy lunches at Casa Cugat, a Latin restaurant on La Cienega owned by ex-bandleader Xavier Cugat. "They were known for their strawberry margaritas," recalls Flaherty. "So we'd have a bunch of those and kick around ideas. You know what I never saw with Doug? The depression. But I saw the drinking side. He was pretty good at that. Anyway, I think the studio did it just to be nice to Doug and Harold. 'Sure, we'll let you have input!' But they didn't use anything we came up with. Our ideas might have been too strange. It's advertising; they'll always go with something safe rather than something good."

Something safe is putting it mildly. Even with an edgier comedy like *Caddyshack*, Orion's marketing team aimed straight for the bland bull's-eye of Middle America with its promotional campaign. One idea that they thought would dazzle the media involved throwing the First Annual Hollywood Fun Drive Invitational Golf Tournament in the less-than-iconic parking lot of the iconic Mann's Chinese Theatre in Hollywood. Set to take place on July 24, one day before *Caddyshack* opened, the event was scheduled to kick off right after Rodney Dangerfield's handprints were immortalized in cement outside the theater.

A so-called "mad cap" golf tournament played with whiffle balls, the Invitational was a Who's Who of Hollywood's C- and D-list "celebrities" competing against one another as they desperately grasped for a few fleeting moments in the public spotlight. The invitees included Buzz Aldrin, Bob Barker, Cathy Lee Crosby, Scatman Crothers, Phyllis Diller, Don Knotts, Jack Klugman, Karl Malden, Valerie Perrine, Telly Savalas, Robert Wagner, and Dionne Warwick. Clearly, the studio had no clue who the audience for their own film was.

◆ ◆

Two weeks before its release, the nation's film critics and entertainment journalists finally got their first chance to see *Caddyshack* during a splashy two-day press junket in New York City. A Friday-night screening at the Loew's State Theatre in Times Square would be followed by a Saturday morning press conference and series of round-robin interviews with the film's stars at Dangerfield's comedy club on the Upper East Side.

The studio's publicity team working the event had been instructed in a strongly worded memo that despite all of the stars in the picture, no *one* star should be favored. "*Caddyshack*'s comedy involves the combined talents of *four* of today's most popular comedians: Chevy Chase, Bill Murray, Rodney Dangerfield, and Ted Knight. We do not want to spotlight any one personality. . . . *Caddyshack* should not be sold (or seem to be sold), for example, as just a Chevy Chase film, or a Rodney Dangerfield comedy. Rather, all four comedians should be treated as a comedic ensemble. . . ." It would be a long weekend of careful ego-massaging.

Back in LA, as the junket weekend approached, *Caddyshack* still wasn't quite finished or "locked." And it wasn't clear whether it would be in time. They were still correcting the film at Technicolor. When that was done, the negative still had to be developed and then a print had to be made. It was going to go right down to the wire. In the end, Rusty Lemorande would end up carrying what they call a "green print" as checked baggage on a plane to New York, just ahead of the press screening (a green print is basically a still-wet copy of the film that's right out of the lab and still has a greenish tint which fades over the course of a few days—days that they did not have). The green print is what the critics would end up seeing, which was, of course, less than ideal.

The reaction to the press screening on the evening of Friday, July 11, was neither through-the-roof good nor tomato-tossing bad. The film just sort of played to a sea of indifference. There were some laughs (how could there not be?), but not nearly as many or as loud as the studio, the cast, and the filmmakers had been hoping for. "It was clear that people were not crazy for the film," recalls Lemorande. Orion was beginning to realize that *Caddyshack* was *not* going to be its summer savior, never mind another *Animal House*–size blockbuster. Maybe if everything went well with the media the next day at Dangerfield's, and the stars really puckered up and schmoozed the roomful of journalists, that might steer reviews in a more positive direction.

At the ungodly hour of nine the following morning, Kenney, who had been up all night getting loaded, trying to numb his own sense of failure and drown out all of the creative concessions he'd made and battles he'd surrendered over the previous six months, stood on the corner of First Avenue and 61st Street. The blinding midsummer sunlight was like a pickax to his throbbing skull. He looked across the street at the entrance to Dangerfield's comedy club and began the forced march to what he believed would be his professional execution.

The film's stars were already there: Bill Murray in his pink shorts and rumpled polo shirt, hiding behind sunglasses; Chevy Chase in his cream-colored linen pants and matching silk shirt and driving cap, getting surlier by the moment; Rodney Dangerfield, as wired as a downed power line in his khaki cabana shirt; and Ted Knight, with his silver-fox hair and natty Brahmin pocket square.

Kenney slipped in and made a beeline for a table in the back, where he began drinking—or, to be more accurate, continued drinking from the previous night. The sunny young Warner Bros. publicist in charge of the event welcomed the media from the club's seedy stage and asked, with all of the mock enthusiasm he could muster, if they'd enjoyed the previous evening's screening? That's when Kenney, who couldn't swallow the rage that constricted his throat anymore, began to heckle both the studio flack and the movie—*his movie*. Kenney let the room know how much he thought *Caddyshack* sucked before telling everyone, including the press he was ostensibly there to woo, to go fuck themselves. He then passed out cold, facedown on the table. "He was dead drunk," recalls Chase, still wincing at the memory. Added the equally shocked Ramis, "Doug was very depressed, and I think his substance abuse was peaking. Someone once said to me, 'You can never get enough of what you don't really need.' And Doug kept going to his substance abuse for comfort, and there's no comfort there. It was a pretty bad scene."

After Kenney was escorted from the club's main room by his concerned and red-faced parents, it was clear to everyone that he hadn't done *Caddyshack* any favors by verbally assaulting the people who held its fate in their hands. It was an act of pure self-destruction. Meanwhile, the film's stars didn't exactly go out of their way to salvage the morning, either. Chase was glib and smarmy with interviewers, Murray basically clammed up and offered clipped, unfunny answers, and Dangerfield seemed uncharacteristically serious and defensive. The three funniest men on the planet temporarily forgot how to be funny. Only Knight, the old pro, seemed willing to make a halfhearted effort. During one particularly awkward group interview with Bobbie Wygant, a veteran television correspondent from the NBC affiliate in Dallas, the four *Caddyshack* stars could barely conceal their hostility and discomfort.

With a Betty Ford meringue hairdo, troweled-on makeup, and a *Good Housekeeping* smile permanently pressed on her face, Wygant looked like a caricature of an aging Southern belle. If she'd actually seen the film, you wouldn't have known it from her questions. Chase, Murray, and Dangerfield were clearly in no mood to suffer fools. They looked like they were caught in a hostage video—curt, defensive, and smug. It was the definition of cringe-inducing. The six-minute interview ended with Chase's cracking a joke about having sex with the entire Osmond family. The final silent seconds seem to last an eternity—a fitting coda to an excruciating morning.

"The next day someone sent me a clipping from the event that said, 'If this is the new Hollywood, let's have the old Hollywood back,' " said Ramis.

◆ ◆

A little more than a week later, on the eve of the film's official release, Orion threw a splashy red-carpet premiere at a Times Square theater followed by an after-party at the Rockefeller Center skating rink. If the studio knew that it was in possession of a DOA flop, it didn't act like it. No expense was spared. True to his threats back in Florida, Jon Peters ended up not inviting Cindy Morgan to the event. The actress, who was now dating her *Caddyshack* costar Scott Colomby, would attend only after Kenney personally reached into his pocket and bought her two first-class air tickets from LA. At the premiere, Morgan remembers, she spotted Peters at the concession stand, walked up to him, and flippantly asked him what he was doing there. She thought that was something Lacey would do. She says he was so surprised to see her, he spilled his popcorn.

Peter Berkrot, the young actor who'd been on the business end of Bill Murray's menacing pitchfork in the Dalai Lama scene, wasn't invited to the premiere either. But he finagled a pair of tickets from the Warner Bros. publicity office. "I remember that night like a Polaroid," he says. "I remember sitting in the theater and being astonished that all of the scenes I'd done ended up in the movie. But then I saw how upset some other people were because so much of their stuff was cut." After the screening was over, an ashen Scott Colomby trudged into the lobby looking stunned. "I was pissed," he says. "I was one of the stars replaced by a gopher."

At the after-party, top-shelf vodka flowed. Everyone seemed to get wasted. Rodney Dangerfield staggered out onto the ice skating rink and proceeded to slip and slide around before falling ass-over-teakettle so many times that some onlookers thought he was doing a routine. He wasn't. Kenney ended up getting so drunk that at one point, he ran through the crowd as his parents were leaving, loudly begging his mother to let him suckle at her teat one last time. "I'm sure he was kidding," says Brian McConnachie. "But I guess he thought that if he could do that, it would make everything good again."

Morgan was one of the many revelers there who recognized that Kenney was in a scary state—even for him. She walked up to Kenney's parents and introduced herself, before saying, "I don't normally stick my nose into other people's business, but please take care of your son."

◆ ◆

The first review of *Caddyshack* appeared in the July 23, 1980, edition of *Variety*. It began: "In its unabashed bid for the mammoth audience which responded to the anti-establishment outrageousness of *National Lampoon's Animal House*, this vaguely likable, too-tame comedy stands to fall short of the mark. . . ." It didn't get better from there. The industry paper's critic mentioned the film's "thinly plotted shenanigans" and "stock characters."

In *The Washington Post*, Gary Arnold wrote that the "latest misbegotten spawn of *National Lampoon's Animal House*" was "shabbily photographed, and raggedly assembled," adding that "*Caddyshack* is hanging evidence that Ramis wasn't prepared for the assignment or clever enough to fake it" before labeling it a "stinky, dismembered heap." *The Hollywood Reporter*'s Arthur Knight began his review: "To attempt a critical evaluation of Orion's new *Caddyshack* is a little like describing the esthetic qualities of an outhouse."

The Boston Globe delivered possibly the harshest verdict of all, saying, "*Caddyshack* represents everything that is wrong with contemporary film comedy. It relies on stock television characters and a stale sitcom style. It is an unoriginal pastiche of other slapstick farces such as *Meatballs*, and it presupposes an audience with the collective intelligence of a lobotomized ape." Only Roger Ebert, in his two-and-a-half-out-of-four-stars review, seemed to get to the nub of what had actually happened during the making of the film: "*Caddyshack* feels more like a movie that was written rather loosely, so that when shooting began there was freedom, too much freedom, for it to wander off in all directions in search of comic inspiration." The Zen-like Ramis seemed to take the negative reviews in stride, but he says that Kenney took them more personally.

Despite the critical dog-piling, the audience polling firm CinemaScore gave *Caddyshack* a B rating on its generous A-to-F scale. Not surprisingly, it scored highest with male moviegoers under the age of twenty-five. During its opening weekend, from July 25 to July 27, 1980, *Caddyshack* made $3.1 million in 656 theaters, finishing in second place behind *The Empire Strikes Back*, which was still a juggernaut in its tenth week.

After Kenney's embarrassing display at the film's junket, one of his concerned friends (no one recalls who) pulled Chevy Chase aside and suggested that he take Kenney somewhere where he could dry out and straighten up. With the second wave of reviews about to hit newsstands in the coming days and weeks, it seemed like a good time to get out of town. Chase understood the sentiment behind the suggestion. Part of him even agreed that it was a good idea to get Kenney the hell out of Hollywood. But he was hardly a role model for sober living at the time. "I was the last guy to ask!" Chase says. "But they knew Doug and I were close. And I could immediately see what they were talking about. The idea was to dry out, but why would that happen? Look at us at that age at that time, and the idea of *me* suddenly being a priest!"

Chase and Kenney headed down to Vic Braden's tennis camp,

about eighty miles south of Los Angeles, for two weeks of exercise, healthy living, and blocking out the white noise of malicious industry chatter and the jabs of sharp-shivved critics. After that, they decided to fly to Maui for a few weeks. Said Ramis, "That's when Doug went to Hawaii with Chevy, and Chevy came back and Doug didn't. . . ."

• •

Doug Kenney and Chevy Chase checked into the Hyatt Regency in Maui for their self-imposed period of relaxation and recovery. But their attempt at abstinence wouldn't last very long. While in Hawaii, Kenney had become obsessed with tracking the box office numbers for *Caddyshack*. At one point, Chase said he couldn't take it anymore and went back to his room across the hall from Kenney's on the fifteenth floor. Chase placed his cowboy boots on his balcony and screamed as if he'd jumped. Kenney rushed across the hall, busted into Chase's room, and looked in horror over the ledge. Chase was hiding behind the curtains and began laughing so hard that he gave himself away.

It didn't take long for Kenney and Chase to give in to temptation on Maui. When Kenney's Three Wheel producing partner, Alan Greisman, joined them after a few days, he quickly noticed that there wasn't much drying out going on. "Drying out? That is the exact *opposite* of what happened," Greisman says "They had a suite for two weeks and they never let the maid in once. I don't think they were clean for a minute." Dutiful assistants back in LA shipped cocaine to Chase and Kenney by FedEx, stuffing envelopes of white powder inside cut-out books and tennis balls. Getting drugs would prove to be a lot easier than giving them up.

Greisman recalls taking a long walk on the beach with Kenney in Hawaii, where he opened up about how sad he was that *Caddyshack* didn't turn out better. "He had this criteria of always being on the cutting edge with the *Lampoon* and then *Animal House*," says Greisman. "I was shocked because it sure seemed like a success to me." After a couple of weeks, Kenney's girlfriend, Kathryn Walker, flew in having just finished shooting a TV movie in Newfoundland. She and Kenney seemed to be in a good place. They talked about their plans for the future. They were putting in a swimming pool at the new house on Outpost Drive and they'd ordered grown-up furniture, planning to live there together as a couple. They both seemed committed to making it work.

In mid-August, Chase had to return to Los Angeles for work. Walker left a few days later so that she could be home when the furniture deliverymen arrived. Greisman would eventually head back to LA as well. But Kenney decided that he wanted to stay on a little longer to do some sightseeing and enjoy some time alone. He called Chase one night and asked him to come back, sounding lonely. He called Brian Doyle-Murray and apologized that *Caddyshack* hadn't turned out to be a bigger hit. He wrote a chatty letter to John Landis about a movie idea he was working on for John Belushi to star in. Even Rachel Igel, *Caddyshack*'s assistant editor, got a postcard in which Kenney joked about the jacket he always wore that she made no secret about coveting. "He had this red jacket like the one James Dean wore in *Rebel Without a Cause*, and I really loved it," she says. "The postcard said, 'Me and the jacket are having a great time!'"

Now alone, Kenney took a ferry from Maui roughly two hundred miles northwest to the island of Kauai. He checked in to the Coco Palms Resort in Wailua on August 26 and rented a Jeep. He intended to go off-roading on the island's back trails and enjoy the views. He had told Walker that he would be flying back to LA in time for Labor Day weekend, which began on August 29. But the 29th came and went. Then the 30th. "I got

a call from Kathryn saying that no one could find Doug," says
Greisman. "So everyone went over to his house to be with
Kathryn. Eventually we called the police."

Kenney had pulled vanishing acts before, but for some reason
it felt different this time, between the drugs and the disappointment of the film. "Peter and I were on Martha's Vineyard, and
we got a call from Kathryn saying that Doug was missing," says
Lucy Fisher. "The longer it went on, the scarier it got."

Soon, all of Kenney's friends were holding vigil at his home.
Then the call came.

• •

The Hanapepe Lookout is an off-the-beaten-track spot high up
in the southernmost hills of Kauai. It has staggering views of the
lush tropical valley below. The quiet there can be almost deaf-
ening. The local police spotted Kenney's rented Jeep abandoned
by the side of the road shortly after receiving the missing per-
sons call from the mainland. They walked slowly along a worn dirt
footpath, through briars and brambles, and past a well-marked
orange sign that reads: "DANGER: Do Not Go Beyond Guard-
rail." For someone like Doug Kenney, that might have been a
warning too tempting to heed. At the rim of the cliff, the police
noticed a pair of shoes and a pair of round wire-rimmed glasses.

Kenney had last been spotted at the Coco Palms on the evening
of August 28. It was now September 1. As the police lowered
themselves forty feet into the ravine, they spotted the twisted,
sunburned body of a man wedged between two large jagged
rocks. His skull had been fractured and his ribs broken. The coroner would later rule Doug Kenney's death an accident, adding
that he most likely died upon impact. He was thirty-three years
old.

Alan Greisman, the last of Kenney's friends to see him alive,
identified the body over the phone. "I asked if they found wire-

rimmed glasses. They said yeah. Then I asked if the right-hand side of the glasses bent out all the way perpendicular to the lens? They said yeah. . . . It was Doug."

In the hazy, chaotic days after Kenney's death, some of his friends thought that he had committed suicide. Others simply thought it was an accident. "Some people say he fell; some people say he jumped. I thought he fell looking for a place to jump," said Ramis. "Anything's possible. There were even people who thought he was murdered by drug dealers, but I kind of doubted that."

Ramis, who had become like family with Kenney over the previous four years closely collaborating on two films together, had the unenviable task of calling Kenney's parents and breaking the news.

◆ ◆

Chevy Chase, Kathryn Walker, Alan Greisman, and Kenney's attorney, Joe Shapiro, flew to Kauai the next day to retrieve the body. They drove out to Hanapepe Lookout to try and fill in the tragic picture of what might have happened to their friend. Greisman remembers looking down and thinking: This is not the kind of place where you jump to kill yourself. In his mind, it was settled. Doug was probably high and slipped. He was clumsy. He liked to step over the line. Still, that didn't make the pain any easier to deal with or the task they were about to embark on any less surreal.

They went back to Kenney's hotel room. There, they found two things that only added to the mysterious nature of Kenney's final days. The first was three words scrawled in soap on the bathroom mirror: I Love You. Was it a suicide note, or just the self-affirmation of a depressed man? Maybe it was even a note he'd left for Chase, who had still been flirting with the idea of coming back to Hawaii. The second was a notebook filled with stray

thoughts. It included some ideas for a movie, a couple of random jokes, and one enigmatically composed sentence: "These are some of the happiest days I've ever ignored."

Like Kenney himself, it was cryptic, clever, and hard to pin down. "I thought it just sounded like he was unable to appreciate the fact that he was with friends in a beautiful place and that he otherwise should be happy," says Greisman. Adds Landis, "That was just Doug, just sort of an Algonquin Round Table kind of witty line. He was full of brilliantly witty remarks. It's like that Dorothy Parker line: If all the girls who went to Vassar were laid end to end, I wouldn't be surprised. That's the kind of smarts Doug had."

After Kenney's friends identified and collected his body, they headed to the airport to return to Los Angeles. Chase insisted on taking an earlier flight because he couldn't stand the thought of being on the same plane as his best friend's coffin. According to Greisman, as they were approaching LAX, Walker, devastated by grief, began to have a severe panic attack. As soon as they landed and Kenney's coffin was loaded into a waiting hearse, they drove her to the emergency room at UCLA. The hearse with Kenney's body inside sat parked in the hospital's short-term garage.

"It was just insane," says Greisman. "You have to remember, we were a generation who avoided catastrophe. We avoided the war in Vietnam; we were upper-middle-class kids who were blessed in one way or another. And Doug's death was the first hint of mortality that any of us had ever experienced. Nobody knew what to do. We were like helpless little kids."

17

Welcome, Kenney Mourners!

THE SIGN HAD APPARENTLY BEEN HENRY BEARD'S IDEA. On the roadside marquee in front of the motel where the attendees of Doug Kenney's funeral were staying, it said: "Welcome, Kenney Mourners!" Beard thought his old *National Lampoon* partner would have appreciated the pitch-black sentiment. Kenney's funeral Mass and burial took place on September 8, 1980, in Newtown, Connecticut, not far from the home that he had purchased for his parents. They had made all of the arrangements. They were burying their second son in just over a decade.

The funeral Mass was held on a rainy Monday morning at St. Rose Church, which was filled with four hundred friends from Harvard, the *National Lampoon*, and Hollywood. Joni Mitchell was there. Michael O'Donoghue had arrived in a pink Chevy convertible. Bill Murray cut short a vacation in Bali and showed up at the motel in a wet suit. They all came to pay their respects, in their own way, to the first of their generation to go. Only Kenney, the charmer, the cutup, the chameleon, could have brought these three vastly different worlds together. Murray was one of the only people in the church who knew the Catholic catechism by heart. His brother Brian, along with Harold Ramis and Chevy Chase, was among the pallbearers. People who had not seen one

another—and in some cases had refused to speak to one another—in years, sat together in quiet disbelief. "He was like our
young fallen prince," says Brian McConnachie, who still grows
quiet recalling that afternoon.

The funeral procession slowly snaked through the quiet New
England town's streets to Village Cemetery. It pulled to a stop
at the base of a hill that overlooked a duck pond below. Chevy
Chase delivered a eulogy, barely intelligible through his tears and
quavering voice. One of Kenney's closest friends from Harvard,
playwright Tim Mayer, followed with equally subdued remarks.
"The best thing that happened was Michael O'Donoghue
saying that the biggest tragedy of this was that Doug wasn't
holding hands with Chevy at the time," says *Lampoon* staffer
Sean Kelly.

As the coffin was about to be lowered into the ground, Peter
Ivers, Kenney's best friend from college, pulled out his harmon-
ica and played a plaintive blues version of "Beautiful Dreamer,"
then collapsed to his knees and howled and sobbed as the casket
was lowered into the ground.

"Everybody was devastated," says Michael O'Keefe. "Doug
was the casualty of the high-risk lifestyle and a wake-up call for
everybody. It was like, 'Okay, do you still want to go to the party?
Because this is what can happen.'"

Harold Ramis said that for years after Kenney's death, his
friend would appear to him in his dreams. Ramis would always
ask him: "Doug, where have you been?" Kenney would just flash
him a knowing look and not respond. Alan Greisman says that
ever since Kenney died, he's had a nagging, unshakable feeling
that he didn't really die—that he went away because he couldn't
stand the craziness of Hollywood. "I've had that same dream for
thirty-six years," he says.

At the reception, some of Kenney's friends started a halfhearted, *Animal House*–style food fight in his honor. But nothing seemed funny. Everything felt forced and strained. It was one thing to joke about death as Kenney had done so many times at the *Lampoon*, but in the end, death always got the last laugh. Two years later, John Belushi would be gone, too. On March 5, 1982, Belushi's naked, dead body would be discovered in a room at the Chateau Marmont in Los Angeles—the result of an overdose of cocaine and heroin after a night of partying with Robin Williams, Robert De Niro, and a drug dealer and former consort of the Rolling Stones named Cathy Smith.

Kenney wouldn't live long enough to see that *Caddyshack* wasn't the disaster he'd feared, not even close. It would go on to make $39.8 million at the box office (roughly $124 million today). But its legacy goes far beyond mere numbers. Kenney never got to hear the film's lines—*his lines*—become part of the pop culture vernacular quoted by everyone from professional golfers to US presidents. He never got to see how it helped to revolutionize American comedy for more than one generation of stand-ups and satirists, bringing the underground into the daylight of the mainstream. He never got to see his friends continue to thrive and succeed on screen and off, becoming Hollywood's next era of comedy superstars. He never got to see the long shadow that his "failure" cast, or the rabid devotion it inspired—and continues to inspire—nearly four decades later. He never got to see the end of his Cinderella story.

"Years after Doug died, my wife took me to a medium," says Chase. "Now, I don't believe in that stuff at all. But I said, 'I've never known how my best friend died.' I never gave her more than that. And her feet immediately started going up, sort of raising off the floor where she was sitting. And she said, '*Slipped . . . slipped.*' Then she said, 'He's standing right there. . . . He says it was the stupidest way he could have ever died. . . . And he left you a present.' I said, 'What do you mean "He left me a present"?' And she said, 'His glasses.' Well, Doug's penny loafers and glasses were left at the top of the cliff in Hawaii. I mean, *whoa!* That conversation absolutely convinced me that Doug's death was an accident."

Chase pauses for a moment in retelling the story and exhales long and deep. For a few silent seconds, he seems to be searching for some sort of silver lining, but fails to find one. "You know, it's really a shame. If Doug were alive today, he would've seen that *Caddyshack* became a big deal. I miss him for a lot of other reasons, but that would have been really nice. . . ."

Epilogue

CHEVY CHASE returned to the *Lampoon* fold as the clueless suburban patriarch Clark Griswold in *National Lampoon's Vacation* (1983) and its three sequels. In the mid-'80s he checked in to the Betty Ford Clinic to kick an addiction to painkillers that he claimed was the result of years of pratfalls and punishing physical comedy. For the remainder of the '80s—in such films as *Fletch* (1985) and *Three Amigos* (1986)—he remained one of the biggest movie stars in Hollywood before a career downturn in the '90s. From 2009 to 2013, he was a regular cast member on the NBC sitcom *Community*.

RODNEY DANGERFIELD went on to have an unlikely second act on the big screen in the wake of *Caddyshack* with such hit comedies as *Easy Money* (1983) and *Back to School* (1986), the latter of which was cowritten by Harold Ramis. His self-named New York City comedy club continued to thrive (even after the disastrous *Caddyshack* press junket) and remained a vital launching pad for several generations of young stand-ups, including Jim Carrey. Dangerfield died in 2004 from complications following heart surgery at age eighty-three.

BRIAN DOYLE-MURRAY continued as a writer and performer on *Saturday Night Live* until 1982. He and his distinctively gruff voice have appeared in dozens of television shows and movies, including *Scrooged* (1988), *Groundhog Day* (1993), and the long-running ABC series *The Middle*. Doyle-Murray and his five brothers run an annual *Caddyshack* charity golf tournament and, in 2001, opened a *Caddyshack*-themed restaurant in St. Augustine, Florida.

SARAH HOLCOMB walked away from the industry shortly after *Caddyshack*. Having appeared in four films by the time she was twenty-two, she stopped acting and retreated from the public eye altogether.

DOUG KENNEY died on the island of Kauai on August 29, 1980. His death was officially ruled an accident. He was thirty-three. Kenney was credited as an executive producer on the 1981 Chevy Chase comedy *Modern Problems*, which was in development at his Twentieth Century Fox–based production company, Three Wheel Productions, when he passed away. Director Harold Ramis and writer Chris Miller—Kenney's writing partners on *National Lampoon's Animal House*—paid tribute to Kenney in their 1996 film *Multiplicity*, naming Michael Keaton's lead character "Doug Kinney."

TED KNIGHT lived just down the road from Chevy Chase in Pacific Palisades for years after the making of *Caddyshack*. The Emmy-winning *Mary Tyler Moore Show* star returned to television for the hit series *Too Close for Comfort*, which ran on ABC, then in first-run syndication from 1980 until 1987. Knight died from cancer in 1986. He was sixty-two.

MIKE MEDAVOY continued to be a successful Hollywood executive after leaving Orion in 1990, first as chairman at TriStar Pictures (where he made *Philadelphia, Terminator 2: Judgment Day,* and *Sleepless in Seattle*), then as chairman and CEO at Phoenix Pictures (*The People vs. Larry Flint, Zodiac,* and *Shutter Island*).

CINDY MORGAN followed up her debut as Lacey Underall by starring in the cult science-fiction movie *TRON* (1982). She continues to act and is working on a book about her experiences during the making of *Caddyshack.*

BILL MURRAY went on to star in some of the most iconic movies of the past forty years, including *Ghostbusters* (1984), *Groundhog Day* (1993), and *Rushmore* (1998). He received a Best Actor Oscar nomination for his dry, debauched performance in *Lost in Translation* (2003). He was also the voice of *Garfield* (2004). When he's not acting—or turning up at random kickball games and crashing weddings—he can be found on the links, pursuing his passion on the pro-am circuit.

MICHAEL O'KEEFE has remained an in-demand actor, appearing in such films as *Michael Clayton* (2007) and television shows as *Homeland* (for which he received a Screen Actors Guild Award nomination). O'Keefe married—and divorced—singer Bonnie Raitt and became a Zen priest in the 1990s.

JON PETERS went on to produce such hit movies as *Flashdance* (1983), *Rain Man* (1988), and *Batman* (1989). For a brief period, he also ran Sony Pictures alongside Peter Guber. Their profligate partnership was chronicled in the 1996 book, *Hit and Run: How Jon Peters and Peter Guber Took Sony for a Ride in Hollywood.* After parting ways with the studio, Peters produced several successful films including *Ali* (2001) and *Superman Returns* (2006).

HAROLD RAMIS acted in front of the camera for such generation-defining comedies as *Stripes* (1981), *Ghostbusters* (1984), and *Knocked Up* (2007), and called the shots behind it as the director of *National Lampoon's Vacation* (1983), *Groundhog Day* (1993), and *Analyze This* (1999). His "$6 million scholarship to film school" on *Caddyshack* paid off. Ramis died in 2014 from complications of autoimmune inflammatory vasculitis, a rare disease that involves the swelling of blood vessels. He was sixty-nine.

THE GOPHER was briefly the toast of Hollywood after the release of *Caddyshack*. But his career flamed out after 1988's ill-fated and ill-advised sequel, *Caddyshack II*. In the decades since his film debut, however, he has achieved a measure of wealth and fame licensing his likeness for golf head covers, T-shirts, and book jackets. He is currently retired and resides in Davie, Florida.

Acknowledgments

THE RED LIGHT ON THE PHONE in my office rang at 9:30 p.m. On most nights, I would have been long gone by then. On most nights, I also wouldn't have bothered picking it up. But the deadline on my first feature for *Sports Illustrated*, a magazine that I had subscribed to and devoured since I was eight years old, was closing in fast. A few months earlier I had been assigned to write a six-page oral history on the making of *Caddyshack* by then-editor Terry McDonell. Now I found myself with two short days until the agreed-upon deadline with one glaring piece of the puzzle missing. I had spent the previous weeks in a nearly constant state of anxiety thinking that I was about to screw up an opportunity that I'd dreamed of for decades. And the cause of that anxiety was Bill Murray. I had not yet been able to secure an interview with the film's biggest and most elusive star.

Then the phone rang. The caller ID flashed a number with what I recognized to be a South Carolina prefix. I quickly picked up the receiver before the man on the other end of the line had a chance to change his mind. The voice that greeted me was instantly familiar from a lifetime of watching movies. "Is this Chris?" Yes. "This is Bill Murray. I'm sorry it's taken so long to get back to you . . . so, what do you want to know?" Underneath that voice, I distinctly heard the sound of tinkling ice cubes in what I imagined was a perspiring highball glass.

Let me backtrack a bit. As you may or may not know, getting in touch with Bill Murray is a bit like tracking down Sasquatch. Since the mid '80s, the actor has eschewed all the normal Hollywood publicity machinery. He has no agent. No P.R. rep on retainer. Just an attorney, who will kindly take your interview request while apologizing that it's highly unlikely to ever lead to anything. Half the time, Murray's legal representative doesn't even know what time zone his client is in. The only way to contact Murray if you're a journalist (or a director itching to cast him in your movie) is to call a highly guarded 1-800 number that has no outgoing message, just a beep followed by . . . silence. Leaving a message is like casting a prayer into the void. Murray may respond to your entreaties, but more likely he will not. And should he choose to indulge you, it could take months—or longer. After obtaining the 1-800 number from a friend and acquaintance of the star's, I left more than a dozen messages for Murray, taking an array of varied tacks and shameless displays of flattery. All of them somewhat desperate and embarrassing. I am not proud about the rambling, incoherent monologue I left about my (sincere) passion for his sole directing effort, *Quick Change*, but there it is.

It turned out that Murray was everything I could have hoped for over the course of our hour-long phone call. He answered every question that I tossed his way with good humor and was surprisingly thoughtful, shockingly introspective, and, of course, hilarious. It turns out that *Caddyshack*, one of his earliest films, held a special place for him. Not merely because he'd been a caddie himself as a kid. But also because he had been surrounded by a trio of dear friends on the film that he had looked up to from an early age: Harold Ramis, Doug Kenney, and his older brother Brian Doyle-Murray—the three co-writers of *Caddyshack*. When I eventually hung up the phone, I immediately emailed McDonell, who seemed as genuinely stunned as I was. I had been granted a last-minute, Hail Mary stay of execution.

During the course of reporting that initial magazine story, I was lucky to be on the receiving end of kindnesses, both large and small, from two other people who gave me more time than I could have ever expected: Chevy Chase and Harold Ramis. Chase was candid and sentimental in his recollections of his pal Doug Kenney and a film he'd made decades earlier and the important role it played in his then-fledgling screen career. Ramis, who would pass away in 2014, was a gift, not only in his reflections on the film that would mark his baptism into the world of directing, but also the crazy years leading up to it. During my twenty-five years as a writer at *Entertainment Weekly* magazine, I had the good fortune to interview Ramis several times. Each time, he was unfailingly polite and also proved to be a master storyteller. He was truly one of the few "nice guys" in an industry with too few of them. He is and will continue to be missed.

Writing a book about the making of a Hollywood film, especially one as distant in the rearview mirror as *Caddyshack*, presents a tricky balancing act of separating fact from the foggier realms of fiction. No one goes out of his or her way to remember the past inaccurately, but accounts of certain events and time lines differ, often in an attempt to flatter the teller. It was my job to sort through those varying accounts and determine which side the truth laid on. Not everyone involved with the making of *Caddyshack* will agree on certain points, but I feel confident that I have cast the net wide enough to come down on the side of the facts.

I would like to offer my sincere thanks to the rest of the people who agreed to be interviewed (on and off the record) for this book. In many cases, they shared not only their memories, but also telephone numbers and personal photographs. I am particularly indebted to a group of friends, angels, and colleagues without whose help I could not have completed this book. I would like to single out Elvis Mitchell, who put in a kind word on my behalf with Bill Murray. Elvis is a mysterious guy, and also as well-connected as anyone I've ever met in this business. He possesses that all-too-rare trait of being gracious when it comes to using those connections in the service of others. I would like to thank—in addition to McDonell—Adam Duerson and Chris Stone at *Sports Illustrated*, who not only helped to champion my original *Caddyshack* story but also continued to take a chance on me on several occasions since. At *Entertainment Weekly*, my employer for nearly a quarter of a century, I would like to express my appreciation to managing editor Henry Goldblatt for his remarkable support at every turn, and editors Sean Smith, Jeff Giles, and Jeff Labrecque (my brother-in-arms when it comes to '80s comedies). Plus, photo editor extraordinaire Michele Romero, who in addition to being a true friend, guided me through the maddening ins and outs of tracking down and gaining the rights to many of the photographs that appear in this book.

No author researches, writes, and publishes a book by him- or herself. I am grateful for the assistance of the staff at the Margaret Herrick Library of the Academy of Motion Picture Arts and Sciences in Los Angeles and Second City archivist Chris Pagnozzi in Chicago. I would also like to offer a tip of the cap to John Ptak, who always made himself available to help recall the hazier events of a very hazy period in time. I am also deeply indebted to Kerry Brock and John Seigenthaler, who gave me a private oasis in the woods of Connecticut, which proved invaluable in completing this project.

I offer a deep bow to my agent Farley Chase, whose faith, enthusiasm, and perspective helped me recognize that this was a project worth pursuing. He is the best kind of advocate—supportive, patient, and always available without ever tapping his watch wondering where the manuscript is. At my publisher, Flatiron Books, I would like to express my deepest gratitude to Colin Dickerman, James Melia, and Bob Miller—a publishing triumvirate as passionate about books as anyone I've ever met. I'd also like to single out publicist Steven Boriack, production editor David Lott, and copy editor Bob Ickes, who saved me on too many occasions to count.

I would also like to thank my parents, who never regarded a day spent inside watching movies as a wasted day, and my brother Keith, who was always watching them beside me (and I believe still is). Most of all, I would like to thank my exceedingly patient and loving wife, Jennifer, who sustains me every day, and our two sons, Charlie and Rooney, who I look forward to watching *Caddyshack* with one day. This book would be unimaginable without all of their unconditional love, generosity, encouragement, support, and inspiration.

Notes

Prologue

3   But the stingy smattering of laughs . . . : Ramis, Harold. Interview by Chris Nashawaty. By telephone. New York, NY. May 20, 2010.

4   For his encore . . . : Boxofficemojo.com.

6   Kenney's voice rose . . . : Josh Karp, *A Futile and Stupid Gesture* (Chicago: Chicago Review Press, 2006), 359.

6   Then, just to prove . . . : Kate Meyers, "King of Comedy," *Golf Digest*, May 2004. Accessed online.

6   He was sabotaging . . . : Chase, Chevy. Interview by Chris Nashawaty. By telephone. New York, NY. May 27, 2010.

7   When Kenney asked . . . : Ramis, Harold. Interview by Chris Nashawaty. By telephone. New York, NY. May 20, 2010.

7   By the end . . . : Boxofficemojo.com.

7   David Ansen in . . . : David Ansen, *Newsweek*, August 11, 1980. Accessed online.

7   And in *New York* . . . : David Denby, "In the Rough," *New York*, August 11, 1980. Accessed online.

1. The Algonquin Round Table

13   As they predicted . . . : Beard, Henry. Interview by Chris Nashawaty. By telephone. New York, NY. November 27, 2016.

13   It sold out . . . : Craig Lambert, "Comic Sutra," *Harvard Magazine*, July–August 1992, 26.

13   It opened our . . . : Beard, Henry. Interview by Chris Nashawaty. By telephone. New York, NY. November 27, 2016.

14 In truth, his . . . : Karp, *A Futile and Stupid Gesture*, 6.

16 The *Life* parody . . . : Beard, Henry. Interview by Chris Nashawaty. By telephone. New York, NY. November 27, 2016.

16 Wanting to keep . . . : Simmons, Matty. Interview by Chris Nashawaty. By telephone. New York, NY. August 12, 2016.

17 And Doug . . . : Simmons, Matty. Interview by Chris Nashawaty. By telephone. New York, NY. August 12, 2016.

17 Beard admits that . . . : Beard, Henry. Interview by Chris Nashawaty. By telephone. New York, NY. November 27, 2016.

18 "He went through . . . : Beard, Henry. Interview by Chris Nashawaty. By telephone. New York, NY. November 27, 2016.

19 *Bored of the Rings* . . . : Ellin Stein, *That's Not Funny, That's Sick* (New York: W. W. Norton, 2013), 31–36.

19 To their surprise . . . : Beard, Henry. Interview by Chris Nashawaty. By telephone. New York, NY. November 27, 2016.

20 Thirty-two editions . . . : Beard, Henry. Interview by Chris Nashawaty. By telephone. New York, NY. November 27, 2016.

20 Since they planned . . . : Simmons, Matty. Interview by Chris Nashawaty. By telephone. New York, NY. August 12, 2016.

21 Simmons, desperate for . . . : Simmons, Matty. Interview by Chris Nashawaty. By telephone. New York, NY. August 12, 2016.

21 "Rob Hoffman was . . . : Simmons, Matty. Interview by Chris Nashawaty. By telephone. New York, NY. August 12, 2016.

22 They began casting . . . : Beard, Henry. Interview by Chris Nashawaty. By telephone. New York, NY. November 27, 2016.

22 He had made . . . : Chip Kidd, "Doonesbury Turns 40," *Rolling Stone*, October 27, 2010. Accessed online.

22 But O'Donoghue thought . . . : Dennis Perrin, *Mr. Mike: The Life and Work of Michael O'Donoghue* (New York: Avon Books, 1998), 172.

24 I think he . . . : Kelly, Sean. Interview by Chris Nashawaty. By telephone. New York, NY. August 25, 2016.

24 The *Newsweek* writer . . . : "Postgraduate Humor," *Newsweek*, March 23, 1970, 94.

24 It sold less . . . : Simmons, Matty. Interview by Chris Nashawaty. By telephone. New York, NY. August 12, 2016.

25 The May edition . . . : Samuel Z. Goldhaber, "From the Newsland Poons," *The Harvard Crimson*, April 7, 1970. Accessed online.

26 It was . . . : Beard, Henry. Interview by Chris Nashawaty. By telephone. New York, NY. November 27, 2016.

26 His best man . . . : Josh Frank with Charlie Buckholtz, *In Heaven Everything Is Fine: The Unsolved Life of Peter Ivers and the Lost History of New Wave Theatre* (New York: Soft Skull Press, 2010), xvi.

26 I remember feeling . . . : Fisher, Lucy. Interview by Chris Nashawaty. By telephone. New York, NY. August 29, 2016.

26 One thing leads . . . : Beard, Henry. Interview by Chris Nashawaty. By telephone. New York, NY. September 13, 2016.

27 The Walt Disney Company . . . : Karp, *A Futile and Stupid Gesture* (Chicago: Chicago Review Press, 2006), 79.

28 It was incredible . . . : Beard, Henry. Interview by Chris Nashawaty. By telephone. New York, NY. September 13, 2016.

28 It wasn't like . . . : Miller, Chris. Interview by Chris Nashawaty. By telephone. New York, NY. August 31, 2016.

28 It didn't help . . . : Kelly, Sean. Interview by Chris Nashawaty. By telephone. New York, NY. August 25, 2016.

2. If You Don't Buy This Magazine . . .

31 But there was . . . : Beard, Henry. Interview by Chris Nashawaty. By telephone. New York, NY. September 13, 2016.

32 When they finally . . . : Fisher, Lucy. Interview by Chris Nashawaty. By telephone. New York, NY. August 29, 2016.

32 They had breakfast . . . : Fisher, Lucy. Interview by Chris Nashawaty. By telephone. New York, NY. August 29, 2016.

32 "In our minds . . . : Fisher, Lucy. Interview by Chris Nashawaty. By telephone. New York, NY. August 29, 2016.

32 It consisted of . . . : Simmons, Matty. Interview by Chris Nashawaty. By telephone. New York, NY. August 12, 2016.

33 "They felt Doug . . . : Simmons, Matty. Interview by Chris Nashawaty. By telephone. New York, NY. August 12, 2016.

33 But there was . . . : Beard, Henry. Interview by Chris Nashawaty. By telephone. New York, NY. September 13, 2016.

33 Then write a book . . . : "Doug Kenney Speaking at UCLA 3/6/1972," Youtube, accessed April 4, 2017. https://www.youtube.com/watch?v=xntFghVSVBo

34 Now, with circulation . . . : Beard, Henry. Interview by Chris Nashawaty. By telephone. New York, NY. September 13, 2016.

35 Still, with the . . . : Mopsy Strange Kennedy, "Juvenile, puerile, sopho-moric, jejune, nutty—and funny," *The New York Times*, December 10, 1972. Accessed online.

37 Chevy grew up . . . : Rena Fruchter, *I'm Chevy Chase . . . And You're Not* (London: Virgin Books, 2007), 10–14.

38 He could apologize . . . : Hendra, Tony. Interview by Chris Nashawaty. By telephone. New York, NY. March 23, 2017.

39 And we did . . . : Flaherty, Joe. Interview by Chris Nashawaty. By telephone. New York, NY. August 18, 2016.

39 "But you forgave . . . : Brett Martin, "Harold Ramis Gets the Last Laugh," *GQ*, May 2009. Accessed online.

40 Here was the generation . . . : Hendra, Tony. Interview by Chris Nashawaty. By telephone. New York, NY. March 23, 2017.

40 But, he went on . . . : Mel Gussow, "Lemmings Fails Early, Recovers Later," *The New York Times*, January 26, 1973. Accessed online.

41 I felt like . . . : Tony Schwartz, "College Humor Comes Back," *Newsweek*, October 23, 1978, 97.

41 Especially when the . . . : Simmons, Matty. Interview by Chris Nashawaty. By telephone. New York, NY. August 12, 2016.

42 He would smoke . . . : Kelly, Sean. Interview by Chris Nashawaty. By telephone. New York, NY. August 25, 2016.

42 "It sucks . . . : Beard, Henry. Interview by Chris Nashawaty. By telephone. New York, NY. September 13, 2016.

44 By weight of . . . : Thomas Carney, "They Only Laughed When It Hurt," *New Times*, August 21, 1978. Accessed online.

44 It would go on . . . : Charles Nicol, "Ich bin ein Kefauver Senior," *Harper's Magazine*, April 1975. Accessed online.

45 The idea was . . . : Ramis, Harold. Interview by Chris Nashawaty. By telephone. New York, NY. September, 1998.

46 Second City was . . . : Ramis, Harold. Interview by Chris Nashawaty. By telephone. New York, NY. September, 1998.

46 Like several . . . : Murray, Bill. Interview by Chris Nashawaty. By telephone. New York, NY. June 7, 2010.

47 He could do it . . . : Ramis, Harold. Interview by Chris Nashawaty. By telephone. New York, NY. May 20, 2010.

47 That's how . . . : Kelly, Sean. Interview by Chris Nashawaty. By telephone. New York, NY. August 25, 2016.

3. Live from New York

49   And at Second City . . . : Murray, Bill. Interview by Chris Nashawaty. By telephone. New York, NY. June 7, 2010.

49   That's where Sean . . . : Kelly, Sean. Interview by Chris Nashawaty. By telephone. New York, NY. August 25, 2016.

50   It was an . . . : Murray, Bill. Interview by Chris Nashawaty. By telephone. New York, NY. June 7, 2010.

50   Bill had just . . . : Ramis, Harold. Interview by Chris Nashawaty. By telephone. New York, NY. May 20, 2010.

51   He was in . . . : Murray, Bill. Interview by Chris Nashawaty. By telephone. New York, NY. June 7, 2010.

51   I did do . . . : David Felton, "Bill Murray: Maniac For All Seasons," *Rolling Stone*, April 20, 1978, 29.

51   The bells were . . . : Robert Schnakenberg, *The Big Bad Book of Bill Murray* (Philadelphia: Quirk Books, 2015), 218.

52   What they could . . . : Kelly, Sean. Interview by Chris Nashawaty. By telephone. New York, NY. August 25, 2016.

52   He hired him . . . : Simmons, Matty. Interview by Chris Nashawaty. By telephone. New York, NY. August 12, 2016.

53   That kind of . . . : Jeff Labrecque, "Bill Murray: The Curious Case of Hollywood's White Whale," *Entertainment Weekly*, July 2, 2010, 48.

53   At the *Lampoon* . . . : Murray, Bill. Interview by Chris Nashawaty. By telephone. New York, NY. June 7, 2010.

54   We were taking . . . : Flaherty, Joe. Interview by Chris Nashawaty. By telephone. New York, NY. August 18, 2016.

54   It spoke to . . . : Reitman, Ivan. Interview by Chris Nashawaty. By telephone. New York, NY. September 14, 2016.

55   "But he was . . . : Reitman, Ivan. Interview by Chris Nashawaty. By telephone. New York, NY. September 14, 2016.

56   So Murray jumped . . . : Karp, *A Futile and Stupid Gesture*, 244.

56   In *The New York Times* . . . : Mel Gussow, "Stage: A New Lampoon," *The New York Times*, March 3, 1975. Accessed online.

56   "That somehow our . . . : Ramis, Harold. Interview by Chris Nashawaty. By telephone. New York, NY. May 20, 2010.

57   Thanks to a . . . : Simmons, Matty. Interview by Chris Nashawaty. By telephone. New York, NY. August 12, 2016.

57   I thought about . . . : Beard, Henry. Interview by Chris Nashawaty. By telephone. New York, NY. September 13, 2016.

57　According to Simmons . . . : Simmons, Matty. Interview by Chris Nashawaty. By telephone. New York, NY. August 12, 2016.

58　Said Kenney later . . . : Carney, "They Only Laughed When It Hurt." Accessed online.

58　"Matty would walk . . . : Kelly, Sean. Interview by Chris Nashawaty. By telephone. New York, NY. August 25, 2016.

58　We had to . . . : Kelly, Sean. Interview by Chris Nashawaty. By telephone. New York, NY. August 25, 2016.

59　As they sat . . . : Hendra, Tony. Interview by Chris Nashawaty. By telephone. New York, NY. March 23, 2017.

60　Kenney's reaction . . . : Robert Sam Anson, "The Life and Death of a Comic Genius," *Esquire*, October 1981. Accessed online.

61　But Simmons . . . : Simmons, Matty. Interview by Chris Nashawaty. By telephone. New York, NY. August 12, 2016.

61　In 1968, Michaels . . . : Kliph Nesteroff, *The Comedians* (New York: Grove Press, 2015), 268–9.

62　Michaels was given . . . : Tom Shales and James Andrew Miller, *Live from New York*, (New York: Little, Brown, 2002), 87.

63　Michaels hired Chase . . . : Doug Hill and Jeff Weingrad, *Saturday Night* (New York: Vintage, 1987), 55.

63　The only reason . . . : Charles M. Young, "From Samurai Saturday Night Live to Matinee Idol," *Rolling Stone*, August 10, 1978. Accessed online.

64　So he . . . : Flaherty, Joe. Interview by Chris Nashawaty. By telephone. New York, NY. August 18, 2016.

64　"We wanted to . . . : Shales and Miller, *Live From New York*, 69.

65　But they were . . . : Timothy Crouse, "Bill Murray: The Rolling Stone Interview," *Rolling Stone*, August 16, 1984. Accessed online.

67　For however long . . . : John J. O'Connor, "TV View," *The New York Times*, November 30, 1975. Accessed online.

67　"*SNL* spoke to . . . : Reitman, Ivan. Interview by Chris Nashawaty. By telephone. New York, NY. September 14, 2016.

67　Not everyone was . . . : Landis, John. Interview by Chris Nashawaty. By telephone. New York, NY. August 9, 2016.

69　They throw me . . . : Hill and Weingrad, *Saturday Night*, 218.

69　The article was . . . : Jeff Greenfield, "He's Chevy Chase and You're Not, and He's TV's Hot New Comedy Star," *New York*, December 22, 1975. Accessed online.

70　And he said . . . : Fruchter, *I'm Chevy Chase . . . And You're Not*, 41.

70   Industry sources report . . . : Greenfield, "He's Chevy Chase and You're Not, and He's TV's Hot New Comedy Star." Accessed online.

70   The others are . . . : Greenfield, "He's Chevy Chase and You're Not, and He's TV's Hot New Comedy Star." Accessed online.

71   For its part . . . : Fruchter, *I'm Chevy Chase . . . And You're Not*, 50.

71   I think he'd . . . : Shales and Miller, *Live From New York*, 92.

71   So she gave . . . : Chase, Chevy. Interview by Chris Nashawaty. By telephone. New York, NY. May 27, 2010.

72   It was . . . : Chase, Chevy. Interview by Chris Nashawaty. By telephone. New York, NY. May 27, 2010.

72   "Lorne used to say . . . : Shales and Miller, *Live From New York*, 81.

73   "I knew that . . . : Simmons, Matty. Interview by Chris Nashawaty. By telephone. New York, NY. August 12, 2016.

4. Knowledge Is Good

75   As part of . . . : Reitman, Ivan. Interview by Chris Nashawaty. By telephone. New York, NY. September 14, 2016.

75   He paid Ramis . . . : Ramis, Harold. Interview by Chris Nashawaty. By telephone. New York, NY. September 1998.

75   So we tried . . . : Reitman, Ivan. Interview by Chris Nashawaty. By telephone. New York, NY. September 14, 2016.

76   He was just . . . : Ramis, Harold. Interview by Chris Nashawaty. By telephone. New York, NY. May 20, 2010.

76   They called it . . . : Ramis, Harold. Interview by Chris Nashawaty. By telephone. New York, NY. September 1998.

76   So I said . . . : Simmons, Matty. Interview by Chris Nashawaty. By telephone. New York, NY. August 12, 2016.

77   They offered to . . . : Miller, Chris. Interview by Chris Nashawaty. By telephone. New York, NY. August 31, 2016.

77   And there was . . . : Miller, Chris. Interview by Chris Nashawaty. By telephone. New York, NY. August 31, 2016.

78   And, in our . . . : Ramis, Harold. Interview by Chris Nashawaty. By telephone. New York, NY. September 1998.

78   "It was funny . . . : Simmons, Matty. Interview by Chris Nashawaty. By telephone. New York, NY. August 12, 2016.

78   Whenever Belushi would . . . : Miller, Chris. Interview by Chris Nashawaty. By telephone. New York, NY. August 31, 2016.

79   "Even when you . . . : Reitman, Ivan. Interview by Chris Nashawaty. By telephone. New York, NY. September 14, 2016.

79   "He really thought . . . : Simmons, Matty. Interview by Chris Nashawaty. By telephone. New York, NY. August 12, 2016.

79   But Mount and Daniel . . . : Simmons, Matty. Interview by Chris Nashawaty. By telephone. New York, NY. August 12, 2016.

80   Ramis, Kenney, and Miller . . . : Ramis, Harold. Interview by Chris Nashawaty. By telephone. New York, NY. September 1998.

80   "Chris said . . . : Mount, Thom. Interview by Chris Nashawaty. By telephone. New York, NY. August 24, 2016.

80   "And I remember . . . : Ramis, Harold. Interview by Chris Nashawaty. By telephone. New York, NY. September 1998.

81   They had four . . . : Flaherty, Joe. Interview by Chris Nashawaty. By telephone. New York, NY. August 18, 2016.

82   "We thought . . . : Sheldon Patinkin, *The Second City: Backstage at the World's Greatest Comedy Theater* (Naperville, IL: Sourcebooks, 2000), 119.

82   He kept saying . . . : Reitman, Ivan. Interview by Chris Nashawaty. By telephone. New York, NY. September 14, 2016.

82   Of course . . . : Reitman, Ivan. Interview by Chris Nashawaty. By telephone. New York, NY. September 14, 2016.

82   Back in LA . . . : Daniel, Sean. Interview by Chris Nashawaty. By telephone. New York, NY. September 8, 2016.

83   At twenty-one . . . : Landis, John. Interview by Chris Nashawaty. By telephone. New York, NY. August 9, 2016.

83   It was . . . : Daniel, Sean. Interview by Chris Nashawaty. By telephone. New York, NY. September 8, 2016.

83   "But it was . . . : Landis, John. Interview by Chris Nashawaty. By telephone. New York, NY. August 9, 2016.

84   "The fact that . . . : Landis, John. Interview by Chris Nashawaty. By telephone. New York, NY. August 9, 2016.

84   "They didn't want . . . : Miller, Chris. Interview by Chris Nashawaty. By telephone. New York, NY. August 31, 2016.

84   But he did . . . : Ramis, Harold. Interview by Chris Nashawaty. By telephone. New York, NY. September 1998.

85   And I'm working . . . : Landis, John. Interview by Chris Nashawaty. By telephone. New York, NY. August 9, 2016.

85   I hadn't lived . . . : Chase, Chevy. Interview by Chris Nashawaty. By telephone. New York, NY. May 27, 2010.

86 Five minutes later . . . : Landis, John. Interview by Chris Nashawaty. By telephone. New York, NY. August 9, 2016.

86 In the end . . . : Schwartz, "College Humor Comes Back," 91.

87 So now comes . . . : Landis, John. Interview by Chris Nashawaty. By telephone. New York, NY. August 9, 2016.

87 But since this . . . : Landis, John. Interview by Chris Nashawaty. By telephone. New York, NY. August 9, 2016.

87 I thought to myself . . . : McGill, Bruce. Interview by Chris Nashawaty. By telephone. New York, NY. September 1998.

87 "I thought . . . : Martin, "Harold Ramis Gets the Last Laugh." Accessed online.

87 In October of 1977 . . . : Landis, John. Interview by Chris Nashawaty. By telephone. New York, NY. August 9, 2016.

88 You can shoot here . . . : Reitman, Ivan. Interview by Chris Nashawaty. By telephone. New York, NY. September 14, 2016.

88 "Doug loved . . . : Reitman, Ivan. Interview by Chris Nashawaty. By telephone. New York, NY. September 14, 2016.

89 I ended up . . . : Widdoes, Jamie. Interview by Chris Nashawaty. By telephone. New York, NY. September 1998.

89 Adds McGill . . . : McGill, Bruce. Interview by Chris Nashawaty. By telephone. New York, NY. September 1998.

89 "If I walked in . . . : Landis, John. Interview by Chris Nashawaty. By telephone. New York, NY. August 9, 2016.

89 "Belushi would have . . . : Matheson, Tim. Interview by Chris Nashawaty. By telephone. New York, NY. September 1998.

90 He truly was . . . : Landis, John. Interview by Chris Nashawaty. By telephone. New York, NY. August 9, 2016.

90 As for Miller . . . : Miller, Chris. Interview by Chris Nashawaty. By telephone. New York, NY. August 31, 2016.

90 They just . . . : Reitman, Ivan. Interview by Chris Nashawaty. By telephone. New York, NY. September 14, 2016.

91 He'd taped . . . : Riegert, Peter. Interview by Chris Nashawaty. By telephone. New York, NY. September 1998.

91 "After that . . . : Landis, John. Interview by Chris Nashawaty. By telephone. New York, NY. August 9, 2016.

91 It was the . . . : Boxofficemojo.com.

91 Roger Ebert gave . . . : Roger Ebert, "Animal House," *The Chicago Sun-Times*, July 28, 1978. Accessed online.

91 By the end . . . : Boxofficemojo.com.

91 We wanted to . . . : Mount, Thom. Interview by Chris Nashawaty. By telephone. New York, NY. August 24, 2016.

91 By late October . . . : Boxofficemojo.com.

5. Tinseltown Gold Rush

94 And then when . . . : Landis, John. Interview by Chris Nashawaty. By telephone. New York, NY. August 9, 2016.

94 Though Kenney . . . : Ramis, Harold. Interview by Chris Nashawaty. By telephone. New York, NY. September 1998.

94 But after the movie . . . : Ramis, Harold. Interview by Chris Nashawaty. By telephone. New York, NY. September 1998.

94 We got some . . . : Miller, Chris. Interview by Chris Nashawaty. By telephone. New York, NY. August 31, 2016.

94 Landis had been . . . : Landis, John. Interview by Chris Nashawaty. By telephone. New York, NY. August 9, 2016.

95 While Simmons would . . . : Matty Simmons, *If You Don't Buy This Book We'll Kill This Dog* (New York: Barricade Books, 1994), 143.

95 And I went . . . : Greisman, Alan. Interview by Chris Nashawaty. By telephone. New York, NY. August 9, 2016.

95 The guy laughed . . . : Ramis, Harold. Interview by Chris Nashawaty. By telephone. New York, NY. May 20, 2010.

96 And John Belushi . . . : Schwartz, "College Humor Comes Back," 91.

96 We all had . . . : Reitman, Ivan. Interviewed by Chris Nashawaty. By telephone. New York, NY. September 14, 2016.

97 By 1979 . . . : Peter Biskind, *Easy Riders, Raging Bulls* (New York: Simon & Schuster, 1998), 433.

97 "To us . . . : Ramis, Harold. Interview by Chris Nashawaty. By telephone. New York, NY. May 20, 2010.

97 "After *Animal House* . . . : Daniel, Sean. Interview by Chris Nashawaty. By telephone. New York, NY. September 8, 2016.

98 And that was . . . : Miller, Chris. Interview by Chris Nashawaty. By telephone. New York, NY. August 31, 2016.

99 It was a lot . . . : Greisman, Alan. Interview by Chris Nashawaty. By telephone. New York, NY. August 9, 2016.

99 It stood for . . . : Geoff Edgers, "The Greatest Role of Bill Murray's Life Has Been Playing Bill Murray," *The Washington Post*, October 19, 2016. Accessed online.

100   Made for just . . . : Boxofficemojo.com.

101   There he found . . . : Nancy Griffin and Kim Masters, *Hit & Run: How Jon Peters and Peter Guber Took Sony for a Ride in Hollywood* (New York: Simon & Schuster, 1996), 13–15.

101   He would soon . . . : Griffin and Masters, *Hit & Run: How Jon Peters and Peter Guber Took Sony for a Ride in Hollywood*, 22.

102   He told her . . . : Griffin and Masters, *Hit & Run: How Jon Peters and Peter Guber Took Sony for a Ride in Hollywood*, 29.

102   At one point . . . : Cameron Crowe, "The Kristoffersons Make It," *Rolling Stone*, February 23, 1978. Accessed online.

102   *A Star Is Born* . . . : Boxofficemojo.com.

103   He followed it . . . : Boxofficemojo.com.

103   In April 1978 . . . : Griffin and Masters, *Hit & Run: How Jon Peters and Peter Guber Took Sony for a Ride in Hollywood*, 57.

104   He was a . . . : Mike Medavoy with Josh Young, *You're Only As Good As Your Next One* (New York: Atria Books, 2002), 98–99.

104   Peters just happened . . . : Ramis, Harold. Interview by Chris Nashawaty. By telephone. New York, NY. May 20, 2010.

106   I wanted to look . . . : Ramis, Harold. Interview by Chris Nashawaty. By telephone. New York, NY. May 20, 2010.

106   You look like . . . : Ramis, Harold. Interview by Chris Nashawaty. By telephone. New York, NY. May 20, 2010.

106   Still, it wouldn't . . . : Boxofficemojo.com.

107   "Harold pitched his . . . : Medavoy, Mike. Interview by Chris Nashawaty. By telephone. New York, NY. August 15, 2016.

107   And I'll never forget . . . : Ramis, Harold. Interview by Chris Nashawaty. By telephone. New York, NY. May 20, 2010.

107   But he figured . . . : Ramis, Harold. Interview by Chris Nashawaty. By telephone. New York, NY. May 20, 2010.

107   "Doug was going . . . : Doyle-Murray, Brian. Interview by Chris Nashawaty. By telephone. New York, NY. August 9, 2016.

6. Like The Dick Van Dyke Show

109   "To my regret . . . : Medavoy, Mike. Interview by Chris Nashawaty. By telephone. New York, NY. August 15, 2010.

109   "I must say . . . : Mount, Thom. Interview by Chris Nashawaty. By telephone. New York, NY. August 24, 2016.

110   I think he . . . : Reitman, Ivan. Interview by Chris Nashawaty. By telephone. New York, NY. September 14, 2016.

110   Peters told them . . . : Peters, Jon. Interview by Chris Nashawaty. By telephone. New York, NY. May 24, 2010.

112   No one I knew . . . : Ramis, Harold. Interview by Chris Nashawaty. By telephone. New York, NY. May 20, 2010.

112   We switched off . . . : Ramis, Harold. Interview by Chris Nashawaty. By telephone. New York, NY. May 20, 2010.

112   I thought . . . : Albert, Trevor. Interview by Chris Nashawaty. By telephone. New York, NY. August 31, 2016.

113   I wasn't sure . . . : Albert, Trevor. Interview by Chris Nashawaty. By telephone. New York, NY. August 31, 2016.

114   I always suspected . . . : Ramis, Harold. Interview by Chris Nashawaty. By telephone. New York, NY. May 20, 2010.

114   It's its own . . . : "Caddyshack Production Information," accessed October 13, 2016, from the Academy of Motion Pictures Arts and Sciences, Margaret Herrick Library Archives.

115   "I didn't know . . . : Canton, Mark. Interview by Chris Nashawaty. By telephone. New York, NY. August 24, 2016.

116   Seventeen million people . . . : Hill and Weingrad, *Saturday Night*, 307.

117   "So he ran . . . : Ptak, John. Interview by Chris Nashawaty. By telephone. New York, NY. August 23, 2016.

117   In the end . . . : Ptak, John. Interview by Chris Nashawaty. By telephone. New York, NY. August 23, 2016.

119   We would do . . . : Miller, Chris. Interview by Chris Nashawaty. By telephone. New York, NY. August 31, 2016.

119   Still, it's not . . . : "Frat Brats Stand Pat," *New York*, February 26, 1979. Accessed online.

120   "We just thought . . . : Fisher, Lucy. Interview by Chris Nashawaty. By telephone. New York, NY. August 29, 2016.

120   She thought . . . : Fisher, Lucy. Interview by Chris Nashawaty. By telephone. New York, NY. August 29, 2016.

121   The marriage wasn't . . . : Ptak, John. Interview by Chris Nashawaty. By telephone. New York, NY. August 23, 2016.

121   "Mel said . . . : Fisher, Lucy. Interview by Chris Nashawaty. By telephone. New York, NY. August 29, 2016.

122   And he was . . . : Shamberg, Michael. Interview by Chris Nashawaty. By telephone. New York, NY. August 17, 2016.

122 And there was . . . : Shamberg, Michael. Interview by Chris Nashawaty. By telephone. New York, NY. August 17, 2016.

7. Finally, Some Respect

127 That's the day . . . : *Variety*, June 25, 1979. Accessed online.

128 (it would grow . . . : Ned Zeman, "Soul Men: The Making of *The Blues Brothers*," *Vanity Fair*, December 2012. Accessed online.

128 budget at $6 million . . . : Ramis, Harold. Interview by Chris Nashawaty. By telephone. New York, NY. May 20, 2010.

128 We all socialized . . . : Nicita, Wallis. Interview by Chris Nashawaty. By telephone. New York, NY. August 10, 2016.

128 "It wasn't Paddy Chayefsky . . . : Nicita, Wallis. Interview by Chris Nashawaty. By telephone. New York, NY. August 10, 2016.

129 We had all . . . : Nicita, Wallis. Interview by Chris Nashawaty. By telephone. New York, NY. August 10, 2016.

129 "With any big . . . : Ramis, Harold. Interview by Chris Nashawaty. By telephone. New York, NY. May 20, 2010.

129 The soft-boiled . . . : Boxofficemojo.com.

130 Walking around like . . . : Chase, Chevy. Interview by Chris Nashawaty. By telephone. New York, NY. May 27, 2010.

130 "He had the . . . : Ramis, Harold. Interview by Chris Nashawaty. By telephone. New York, NY. May 20, 2010.

131 "He was just . . . : Ramis, Harold. Interview by Chris Nashawaty. By telephone. New York, NY. May 20, 2010.

131 The ideas of . . . : Nicita, Wallis. Interview by Chris Nashawaty. By telephone. New York, NY. August 10, 2016.

132 He finally became . . . : Rodney Dangerfield, *It's Not Easy Bein' Me* (New York: Perennial Currents, 2004), 137.

132 "No one knew . . . : Albert, Trevor. Interview by Chris Nashawaty. By telephone. New York, NY. August 31, 2016.

132 He sniffs . . . : Peters, Jon. Interview by Chris Nashawaty. By telephone. New York, NY. May 24, 2010.

132 And though he . . . : Dangerfield, *It's Not Easy Bein' Me*, 193.

134 Then the guerrillas . . . : "Caddyshack Production Information," accessed October 13, 2016, from the Academy of Motion Pictures Arts and Sciences, Margaret Herrick Library Archives.

134 He came back . . . : Jennifer Keishin Armstrong, *Mary and Lou and Rhoda and Ted* (New York: Simon & Schuster, 2013), 61.

134 "That would have . . . : Nicita, Wallis. Interview by Chris Nashawaty. By telephone. New York, NY. August 10, 2016.

135 "It gives you . . . : Nicita, Wallis. Interview by Chris Nashawaty. By telephone. New York, NY. August 10, 2016.

135 "Mickey made sense . . . : Nicita, Wallis. Interview by Chris Nashawaty. By telephone. New York, NY. August 10, 2016.

135 Mickey Rourke was . . . : Ramis, Harold. Interview by Chris Nashawaty. By telephone. New York, NY. May 20, 2010.

136 Doug wanted . . . : O'Keefe, Michael. Interview by Chris Nashawaty. By telephone. New York, NY. August 15, 2016.

136 I guess I . . . : O'Keefe, Michael. Interview by Chris Nashawaty. By telephone. New York, NY. August 15, 2016.

136 Clearly, it would . . . : O'Keefe, Michael. Interview by Chris Nashawaty. By telephone. New York, NY. August 15, 2016.

137 Bill Murray, who . . . : Bill Murray with George Peper, *Cinderella Story: My Life in Golf* (New York: Broadway Books, 1999), 33.

138 "We were trying . . . : Ramis, Harold. Interview by Chris Nashawaty. By telephone. New York, NY. May 20, 2010.

139 Murray almost drowned . . . : Schnakenberg, *The Big Bad Book of Bill Murray*, 252.

139 I think they just . . . : Murray, Bill. Interview by Chris Nashawaty. By telephone. New York, NY. June 7, 2010.

140 If true, Murray . . . : *The Hollywood Reporter*, September 21, 1979. Accessed online.

140 "It was like . . . : Lemorande, Rusty. Interview by Chris Nashawaty. By telephone. New York, NY. October 7, 2016.

140 I mean . . . : Nicita, Wallis. Interview by Chris Nashawaty. By telephone. New York, NY. August 10, 2016.

141 They'd said . . . : Morgan, Cindy. Interview by Chris Nashawaty. By telephone. New York, NY. September 9, 2016.

141 But I thought . . . : Morgan, Cindy. Interview by Chris Nashawaty. By telephone. New York, NY. September 9, 2016.

141 "But something special . . . : Albert, Trevor. Interview by Chris Nashawaty. By telephone. New York, NY. August 31, 2016.

142 She'd been in . . . : Morgan, Cindy. Interview by Chris Nashawaty. By telephone. New York, NY. September 9, 2016.

142 "I remember saying . . . : Berkrot, Peter. Interview by Chris Nashawaty. By telephone. New York, NY. August 30, 2016.

143   He was the one . . . : Murray, Bill. Interview by Chris Nashawaty. By telephone. New York, NY. June 7, 2010.

144   Not bad . . . : McConnachie, Brian. Interview by Chris Nashawaty. By telephone. New York, NY. August 29, 2016.

8. Rolling Hills . . . and Action!

146   Instead, he planted . . . : "Caddyshack Production Information," accessed October 13, 2016, from the Academy of Motion Pictures Arts and Sciences, Margaret Herrick Library Archives.

146   But this place . . . : Ramis, Harold. Interview by Chris Nashawaty. By telephone. New York, NY. May 20, 2010.

147   Lewis's financiers had . . . : *Variety*, October 31, 1979. Accessed online.

147   In the end . . . : *Variety*, October 31, 1979. Accessed online.

148   In the '60s . . . : Scott Martin, *The Book of Caddyshack* (Lanham, MD: Taylor Trade Publishing, 2007), 37.

148   Michael O'Keefe . . . : O'Keefe, Michael. Interview by Chris Nashawaty. By telephone. New York, NY. August 15, 2016.

149   "Everyone else was . . . : Albert, Trevor. Interview by Chris Nashawaty. By telephone. New York, NY. August 31, 2016.

150   I mean, if . . . : Lemorande, Rusty. Interview by Chris Nashawaty. By telephone. New York, NY. October 7, 2016.

150   Rodney Dangerfield was . . . : *Caddyshack: The Inside Story*, A&E TV documentary, 2009.

150   He took one lesson . . . : Ramis, Harold. Interview with Chris Nashawaty. By telephone. New York, NY. May 20, 2010.

151   After a few minutes . . . : Berkrot, Peter. Interview by Chris Nashawaty. By telephone. New York, NY. August 30, 2016.

151   Our table was . . . : Berkrot, Peter. Interview by Chris Nashawaty. By telephone. New York, NY. August 30, 2016.

151   "You couldn't find . . . : Ryerson, Ann. Interview by Chris Nashawaty. By telephone. New York, NY. August 18, 2016.

152   I never judged . . . : Ramis, Harold. Interview by Chris Nashawaty. By telephone. New York, NY. May 20, 2010.

152   I didn't know . . . : Ramis, Harold. Interview by Chris Nashawaty. By telephone. New York, NY. May 20, 2010.

153   And that was . . . : Albert, Trevor. Interview by Chris Nashawaty. By telephone. New York, NY. August 31, 2016.

153 They're going to see . . . : Ramis, Harold. Interview by Chris Nashawaty. By telephone. New York, NY. May 20, 2010.

154 Says Michael O'Keefe . . . : O'Keefe, Michael. Interview by Chris Nashawaty. By telephone. New York, NY. August 15, 2016.

154 "Anything beyond that . . . : Ramis, Harold. Interview by Chris Nashawaty. By telephone. New York, NY. May 20, 2010.

154 He'd later say . . . : *Caddyshack: The Inside Story,* A&E TV documentary, 2009.

9. Rappin' Rodney

155 Years later he . . . : "Caddyshack Production Information," accessed October 13, 2016, from the Academy of Motion Pictures Arts and Sciences, Margaret Herrick Library Archives.

158 Ramis had finally . . . : Ramis, Harold. Interview by Chris Nashawaty. By telephone. New York, NY. May 20, 2010.

158 People who are funny . . . : Morgan, Cindy. Interview by Chris Nashawaty. By telephone. New York, NY. September 9, 2016.

158 "Rodney needed . . . : Ramis, Harold. Interview by Chris Nashawaty. By telephone. New York, NY. May 20, 2010.

159 He was not familiar . . . : Chase, Chevy. Interview by Chris Nashawaty. By telephone. New York, NY. May 27, 2010.

160 Nothing was hidden . . . : Lemorande, Rusty. Interview by Chris Nashawaty. By telephone. New York, NY. October 7, 2016.

161 Without that process . . . : Lemorande, Rusty. Interview by Chris Nashawaty. By telephone. New York, NY. February 28, 2017.

162 Lemorande went back . . . : Lemorande, Rusty. Interview by Chris Nashawaty. By telephone. New York, NY. February 28, 2017.

162 You have to follow . . . : Ryerson, Ann. Interview by Chris Nashawaty. By telephone. New York, NY. August 18, 2016.

162 Well, Scott Colomby . . . : Barmon, John. Interview by Chris Nashawaty. By telephone. New York, NY. August 19, 2016.

162 He loved to . . . : Barmon, John. Interview by Chris Nashawaty. By telephone. New York, NY. August 19, 2016.

163 The only person . . . : Berkrot, Peter. Interview by Chris Nashawaty. By telephone. New York, NY. August 30, 2016.

163 After about a week . . . : Barmon, John. Interview by Chris Nashawaty. By telephone. New York, NY. August 19, 2016.

164 "Well, they practiced . . . : Albert, Trevor. Interview by Chris Nashawaty. By telephone. New York, NY. August 31, 2016.

164 It's the one thing . . . : Berkrot, Peter. Interview by Chris Nashawaty. By telephone. New York, NY. August 30, 2016.

164 Later, he would say . . . : "Caddyshack Production Information," accessed October 13, 2016, from the Academy of Motion Pictures Arts and Sciences, Margaret Herrick Library Archives.

165 "People like Doug . . . : Albert, Trevor. Interview by Chris Nashawaty. By telephone. New York, NY. August 31, 2016.

165 His training was . . . : Lemorande, Rusty. Interview by Chris Nashawaty. By telephone. New York, NY. October 7, 2016.

166 Ted was really angry . . . : Morgan, Cindy. Interview by Chris Nashawaty. By telephone. New York, NY. September 9, 2016.

166 Harold liked to . . . : Barmon, John. Interview by Chris Nashawaty. By telephone. New York, NY. August 19, 2016.

167 I tried to give . . . : Ramis, Harold. Interview by Chris Nashawaty. By telephone. New York, NY. May 20, 2010.

10. The Pizza Man

169 "The whole time . . . : Chase, Chevy. Interview by Chris Nashawaty. By telephone. New York, NY. May 27, 2010.

170 But then Chase . . . : Ptak, John. Interview by Chris Nashawaty. By telephone. New York, NY. August 23, 2016.

170 And smoking pot . . . : Chase, Chevy. Interview by Chris Nashawaty. By telephone. New York, NY. May 27, 2010.

171 "Being with Doug . . . : Chase, Chevy. Interview by Chris Nashawaty. By telephone. New York, NY. May 27, 2010.

171 "Doug had an idea . . . : Murray with Peper, *Cinderella Story: My Life in Golf*, 190.

172 You could give Chevy . . . : Ramis, Harold. Interview by Chris Nashawaty. By telephone. New York, NY. May 20, 2010.

173 So with Chevy . . . : O'Keefe, Michael. Interview by Chris Nashawaty. By telephone. New York, NY. August 15, 2016.

174 Years later . . . : Ptak, John. Interview by Chris Nashawaty. By telephone. New York, NY. August 18, 2016.

175 I'm not Lacey . . . : Morgan, Cindy. Interview by Chris Nashawaty. By telephone. New York, NY. September 9, 2016.

175 "So I went . . . : Morgan, Cindy. Interview by Chris Nashawaty. By telephone. New York, NY. September 9, 2016.

175 And that's how . . . : Morgan, Cindy. Interview by Chris Nashawaty. By telephone. New York, NY. September 9, 2016.

11. Total Consciousness

177 Problem was, Bill Murray didn't . . . : Lynn Hirschberg, "Bill Murray, In All Seriousness," *The New York Times*, January 31, 1999. Accessed online.

177 Or a week later . . . : Hirschberg, "Bill Murray, In All Seriousness." Accessed online.

178 "He's just a moody guy . . . : Ramis, Harold. Interview by Chris Nashawaty. By telephone. New York, NY. May 20, 2010.

179 Either way . . . : Hill and Weingrad, *Saturday Night*, 256–7.

180 I was like . . . : Landis, John. Interview by Chris Nashawaty. By telephone. New York, NY. August 9, 2016.

180 Because we all . . . : Nick De Semlyen, "Bill Murray on Fighting Chevy Chase," *Empire,* May 18, 2012. Accessed online.

180 Everyone seemed to . . . : Canton, Mark. Interview by Chris Nashawaty. By telephone. New York, NY. August 24, 2016.

180 "I felt like . . . : McConnachie, Brian. Interview by Chris Nashawaty. By telephone. New York, NY. August 29, 2016.

181 As soon as Bill . . . : Ramis, Harold. Interview by Chris Nashawaty. By telephone. New York, NY. May 20, 2010.

182 And that's what . . . : Berkrot, Peter. Interview by Chris Nashawaty. By telephone. New York, NY. August 30, 2016.

183 He was totally . . . : Berkrot, Peter. Interview by Chris Nashawaty. By telephone. New York, NY. August 30, 2016.

184 That's part of . . . : Albert, Trevor. Interview by Chris Nashawaty. By telephone. New York, NY. August 31, 2016.

184 I guess they . . . : Murray, Bill. Interview by Chris Nashawaty. By telephone. New York, NY. June 7, 2010.

184 It's not grabbed . . . : Ramis, Harold. Interview by Chris Nashawaty. By telephone. New York, NY. May 20, 2010.

185 "All it said . . . : Ramis, Harold. Interview by Chris Nashawaty. By telephone. New York, NY. May 20, 2010.

185 And he said . . . : Ramis, Harold. Interview by Chris Nashawaty. By telephone. New York, NY. May 20, 2010.

187   You made your bones . . . : Murray, Bill. Interview by Chris Nashawaty. By telephone. New York, NY. June 7, 2010.

187   Those are the guys . . . : Murray, Bill. Interview by Chris Nashawaty. By telephone. New York, NY. June 7, 2010.

188   That's how he worked . . . : Ramis, Harold. Interview by Chris Nashawaty. By telephone. New York, NY. May 20, 2010.

189   There was no sign . . . : Lemorande, Rusty. Interview by Chris Nashawaty. By telephone. New York, NY. October 7, 2016.

189   And if I'm . . . : Murray, Bill. Interview by Chris Nashawaty. By telephone. New York, NY. June 7, 2010.

189   Recalls Cindy Morgan . . . : Morgan, Cindy. Interview by Chris Nashawaty. By telephone. New York, NY. September 9, 2016.

190   Peters thought . . . : Peters, Jon. Interview by Chris Nashawaty. By telephone. New York, NY. May 24, 2010.

190   And he goes . . . : Morgan, Cindy. Interview by Chris Nashawaty. By telephone. New York, NY. September 9, 2016.

191   Jon's Old Hollywood . . . : Ramis, Harold. Interview by Chris Nashawaty. By telephone. New York, NY. May 20, 2010.

191   "I don't have a problem . . . . : Morgan, Cindy. Interview by Chris Nashawaty. By telephone. New York, NY. September 9, 2016.

191   I wanted her to . . . : Peters, Jon. Interview by Chris Nashawaty. By telephone. New York, NY. May 24, 2010.

191   "He said, 'Honey . . . : Morgan, Cindy. Interview by Chris Nashawaty. By telephone. New York, NY. September 9, 2016.

192   They did . . . : O'Keefe, Michael. Interview by Chris Nashawaty. By telephone. New York, NY. August 15, 2016.

193   "I felt like . . . : Morgan, Cindy. Interview by Chris Nashawaty. By telephone. New York, NY. September 9, 2016.

193   "He's difficult . . . : Ramis, Harold. Interview by Chris Nashawaty. By telephone. New York, NY. May 20, 2010.

193   So after a forty-five minute . . . . : Morgan, Cindy. Interview by Chris Nashawaty. By telephone. New York, NY. September 9, 2016.

194   And that was . . . : Morgan, Cindy. Interview by Chris Nashawaty. By telephone. New York, NY. September 9, 2016.

194   I went a little . . . : Chase, Chevy. Interview by Chris Nashawaty. By telephone. New York, NY. May 27, 2010.

194   But during the . . . : Morgan, Cindy. Interview by Chris Nashawaty. By telephone. New York, NY. September 9, 2016.

196 And those are qualities . . . : Robert Osborne, "On Location," *The Hollywood Reporter*, October 19, 1979. Accessed online.

196 It also alludes . . . : *Variety*, October 31, 1979. Accessed online.

12. Pool or the Pond

197 "I had never seen cocaine . . . : Berkrot, Peter. Interview by Chris Nashaway. By telephone. New York, NY. August 30, 2016.

198 Hamilton Mitchell, who . . . : Mitchell, Hamilton. Interview by Chris Nashaway. By telephone. New York, NY. March 13, 2017.

198 Pure, like they . . . : Mitchell, Hamilton. Interview by Chris Nashawaty. By telephone. New York, NY. March 13, 2017.

198 Those of us . . . : O'Keefe, Michael. Interview by Chris Nashawaty. By telephone. New York, NY. August 15, 2017.

198 By the time . . . : John Blumenthal, "Playboy Interview: Chevy Chase," *Playboy*, June 1988, 65.

199 Get your per diems . . . : Morgan, Cindy. Interview by Chris Nashawaty. By telephone. New York, NY. September 9, 2016.

199 And he would just . . . : O'Keefe, Michael. Interview by Chris Nashawaty. By telephone. New York, NY. August 15, 2016.

199 By the late '70s . . . : Biskind, *Easy Riders, Raging Bulls*, 382.

200 Coke use . . . : Hill and Weingrad, *Saturday Night*, 322.

200 "One would say . . . : McConnachie, Brian. Interview by Chris Nashawaty. By telephone. New York, NY. August 29, 2016.

200 The delays caused . . . : Zeman, "Soul Men: The Making of *The Blues Brothers*." Accessed online.

201 "And I think anybody . . . : Medavoy, Mike. Interview by Chris Nashawaty. By telephone. New York, NY. August 15, 2016.

201 It was a huge . . . : Peters, Jon. Interview by Chris Nashawaty. By telephone. New York, NY. May 24, 2010.

201 What got in the way . . . : Ramis, Harold. Interview by Chris Nashawaty. By telephone. New York, NY. May 20, 2010.

201 What I think is . . . : Karp, *A Futile and Stupid Gesture,* 344.

202 "We had two . . . : Peters, Jon. Interview by Chris Nashawaty. By telephone. New York, NY. May 24, 2010.

202 "They just kept . . . : Murray, Bill. Interview by Chris Nashawaty. By telephone. New York, NY. June 7, 2010.

203 Once again . . . : Murray, Bill. Interview by Chris Nashawaty. By telephone. New York, NY. June 7, 2010.

203 "It has nothing . . . : Ramis, Harold. Interview by Chris Nashawaty. By telephone. New York, NY. May 20, 2010.

203 They didn't really . . . : Murray, Bill. Interview by Chris Nashawaty. By telephone. New York, NY. June 7, 2010.

203 I remember he . . . : Chase, Chevy. Interview by Chris Nashawaty. By telephone. New York, NY. May 27, 2010.

204 They were given . . . : Ramis, Harold. Interview by Chris Nashawaty. By telephone. New York, NY. May 20, 2010.

204 So he sees me . . . : Chase, Chevy. Interview by Chris Nashawaty. By telephone. New York, NY. May 27, 2010.

204 It's a really fun . . . : Murray, Bill. Interview by Chris Nashawaty. By telephone. New York, NY. June 7, 2010.

205 Harold had to   : Chase, Chevy. Interview by Chris Nashawaty. By telephone. New York, NY. May 27, 2010.

205 Even though . . . : Chase, Chevy. Interview by Chris Nashawaty. By telephone. New York, NY. May 27, 2010.

13. The Dynamite Caper

208 By some accounts . . . : *Variety*, October 31, 1979. Accessed online.

208 Others say . . . : Lemorande, Rusty. Interview by Chris Nashawaty. By telephone. New York, NY. February 28, 2017.

208 "I've got pictures . . . : Morgan, Cindy. Interview by Chris Nashawaty. By telephone. New York, NY. September 9, 2016.

208 He asked them . . . : *Caddyshack: The Inside Story*, A&E TV documentary, 2009.

208 "Jon was going to . . . : O'Keefe, Michael. Interview by Chris Nashawaty. By telephone. New York, NY. August 15, 2016.

209 There's no improvisation . . . : Albert, Trevor. Interview by Chris Nashawaty. By telephone. New York, NY. August 31, 2016.

209 Ramis said that . . . : Ramis, Harold. Interview by Chris Nashawaty. By telephone. New York, NY. May 20, 2010.

209 You couldn't fake . . . : Berkrot, Peter. Interview by Chris Nashawaty. By telephone. New York, NY. August 30, 2016.

209 Still, no one . . . : *Caddyshack: The Inside Story*, A&E TV documentary, 2009.

210   It makes absolutely no sense . . . : Ramis, Harold. Interview by Chris Nashawaty. By telephone. New York, NY. May 20, 2010.

210   Ramis would shoot . . . : Lemorande, Rusty. Interview by Chris Nashawaty. By telephone. New York, NY. February 28, 2017.

211   So at the wrap party . . . : *Caddyshack: The Inside Story,* A&E TV documentary, 2009.

212   I couldn't wait . . . : Morgan, Cindy. Interview by Chris Nashawaty. By telephone. New York, NY. September 9, 2016.

212   "I told Doug . . . : Albert, Trevor. Interview by Chris Nashawaty. By telephone. New York, NY. August 31, 2016.

14. The Unkindest Cut

213   The cutting room becomes . . . : Ralph Rosenblum and Robert Karen, *When the Shooting Stops . . . The Cutting Begins* (New York: Da Capo Press, 1979), 1.

214   There's no way . . . : Albert, Trevor. Interview by Chris Nashawaty. By telephone. New York, NY. August 31, 2016.

215   You go from . . . : Igel, Rachel. Interview by Chris Nashawaty. By telephone. New York, NY. September 21, 2016.

215   They weren't lectures . . . : Igel, Rachel. Interview by Chris Nashawaty. By telephone. New York, NY. September 21, 2016.

215   In Hollywood, when . . . : Igel, Rachel. Interview by Chris Nashawaty. By telephone. New York, NY. September 21, 2016.

216   "We had a bunch . . . : Peters, Jon. Interview by Chris Nashawaty. By telephone. New York, NY. May 24, 2010.

216   That first cut . . . : Lemorande, Rusty. Interview by Chris Nashawaty. By telephone. New York, NY. October 7, 2016.

216   "He listened to . . . : Ramis, Harold. Interview by Chris Nashawaty. By telephone. New York, NY. May 20, 2010.

217   "Hey, at least . . . : Simmons, *If You Don't Buy This Book We'll Kill This Dog,* 198–9.

218   Rodney had funny things . . . : Ramis, Harold. Interview by Chris Nashawaty. By telephone. New York, NY. May 20, 2010.

218   And nobody has . . . : Igel, Rachel. Interview by Chris Nashawaty. By telephone. New York, NY. September 21, 2016.

219   They were really . . . : Kelly, Sean. Interview by Chris Nashawaty. By telephone. New York, NY. August 25, 2016.

219   When he left . . . : Lemorande, Rusty. Interview by Chris Nashawaty. By telephone. New York, NY. October 7, 2016.

220 He was our savior . . . : Lemorande, Rusty. Interview by Chris Nashawaty. By telephone. New York, NY. October 7, 2016.

220 That's the toughest . . . : Canton, Mark. Interview by Chris Nashawaty. By telephone. New York, NY. August 24, 2016.

220 Adds Trevor Albert . . . : Albert, Trevor. Interview by Chris Nashawaty. By telephone. New York, NY. August 31, 2016.

221 We thought, OK . . . : Greisman, Alan. Interview by Chris Nashawaty. By telephone. New York, NY. August 9, 2016.

15. Enter the Gopher

223 According to Ramis . . . : Ramis, Harold. Interview by Chris Nashawaty. By telephone. New York, NY. May 20, 2010.

224 Peters was going to need . . . : Lemorande, Rusty. Interview by Chris Nashawaty. By telephone. New York, NY. October 7, 2016.

224 And in Hollywood . . . : Medavoy, Mike. Interview by Chris Nashawaty. By telephone. New York, NY. August 15, 2016.

224 "But the characters . . . : Albert, Trevor. Interview by Chris Nashawaty. By telephone. New York, NY. August 31, 2016.

224 Dykstra agreed . . . : Dykstra, John. Interview by Chris Nashawaty. By telephone. September 6, 2016.

224 For us, it was . . . : Dykstra, John. Interview by Chris Nashawaty. By telephone. September 6, 2016.

226 According to Lemorande . . . : Lemorande, Rusty. Interview by Chris Nashawaty. By telephone. New York, NY. October 7, 2016.

226 The dolphin-like sounds . . . : Dykstra, John. Interview by Chris Nashawaty. By telephone. September 6, 2016.

227 We were just . . . : Dykstra, John. Interview by Chris Nashawaty. By telephone. September 6, 2016.

227 Finally, Ramis offered . . . : *Caddyshack: The Inside Story,* A&E TV documentary, 2009.

227 Instead, Peters reached out . . . : Loggins, Kenny. Interview by Chris Nashawaty. By telephone. New York, NY. August 24, 2016.

227 "He was a Hollywood . . . : Loggins, Kenny. Interview by Chris Nashawaty. By telephone. New York, NY. August 24, 2016.

228 Stupid or not . . . : Loggins, Kenny. Interview by Chris Nashawaty. By telephone. New York, NY. August 24, 2016.

228 I felt like the song . . . : Loggins, Kenny. Interview by Chris Nashawaty. By telephone. New York, NY. August 24, 2016.

228   I just listened . . . : Loggins, Kenny. Interview by Chris Nashawaty. By telephone. New York, NY. August 24, 2016.

229   He felt that . . . : Lemorande, Rusty. Interview by Chris Nashawaty. By telephone. New York, NY. October 7, 2016.

229   On April 25 . . . : Boxofficemojo.com.

230   In what was . . . : Roger Ebert, "Review: Where the Buffalo Roam," *The Chicago Sun-Times*, April 29, 1980. Accessed online.

230   Universal quickly yanked . . . : Boxofficemojo.com.

230   Thompson himself would . . . : Schnakenberg, *The Big Bad Book of Bill Murray*, 252.

230   He would not stop . . . : Hill and Weingrad, *Saturday Night*, 379.

231   Ramis and . . . : *The Hollywood Reporter*, June 5, 1980. Accessed online.

231   "He'd been up . . . : Ramis, Harold. Interview by Chris Nashawaty. By telephone. New York, NY. May 20, 2010.

231   And *they* started . . . : Ramis, Harold. Interview by Chris Nashawaty. By telephone. New York, NY. May 20, 2010.

231   I thought the whole . . . : Medavoy, Mike. Interview by Chris Nashawaty. By telephone. New York, NY. August 15, 2016.

233   I was shocked . . . : Miller, Chris. Interview by Chris Nashawaty. By telephone. New York, NY. August 31, 2016.

233   That's a death wish . . . : Kelly, Sean. Interview by Chris Nashawaty. By telephone. New York, NY. August 25, 2016.

16. Judgment Day

235   "I think we felt . . . : Lemorande, Rusty. Interview by Chris Nashawaty. By telephone. New York, NY. October 7, 2016.

236   It was my $6 million scholarship . . . : Ramis, Harold. Interview by Chris Nashawaty. By telephone. New York, NY. May 20, 2010.

236   For his part . . . : Peters, Jon. Interview by Chris Nashawaty. By telephone. New York, NY. May 24, 2010.

236   The critics were unkind . . . : Boxofficemojo.com.

237   He just didn't think . . . : Fisher, Lucy. Interview by Chris Nashawaty. By telephone. New York, NY. August 29, 2016.

237   *Airplane!* would end up . . . : Boxofficemojo.com.

237   It's advertising . . . : Flaherty, Joe. Interview by Chris Nashawaty. By telephone. New York, NY. August 18, 2016.

238 The invitees included . . . : "Caddyshack Marketing and Promotion Brochure," accessed October 13, 2016, from the Academy of Motion Pictures Arts and Sciences, Margaret Herrick Library Archives.

238 A Friday-night screening . . . : "Caddyshack Marketing and Promotion Brochure," accessed October 13, 2016, from the Academy of Motion Pictures Arts and Sciences, Margaret Herrick Library Archives.

239 We do not want . . . : "Caddyshack Marketing and Promotion Brochure," accessed October 13, 2016, from the Academy of Motion Pictures Arts and Sciences, Margaret Herrick Library Archives.

239 The green print . . . : Lemorande, Rusty. Interview by Chris Nashawaty. By telephone. New York, NY. October 7, 2016.

239 "It was clear . . . : Lemorande, Rusty. Interview by Chris Nashawaty. By telephone. New York, NY. October 7, 2016.

240 "He was dead drunk . . . : Chase, Chevy. Interview by Chris Nashawaty. By telephone. New York. May 27, 2010.

241 It was a pretty bad scene . . . : Ramis, Harold. Interview by Chris Nashawaty. By telephone. New York, NY. May 20, 2010.

241 The six-minute interview . . . : "Rodney Dangerfield, Chevy Chase, Bill Murray, Ted Knight (Caddyshack Interview 1980)," Youtube.com, accessed on April 10, 2017.

241 "The next day . . . : Judd Apatow, *Sick in the Head: Conversations About Life and Comedy* (New York, Random House, 2015), 121.

242 She says he . . . : Morgan, Cindy. Interview by Chris Nashawaty. By telephone. New York, NY. September 9, 2016.

242 But then I saw . . . . Berkrot, Peter. Interview by Chris Nashawaty. By telephone. New York, NY. August 30, 2016.

242 "I was one . . . : *Caddyshack: The Inside Story,* A&E TV documentary, 2009.

242 Rodney Dangerfield staggered . . . : Canton, Mark. Interview by Chris Nashawaty. By telephone. New York, NY. August 24, 2016.

243 "But I guess . . . : McConnachie, Brian. Interview by Chris Nashawaty. By telephone. New York, NY. August 29, 2016.

243 "She walked up . . . : Morgan, Cindy. Interview by Chris Nashawaty. By telephone. New York, NY. September 9, 2016.

243 The industry paper's . . . : *Variety,* July 23, 1980. Accessed online.

243 In *The Washington Post* . . . : Gary Arnold, "Caddy Capers," *The Washington Post,* July 26, 1980. Accessed online.

243 *The Hollywood Reporter's* Arthur Knight . . . : Arthur Knight, "Movie Review: *Caddyshack,*" *The Hollywood Reporter,* July 25, 1980. Accessed online.

243   It is an unoriginal . . . : Schnakenberg, *The Big Bad Book of Bill Murray*, 37.

244   Only Roger Ebert . . . : Roger Ebert, "Caddyshack," *The Chicago Sun-Times*, 1980. Accessed online.

244   During its opening weekend . . . : Boxofficemojo.com.

244   Look at us . . . : Chase, Chevy. Interview by Chris Nashawaty. By telephone. New York, NY. May 27, 2010.

245   That's when Doug . . . : Ramis, Harold. Interview by Chris Nashawaty. By telephone. New York, NY. May 20, 2010.

245   Chase was hiding . . . : Chase, Chevy. Interview by Chris Nashawaty. By telephone. New York, NY. May 27, 2010.

245   Getting drugs would . . . : Greisman, Alan. Interview by Chris Nashawaty. By telephone. New York, NY. August 9, 2016.

246   "I was shocked . . . : Greisman, Alan. Interview by Chris Nashawaty. By telephone. New York, NY. August 9, 2016.

246   "The postcard said . . . : Igel, Rachel. Interview by Chris Nashawaty. By telephone. New York, NY. September 21, 2016.

247   "So everyone went . . . : Greisman, Alan. Interview by Chris Nashawaty. By telephone. New York, NY. August 9, 2016.

247   "The longer it . . . : Fisher, Lucy. Interview by Chris Nashawaty. By telephone. New York, NY. August 29, 2016.

247   The coroner would . . . : "Obituary: Douglas Kenney," *The Los Angeles Herald Examiner,* September 4, 1980. Accessed online.

247   Alan Greisman . . . : Greisman, Alan. Interview by Chris Nashawaty. By telephone. New York, NY. August 9, 2016.

248   There were even people . . . : Ramis, Harold. Interview by Chris Nashawaty. By telephone. New York, NY. May 20, 2010.

249   "These are some . . . : Greisman, Alan. Interview by Chris Nashawaty. By telephone. New York, NY. August 9, 2016.

249   "I thought it . . . : Greisman, Alan. Interview by Chris Nashawaty. By telephone. New York, NY. August 9, 2016.

249   That's the kind . . . : Landis, John. Interview by Chris Nashawaty. By telephone. New York, NY. August 9, 2016.

249   The hearse with . . . : Greisman, Alan. Interview by Chris Nashawaty. By telephone. New York, NY. August 9, 2016.

249   We were like . . . : Greisman, Alan. Interview by Chris Nashawaty. By telephone. New York, NY. August 9, 2016.

17. Welcome, Kenney Mourners!

252   He was like . . . : McConnachie, Brian. Interview by Chris Nashawaty.
      By telephone. New York, NY. August 29, 2016.

252   "The best thing . . . : Kelly, Sean. Interview by Chris Nashawaty. By
      telephone. New York, NY. August 25, 2016.

252   "Everybody was devastated . . . : O'Keefe, Michael. Interview by Chris
      Nashawaty. By telephone. New York, NY. August 15, 2016.

252   Kenney would just flash . . . : Ramis, Harold. Interview by Chris
      Nashawaty. By telephone. New York, NY. May 20, 2010.

252   "I've had that . . . : Greisman, Alan. Interview by Chris Nashawaty.
      By telephone. New York, NY. August 9, 2016.

253   It would go on . . . : Boxofficemojo.com.

254   That conversation . . . : Chase, Chevy. Interview by Chris Nashawaty.
      By telephone. New York, NY. May 27, 2010.

254   I miss him . . . : Chase, Chevy. Interview by Chris Nashawaty. By
      telephone. New York, NY. May 27, 2010.

Bibliography

Apatow, Judd. *Sick in the Head: Conversations About Life and Comedy.* New York: Random House, 2015.

Armstrong, Jennifer Keishin. *Mary and Lou and Rhoda and Ted.* New York: Simon and Schuster, 2013.

Beard, Henry N., and Douglas C. Kenney. *Bored of the Rings.* New York: Signet, 1969.

Biskind, Peter. *Easy Riders, Raging Bulls: How the Sex-Drugs-and-Rock 'n' Roll Generation Saved Hollywood.* New York: Simon and Schuster, 1998.

Dangerfield, Rodney. *It's Not Easy Bein' Me: A Lifetime of No Respect but Plenty of Sex and Drugs.* New York: Harper Collins, 2004.

Davis, Tom. *Thirty-Nine Years of Short-Term Memory Loss: The Early Days of SNL from Someone Who Was There.* New York: Grove Press, 2009.

Edwards, Gavin. *The Tao of Bill Murray.* New York: Random House, 2016.

Frank, Josh, with Charlie Buckholtz. *In Heaven Everything Is Fine: The Unsolved Life of Peter Ivers and the Lost History of New Wave Theatre.* New York: Soft Skull Press, 2010.

Fruchter, Rena. *I'm Chevy Chase . . . and You're Not.* London: Virgin Books, 2007.

Griffin, Nancy, and Kim Masters. *Hit & Run: How Jon Peters and Peter Guber Took Sony for a Ride in Hollywood.* New York: Simon and Schuster, 1996.

Hendra, Tony. *Going Too Far: The Rise and Demise of Sick, Gross, Black, Sophomoric, Weirdo, Pinko, Anarchist, Underground, Anti-Establishment Humor.* New York: Dolphin/Doubleday, 1987.

Hill, Doug, and Jeff Weingrad. *Saturday Night: A Backstage History of Saturday Night Live.* New York: Vintage Books, 1987.

Karp, Josh. *A Futile and Stupid Gesture: How Doug Kenney and National Lampoon Changed Comedy Forever.* Chicago: Chicago Review Press, 2006.

Martin, Scott. *The Book of Caddyshack: Everything You Always Wanted to Know about the Greatest Movie Ever Made.* Lanham, MD: Taylor Trade Publishing, 2007.

Medavoy, Mike, with Josh Young. *You're Only as Good as Your Next One.* New York: Atria, 2002.

Meyerowitz, Rick. *Drunk Stoned Brilliant Dead: The Writers and Artists Who Made the National Lampoon Insanely Great.* New York: Abrams, 2010.

Murray, Bill, with George Peper. *Cinderella Story: My Life in Golf.* New York: Broadway, 2000.

Miller, Chris. *The Real Animal House.* New York: Little, Brown, 2006.

Nesteroff, Kliph. *The Comedians: Drunks, Thieves, Scoundrels and the History of American Comedy.* New York: Grove Press, 2015.

Patinkin, Sheldon. *Second City: Backstage at the World's Greatest Comedy Theater.* Naperville, IL: Sourcebooks, 2000.

Perrin, Dennis. *Mr. Mike: The Life and Work of Michael O'Donoghue.* New York: Avon Books, 1998.

Rosenblum, Ralph, and Robert Karen. *When the Shooting Stops . . . The Cutting Begins: A Film Editor's Story.* New York: Da Capo, 1979.

Sacks, Mike. *Poking a Dead Frog: Conversations with Today's Top Comedy Writers.* New York: Penguin, 2014.

Schnakenberg, Robert. *The Big Bad Book of Bill Murray.* Philadelphia: Quirk Books, 2015.

Shales, Tom, and James Andrew Miller. *Live From New York: An Uncensored History of Saturday Night Live.* New York: Little, Brown, 2002.

Simmons, Matty. *If You Don't Buy This Book We'll Kill This Dog: Life, Laughs, Love and Death at National Lampoon.* New York: Barricade Books, 1994.

Simmons, Matty. *Fat, Drunk, & Stupid: The Inside Story behind the Making of Animal House.* New York: St. Martin's, 2012.

Stein, Ellin. *That's Not Funny, That's Sick: The National Lampoon and the Comedy Insurgents Who Captured the Mainstream.* New York: W. W. Norton, 2013.